Speaking ill of the Dead

edited by

MYLES DUNGAN

NEW
ISLAND

CONTENTS

Foreword

How thousands, if not millions, of the subjects of some of the deceased leaders of totalitarian regimes, who were anything but the paragons of wisdom and virtue their citizens were forced to consider them, must yearn, literally, to speak out and tell it as it was by speaking ill of them. Many of us do this regularly with our living political and sporting heroes. (What do you mean? Sure, that fellow couldn't kick snow off a rope or such and such a team couldn't hurl the Sisters of Mercy!)

Even in Western democracies where relatively greater freedom of expression is enjoyed, there are countless historic figures who enjoy enormous reputations which not everyone accepts. Speaking ill of the dead allows the questioning of reputations and, in the extreme expression of the process, allows one to question the reputation of someone they consider should be challenged and even reassessed.

Rather in the way that the 'what if' (things had been different) approach makes the student return to first principles and the primary evidence to see how various events, movements and even personalities really developed, the what may be called 'speaking ill of the dead' method is also an invitation to revisit and question historical convictions. Not only does it result in taking heroes down from their pedestals, allowing analysis of the wart component of 'warts and all', but also, by posing another way of looking at things, it may be said to fulfil the historian's goal of getting nearer the truth.

The 'speaking ill' exercise should not be a vehicle for the release of spleen, vindictiveness or the settling of political scores. It is best if the questioner doesn't bring too much bias to his or her examination of the chosen figure because the conclusion has to be informed by the facts and balanced by reasonably objective judgement. Of course there is a place in all of this for subjective interest as well as for documented, if unpublished, scandal and, especially when dealing with historically less richly endowed eras, for reasoned hunches.

Conclusions or reservations about historical personalities must be able to stand up after the 'speaking ill' process. It is not about damaging reputations or having an unrestrained go at favourite political targets. It is about revisiting evidence and asking questions in the light of new data or employing contemporary ways of assessment to suggest that there may be more than one way of looking at a particular reputation, possibly leading to the conclusion that the person in question may not have been all they were cracked up to be in the first place.

Over the two days of the Speaking Ill of the Dead conference in March/April 2006, we were challenged and entertained and mostly left with a desire to question former uncontested beliefs. In witnessing the success and entertainment value of the process, many must have been bridling to parade their own favourite targets for reassessment with the relish and aplomb contributors such as Ruth

Foreword

Dudley Edwards and David Norris engaged with theirs. Obviously, speakers on subjects from more recent periods had an advantage over those who questioned the reputations of someone such as the late-medieval Richard FitzRalph or even the late-eighteenth-century double agent Leonard McNally. We were treated to the bad in Gladstone and the good in Balfour and were entertained by witty and probably long overdue assaults on Markievicz and the younger MacBride. The pitfall of selecting one aspect of a reputation which in broad balance would merit a more generous evaluation may be evident in the contribution about Kevin O'Higgins's attitude to women! If only the targets in question had a right of reply! With lively chairing by Michael Laffan, James Maguire and Caitriona Crowe, the conference closed with an invitation to the audience to embark on their own pet rants and this, because of its unprepared nature, allowed for sometimes over-the-top contributions – which were entertaining, if not always in the best tradition of balanced historical analysis.

Our main thanks for such a memorable conference and now for editing the contributions has to go to Myles Dungan, whose idea the whole undertaking was. Myles's work in publicising the event and in making a popular radio series of it is much appreciated, as is his selection of the Collins Barracks branch of the National Museum of Ireland at which to stage it. Thanks, too, to RTÉ and to Helen Beaumont of the Museum's Education Department and her colleagues who stewarded events for the two days. Our collective thanks to the contributors, the conference members and the RTÉ Radio 1 listeners.

A sad endnote to the conference and now to the publication of its proceedings is the passing in the interim of

Foreword

David Walter, the historian and member of the Montana Historical Society who originated the Speaking Ill of the Dead concept around 1990 and annually followed it up thereafter. Walter's own talk on Sir St George Gore was screened at the conference. Ar dheis Dé go raibh a anam uasal.

Pat Wallace
Director
National Museum of Ireland
August 2007

Preface

Mark Antony, or Shakespeare if you prefer, was unerringly accurate in his observation that 'the evil that men do lives after them'. Special pleading, unctuous memoirs, *ex post facto* diaries and the establishment of charitable foundations notwithstanding, a dubious or downright iniquitous past is rarely kept under wraps for long.

Of course, there are gradations of wickedness. The politician who employs an illegal immigrant to tend his garden is hardly on a par with the Unabomber or a genocidal despot. While some appear to be born evil, others have evil thrust upon them (quite literally in the case of that great Irish tradition, the brown envelope).

On the eve of April Fool's Day 2006, a group of polemicists convened in the National Museum intent on interring the good with the bones of a number of individuals deemed worthy of disparagement. Some of the proposed victims were famous, others merely infamous.

The brief of the ten distinguished speakers was to choose a figure from Irish history, though not necessarily Irish born, who a) had incurred their displeasure and b) was deceased. They were then asked to deliver their phillipics to a live audience for an RTÉ recording. The event was billed as Speaking Ill of the Dead.

If the over-generous praise of a biographical subject can be characterised as a variation of hagiography, then Speaking Ill of the Dead is counter-hagiography. Among the victims chosen were the likes of Edward Carson, Countess Markievicz, Sean MacBride, Arthur Balfour, Kevin O'Higgins and William Gladstone – in other words, iconic but controversial figures about whom there are many differences of opinion. In this instance the opinions being expressed were largely, though not entirely, negative. In the words of that irritating TV advertisement, Speaking Ill of the Dead did exactly what it said on the tin.

Like all good notions, the idea behind Speaking Ill of the Dead was stolen. In this case the victims of theft were the Montana Historical Society in the USA. Each year at their annual conference, for most of the last two decades, a number of less than entirely serious or worthy papers were delivered under the heading 'Speaking Ill of the Dead: Jerks in Montana History'. In most cases the subjects chosen by Montana's historians were rather more unambiguously vile than those selected by their Irish counterparts. The idea was dreamed up by a Montanan named Dave Walter, who, sadly, himself died in July 2006. We trust that he is gone to a far better place than those appalling individuals whose pasts he and others have been raking over for the edification of Montana Historical Society conference delegates.

With Dave's acquiescence and encouragement we opened the first Speaking Ill of the Dead franchise operation. We invited the originator to take part and he did so, at least in a virtual sense, providing us with a DVD introduction to the concept and one of his own papers on a highly destructive Irishman, Sir St George Gore, who is not fondly remembered in the American West. Both pieces are reproduced in this volume with the kind permission and creative assistance of his wife, Marcella.

The March/April 2006 conference was a collaborative effort involving RTÉ Radio and the National Museum. It could not have happened without the encouragement and approval of the museum's director, Patrick Wallace (whose essay on his predecessor, Adolf Mahr, kicked off the event), nor could it have taken place without the dedication, hard work, intuition and ideas of the museum's education officer, Helen Beaumont.

For RTÉ, the very notion of the conference and the radio series that followed got an instant 'yes' from Head of Radio Features, Lorelei Harris – the immediacy of the response, I am sure, had nothing to do with the fact that she was well aware that the dead cannot sue.

That the conference was a success (you'll have to take my word for it) was due to the quality of the speakers, the papers and the informed response from the audience. The latter may not have entirely agreed with some of the sentiments about members of the Irish pantheon coming from the platform, but they nobly refrained from chucking anything other than incisive and stimulating questions.

That the papers delivered over those two days have now found their way into published form is down to the willingness of Edwin Higel of New Island and Malachy Moran of RTÉ to take a chance on a reading audience being sufficiently interested in vituperation to guarantee the viability of this volume. That the publication actually happened is due to the co-operation of the conference contributors and the editing skills of Deirdre Nolan of New Island.

On a personal note, had it not been for a steer from the author Joseph O'Connor (Star of the Sea, The Secret Life of the Irish Male) while writing my book How the Irish Won the West, I might never have stumbled across the first volume of the Montana Historical Society's Speaking Ill of the Dead: Jerks in Montana History. Supporters of Gladstone, Carson et al. might have been less irked had that discovery not been made, but a good idea would have been left unconscripted. So Joe must shoulder a small degree of blame for this egregious act of intellectual piracy and the resulting manifestations of disrespect and disdain.

Let the contumely commence.

Myles Dungan, 2007

For the late Dave Walter, distinguished Montanan,
without whom...!

DAVE WALTER

Jerks in Montana History: Speaking Ill of the Dead,
an Introduction

This idea of looking at the 'jerks' in Montana history originated in 1989 during Montana's statehood centennial. Since then, it has become a popular session at the annual Montana History Conference, a book released by Falcon Publishing in 2000, a second book issued in 2005 by Globe Pequot Press and the basis for various talks available from the Montana Committee for the Humanities Speakers' Bureau.

When we began, there were no rules to define who qualified as a 'jerk' so people immediately nominated their spouses, everyone nominated his boss and parents proposed that their kids be considered for the title. Thus we had to institute one rule (and it remains the only criterion for the 'jerks' designation): the nominee must be dead. This restriction also has proved helpful in fighting the inevitable slander and libel suits that have developed.

In 1989, I was sitting on the reference desk in the Montana Historical Society Library. This sounds like a boring job but it was really the best position in the outfit. I fielded all the Montana history questions that came in to the society – whether by mail or by phone or from walk-in traffic or from the staff. I could go home at the end of the day having learned two or three things that I hadn't known when I'd got there in the morning. And there just aren't many good jobs like that around.

As we moved into 1989, it quickly became obvious that Montana's statehood centennial had prompted a good deal of curiosity among out-of-state researchers interested in their Montana ancestors. The calls and letters went something like this: 'Dear Sir, my great-grandfather came to Montana in the 1890s and I think he was the governor.' Or: 'Uncle Fred and Aunt Maude arrived in Butte in 1903. The family thinks he was a "copper king" and maybe a US Senator too.' Apparently no one's ancestor ever had been a clerk in a store, a sheepherder, a homestead wife or – God forbid – a criminal.

The conclusion that one draws is pretty obvious: when looking at our past, we tend to focus on what are the greatest, what are the best and what are the most wonderful things.

The trouble with this approach to history is that it is one-sided, it sanitises our history and, perhaps to me the greatest sin, it takes the humour out of our history. It portrays a past that never was. The real past included real people, like us, people who were a mixture of good and bad. Montana has been the home of some reprehensible characters who were involved in some abhorrent activities and they deserve equal time! Let me give you some examples.

Toussaint Charbonneau was the French trapper/trader who joined the Lewis and Clark Expedition at the Mandan villages, after shamelessly promoting himself as an all-purpose outdoorsman and a highly skilled interpreter. The captains hired him because his young wife, Sacagawea, was a Shoshone. Charbonneau distinguished himself by offering the services of his wives for a bit of cash (it would appear that Charbonneau had at least five wives – this was not that unusual for a professional Mountain Man), swamping one of the pirogues, thereby losing valuable supplies, and abandoning George Drouillard in the face of a grizzly attack. He fed Sacagawea unidentified raw white apples, making her very ill, and he struck her – for which he was reprimanded by Captain Clark. Lewis summarised Charbonneau by noting that he was 'a man of no particular merit'. Why be so obtuse? Toussaint Charbonneau was a wife-beating jerk!

Or we can consider the Reverend Leonard Christler. Reverend Christler was an Episcopalian minister from Havre in the late 1910s and early 1920s. He was responsible for building several of the Episcopal churches along Montana's Hi-Line. He was a dynamic speaker who filled the church, primarily with female parishioners. He was such a remarkable speaker that he joined a Chautauqua company working out of the Midwest. (Chautauqua was a travelling show that brought quality drama, music and oration to small towns; it was called 'culture under canvas'.) After the second summer on the Chautauqua circuit, Reverend Christler returned to Havre with a songstress whom he had met on the road. He deposited her in the spare bedroom in the rectory.

Mrs Reverend Leonard Christler accepted the arrangement for two whole days before she shot them both dead in the parlour ... and never was charged with anything. Evidently that is acceptable behavior in Havre. The Reverend Leonard Christler is a jerk!

So was Ike Gravelle, Montana's first Unabomber. In 1903, Ike held Montana hostage in an attempt to extort $25,000 from the Northern Pacific Railroad. He blew up Northern Pacific bridges and tunnels and mainline track – freezing passenger traffic during the summer of 1903. Ike was finally caught through his lack of education. He began to write his own extortion notes and his spelling errors gave him away. He died by his own hand in the basement of the Montana governor's mansion in Helena, surrounded by a posse. Ike Gravelle is a jerk!

I consider the Carlin hunting party a party of jerks. It included three eastern hunters who, in October 1893, came into the Lochsa Valley right over the hill from Missoula, Montana. They took with them an outfitter/guide and a camptender/cook – a man by the name of George Colgate. They headed in to hunt late in the season. Winter – in the form of snow on the Lolo Trail and rain down in the canyon – came early. Colgate became ill. He'd forgotten to bring his catheters with him and began to fill up with fluids. The outfitter pleaded with the eastern hunters to put Colgate on a horse and get him out. But the eastern hunters said, 'Oh, the elk hunting is so good here. Let's just stay a few more days.' And days turned into weeks. Finally they got Colgate – now immobile – up on a horse. They climbed the three thousand feet onto the Lolo Trail only to discover eight feet of snow. They could not get Colgate out. So they dropped back into the valley, released the horses and spent two weeks building two rafts to float out the Lochsa River. You may remember that the Lochsa River is a river of boulders.

Once the crew got into the water with a delirious Colgate, they made it only about ten miles before the rafts broke up on the rocks. The intrepid hunters went into council and

decided to prop Colgate up against a tree – still alive – and
hike out to save their own lives. I offer a group nomination
for the Carlin hunting party.

You may have noticed that there are not many women on
this list. Now some Montana women claim that's a correct
portrayal of the ratio of jerky women to jerky men. That's
not so. There are just as many jerky women but they suffer
from what women in general suffer from: they just haven't
been as well documented.

But I can tell you about Mary Gleim – a five-foot tall, 270-
pound Missoula madam who ran the Front Street red-light
district from the 1890s to 1914. Mary had three of the best
attorneys in Missoula on retainer because she was constantly in court battling city government and defending herself in aggravated assault cases. Mary's solution to any
personal confrontation was to pummel her opponent with
her fists. In one case, this involved two Jesuit priests from
whom she tried to tear their robes, saying that they did not
deserve to wear them.

I offer Montana's Ku Klux Klan, active in Montana from
1923 until 1931, in a group nomination. In 1924, Montana
hosted more than fifty Klan chapters, comprising more
than five thousand dues-paying members. They gave the
state what you would expect from the Klan: extreme secrecy, hoods, torchlight parades, lots of cross burnings designed to intimidate. In at least one instance, the Montana
KKK was involved in the killing of a black man at Crow
Agency.

Consider, too, Vera Prosser. She was an attractive Seattle
woman in her mid-twenties who had recently divorced her
husband of five years. In June 1910, her ex-husband set out

for Ohio by train with two male companions. Vera followed, in a move that today we would call 'stalking'. The Great Northern train left Spokane, headed east through northern Idaho and north-western Montana. Vera found a way to be alone with her ex-husband in his train compartment.

While we don't know exactly what happened next, we do know that Vera shot her former husband in the head with a small calibre revolver. Train noise muffled the shot. Vera then stripped him of all his clothes and stuffed them out the window of the moving train. Vera got off the train in Libby, Montana. Her husband's friends found the body and wired back to Libby to arrest Vera.

Vera was then held in Libby, which was the county seat for the brand new county of Lincoln. In 1910, there were no facilities for women in the county jail. So Vera was confined to a suite in the Libby Hotel at taxpayer expense. She ate three meals a day in the hotel dining room, again at taxpayer expense. Three times a day, county deputies walked with her up and down the business district, affording her exercise. Vera was young, attractive and personable and she built a following in the community. She was elected mascot of the town's baseball team and cheered the fellows in town and out of town – being allowed to go to Columbia Falls and Missoula.

Vera's trial finally got underway in August 1910. Women did not sit on juries in Montana at that time, so a jury of twelve middle-aged ranchers, miners and loggers – each of whom was deeply in love with Vera – heard the testimony. The trial lasted for six days; the jury was out for six minutes. Vera was found 'not guilty'. She got right back on the Great Northern Railroad and returned to Seattle.

Finally, we need to consider Jacob Thorkelson. Thorkelson was a physician in the 1920s and 1930s. He attempted to start a nudist colony on the flats south of Butte, which, at five thousand feet elevation, was not a successful business venture. Politically, Thorkelson was extremely conservative and, through several misadventures, was elected to the US House of Representatives from Montana in 1938. So on the eve of World War II, what Montana had representing its people in Washington was a Nazi sympathiser. He is the only person in the history of the US House, that I can locate, whose colleagues restricted him from placing his comments in the Congressional Record. And if you know the Record, you know that a congressman can get anything in it: laudatory editorials, letters from his mother, even recipes. 'Thorky' could add nothing.

In 1940, Thorkelson was replaced by Jeannette Rankin – the only person in Congress to vote against US entry into World War II. At that point, Thorkelson received an invitation for an audience with Hitler. Thorkelson and his friends provide just a sampling of Montana's 'jerks'. There is an endless supply.

These examples of 'jerks in Montana history' remind us that history is not an exact science; it is not chemistry; it is not biology; it is not even geology. For most of the public, the best of Montana history remains much closer to the oral tradition – to the art of researched storytelling – than we might want to admit. Without a doubt, this approach to Montana history has its detractors, people who feel that it is disrespectful, that it panders to our basest instinct. My wife is among this group! I counter only that if by looking at some Montana 'jerks' we become more interested in our Montana past, that is justification enough for me.

Of course, this is all in fun – because what we are doing here is using standards from our lives to judge past behaviour. And that constitutes an absolute travesty among historians. Historians maintain that we should strive to judge people in the context of their own time and their own situations. When you enroll in graduate school in history at the University of Montana or Montana State University – on that very first day – you swear that you will never judge past people and events by today's standards. It is your first day and you're scared to death, so you agree. But then, as soon as you settle on a thesis topic, you throw that promise over your shoulder and do what we all do: you judge past events by present criteria.

In 1968, Bobby Kennedy was campaigning in a housing project on the south side of Chicago. Here he was introduced to a ten-year-old girl who was all dressed up to meet him. She had on new black patent leather shoes and a brand-new bright print dress. Her hair was in pigtails and her pigtails were in ribbons. Kennedy posed a question to her that he had used in similar situations during the campaign. He said, 'If all the good things in the world were the color white, and all the bad things in the world were the color black, what would you be?' And without a moment's hesitation, the little girl looked Kennedy right in the eye and she said, 'I'd be striped.'

That's what looking at Montana's 'jerks' is: a survey of some striped people from Montana's past – some Montana history zebras. I urge you to keep an eye out for 'jerks' in your future research. And I urge you, when you encounter them, to embrace them with gusto! 'Jerks' are an important part of our past and they deserve equal time! Thank you.

Note

From 1989, until his death in 2006, Dave wrote and rewrote the introduction to his 'jerks' articles and presentations. He adapted it to fit time available, the host community, his changing sense of audience appeal and — always — new information he'd located about new or already-identified jerks. This introduction is drawn as verbatim as I could muster from Dave's 2006 speech notes. The notes, complete with color-coding and underlining, are hard to duplicate in print. Still, this introduction may communicate the informality and humour Dave employed in his public presentations. To get a sense of how much fun Dave had with this presentation, you need only know that I was the wife standing often at the back of the room — where my job was to look flustered when Dave told the audience I didn't approve.

Marcella S. Walter

PROFESSOR TOM BARTLETT

The Life and Opinions of Leonard MacNally
(1752–1820), Playwright, Barrister, United Irishman
and Informer[1]

U ntil his death in 1820, Leonard MacNally was known
and respected in Dublin as a successful playwright,
whose plays had been performed at Covent Garden
and Drury Lane, as a prominent barrister, whose clients
had included the Sheares brothers and Robert Emmet, and
as an early and leading member of the Society of United
Irishman, which had advocated radical reform in Ireland in
the 1790s and had gone on to promote an ill-fated insurrection in 1798. MacNally's credentials as a patriot up to the
time of his death seemed not only incontestable, but also
impeccable. In 1799, he had taken a stand, along with other
members of the Irish legal profession, against the proposed
Act of Union and he spoke out against it on occasion after
1800. A Protestant, he had been a prominent supporter of
the movement for Catholic Emancipation. In 1811, he had
acted for members of the Catholic Board when they were
arrested under the terms of the Convention Act, and he
numbered Daniel O'Connell and John Philpot Curran
among his friends. A year before he died, he had met John
Devereux, himself a former United Irishman but now recruiting for Simon Bolivar's liberation army in South America, and he had presented him with a powerful talisman,

nothing less than Lord Edward FitzGerald's United Irish badge. Soon after, MacNally passed away in the 'odour of sanctity', hailed in nationalist circles as 'MacNally the incorruptible'.

Shortly after his death, it emerged that MacNally had been for many years in receipt of a secret service pension of £300 bestowed on him as payment for information supplied by him about his friends, colleagues and clients. Sensationally, the man who had been acclaimed by Curran for his 'uncompromising and romantic fidelity' over many years to Ireland turned out to have been Dublin Castle's most important paid informer for over two decades. By interrogating MacNally's letters to Dublin Castle over the period 1795 to 1819, can we assess what damage he did to the patriot cause? Equally, can we discover what lay behind his betrayal?

Details are sketchy about MacNally's early life. He was born in Dublin in 1752 of Catholic stock. His father was a grocer. MacNally appears to have converted to the Established Church in the 1760s.2 He was entirely self-educated and in 1774 he entered the Middle Temple in London to study law.3 In 1776, he was called to the Irish Bar, where he practised for a time, but money proved elusive and he returned to London, where he earned his living by journalism and writing for the stage.

In the late 1770s MacNally wrote a series of forgettable comedies, but in May 1782 he scored his first clear theatrical success. His *Retaliation; or the Citizen a Soldier*, a frivolous tale of intrigue, was performed in the Theatre Royal, Covent Garden, and was regularly listed over the following years. A year later, his *Tristram Shandy: A Sentimental, Shandean Bagatelle ... by the author of Retaliation* was produced at the

11

Theatre Royal and, even though the critics were unenthusiastic, the public liked it and it went on to receive regular productions over the next few years.[4] MacNally followed up this success with his most popular theatrical work, *Robin Hood: or Sherwood Forest, a Comic Opera*, which was first performed at Covent Garden in April 1784. It attracted large audiences, on three occasions taking in more than £200.

However, forsaking his career as a playwright, MacNally returned to Dublin around 1790, where he began to practise once again at the Irish Bar. He also threw himself into radical politics, signalling his arrival on the scene by writing *An Address to the Whig Club*, in which he called for an end to corruption, denounced 'the purchased dependants of the British minister' and urged the newspaper press to 'drag [venal politicians] before the people'.[5] With sentiments such as these, it is not surprising that he found the mildly reformist stance of the Dublin Whig Club uncongenial and that he should gravitate immediately towards the more radical Society of United Irishmen when it was founded in Dublin in November 1791.

MacNally proved an extremely active member of the society, being first noticed by Thomas Collins, a member of the United Irishmen *and* a Dublin Castle spy, in December 1791.[6] From then on, Collins recorded him as attending regularly, speaking frequently and often proposing new members. In June 1792 he was appointed one of a committee (along with William Drennan and Theobald Wolfe Tone) charged with drawing up a congratulatory address to James Napper Tandy on his recent acquittal.[7]

In April 1793, MacNally showed his commitment to the United Irishmen by fighting a duel with a fellow barrister, Jonah Barrington, who had spoken disparagingly of the society's members.[8] (MacNally lost a thumb in this encounter.) Again, MacNally was one of the select group who drew up the United Irish proposals for parliamentary reform. He was also present at the final open meeting of the Society of United Irishmen on 23 May 1794. On that date, Dublin Castle, on foot of information received concerning negotiations between a French agent, the Revd William Jackson and members of the United Irishmen, issued an order supressing the society.

With the outbreak of war between Britain (and Ireland) and revolutionary France in February 1793, Ireland had once again become an object of French military attention. Early in 1794, Jackson had come to Dublin on behalf of the French revolutionary government to investigate the likely reaction in Ireland to the arrival of a French force. Unfortunately for him, from an early date he had been placed under British government surveillance. In particular, he had been accompanied to Ireland by John Cockayne, a London solicitor who was employed as an informer by William Pitt, the prime minister.[9] It appears that both Cockayne and Jackson had known MacNally in London and they made him their first port of call in Dublin. MacNally offered them dinner and facilitated contacts with known radicals including Archibald Hamilton Rowan (then in Newgate Prison) and Theobald Wolfe Tone.[10] When the British government and Dublin Castle had intercepted sufficient incriminating material concerning Jackson, he was seized and put on trial, charged with high treason. Those who had been in contact with him were closely questioned. Rowan acknowledged his guilt by escaping from gaol and fleeing the country. Tone, too, conceded the strength of the case against him by undertaking to go into permanent exile in order to avoid prosecution. MacNally was almost certainly interrogated but, curiously, there was no immediate threat of legal action against him. It was, it seems, some time after the arrest of Jackson in late April 1794 that MacNally embarked on his career as a government informer.

The timing of MacNally's decision to turn informer appears to point to at least one of his motives: self-preservation. MacNally had been gravely compromised by his association with Jackson and there was a chance that he would be taken into custody. Even if he were not charged and put on trial, for a rising barrister to be so closely identified with the 'revolutionary party' in Ireland would inevitably mean that, whatever the outcome, his professional career would be damaged, perhaps irreparably. Did MacNally turn informer in order to head off a crippling prosecution?

It certainly seems probable that MacNally, confronted by evidence of his complicity with Jackson, was induced to turn informer; and it seems likely that it was John Pollock, clerk of the crown on the Leinster circuit (and attorney to the Marquess of Downshire), who 'turned' him and arranged payment for him.

In any discussion of the motivation of an informer, it is inevitable that the question of financial reward will be raised. And there is no doubt that MacNally was persistent (some might say insatiable) in his demands for money. In September 1795, he tactfully reminded his handler of 'a private subject respecting myself' and requested prompt action. By July 1796, he had abandoned delicacy and was even prepared to allow money to be sent directly to his home in Dominick Street. However, a few months later, he complained that he was 'totally exhausted in cash' and petulantly declared 'this is not the way others are treated'.[11] Still aggrieved in May 1797, he then issued an ultimatum: 'I cannot proceed unless what I wrote about is complied with.' By January 1798, he had grown both desperate and piteous in his demands: 'I am in deep distress for want of money … neglect to me is cruelty.'[12] In the event, it was not until June 1801 that MacNally was awarded a secret pension of £300 per annum;[13] until then he had to be content with amounts of between £50 and £300 doled out periodically through Pollock's agency.[14]

Such sums can scarcely be regarded as extravagant and financial inducement can hardly have been the sole motive for MacNally's betrayals, for if money had been his God then he ought to have abandoned radical politics, because his association with the United Irishmen was gravely damaging to his legal career. Such a withdrawal was feasible: William Drennan, one of the founders of the United Irishmen, had backed away from the society after 1795 and, after a lean period, pursued a successful career as an *accoucheur* or lying-in doctor; Peter Burrowes, a lawyer and friend of Tone's, forsook his flirtation with radical politics and made a successful legal career;[15] and John Keogh, the Catholic activist, also distanced himself from his former friends after 1795.[16]

Perhaps MacNally could not in fact escape: once bought, he had no option but to stay bought? Yet there is no indication in any of the 160 or so extant letters from MacNally over the period 1795 to 1815 that he regretted his clandestine activities or that he sought a way out: on the contrary, as the years passed, he evidently warmed to his role as informer. In addition, as, ostensibly, an open and avowed supporter of the United Irishmen, MacNally ran no small risk from the depredations of crown forces in the period of the rebellion. It might be argued that 'MacNally lost much more by his politics than he ever gained from the government … had his politics from the beginning been of a different type his professional talents would probably have raised him to the bench.' MacNally's persistent demands for payment from the Castle have to be viewed in this light. He was a talented – if overly dramatic – barrister and he was a legal scholar with, by the early 1800s, several notable publications to his name. He could legitimately have expected to make his career and his fortune at the Irish Bar: instead he ended up, as William Drennan sniffed, 'a sort of Newgate solicitor much looked down upon by the Bar … a notorious United I[rishman].'[17] MacNally gave up career expectations and he forfeited much peace of mind in return for an annual stipend so meagre that, when it ceased on his death, its absence plunged his family and dependants (eight in all) into penury. What *was* his motivation?

It is possible that principle played some part in MacNally's desertion of the United Irishmen. There is no sign that he ever harboured revolutionary or separatist notions and another informer noted his unease in 1793 at the increasingly subversive tone of discussions among the United Irishmen; for MacNally, the Jackson mission may have proved the last straw.[18] Moreover, MacNally's confidential position with the Castle gave him the opportunity to voice, with impunity, trenchant criticisms of the government's security policy and of the army's activities. There was no dissembling in MacNally's letters and to that extent he retained his earlier radicalism. He pointed out the folly of treating suspects in a cruel manner. He condemned the ghoulish practice of displaying rebel heads on spikes. And he was wholly opposed to the judiciary's policy of exemplary justice. Secure in the belief that he had the ear of the chief secretary and lord lieutenant, MacNally no doubt flattered himself that his strictures on the forces of law and order were being duly noted and even acted upon. In his own lights, he was acting as a patriot: perhaps he justified to himself his betrayals in this way. Perhaps he believed that if he could help prevent an insurrection then he would have done no small service to his country. But there was, inevitably, a very dark side to MacNally's treachery, one which cannot be overlooked in any discussion of his possible principles.

In his brilliant study of the sixteenth-century secret agent Giordano Bruno, John Bossy remarks that the act of informing, 'contrary to an impression which has been put around … always involves betraying your friends or people you have caused to believe your friends'.[19] MacNally's basest betrayals involved those of his clients who knew him and trusted him and who were at their most vulnerable: men charged with high treason, on trial for their lives. He betrayed the secrets and defence strategies of William Jackson, Henry and John Sheares, Robert Emmet – who all paid with their lives – and many others now mostly forgotten. He handed over to the Castle Jackson's last letters to his wife and he held back Emmet's to his brother. He alerted the prosecution at the Maidstone treason trials in early 1798 to the thrust of the Irish defence witnesses' testimony.[20] A few months later, he urged the Sheares brothers to stand trial together, even though the guilt of one would surely seal the fate of the other. Again, when the veracity of the principal prosecution witness against the brothers, Captain J.W. Armstrong, was called into question by his former commanding officer – 'I would not pay much attention to what he did say nor give much credit even to his oath' – MacNally withheld this potentially embarrassing letter from the defence counsel, i.e. himself.[21] Even in relatively minor cases, MacNally appears to have routinely disclosed the defence strategy to the prosecution and he certainly reported his conversations with his clients. All in all, it is difficult to square such treachery and betrayal with any recognised definition of principle.

Could it be that it was the element of risk that attracted MacNally to informing and led him to persist in it? He was, after all, a notorious duellist who had lost a thumb in one encounter and who walked with a pronounced limp after another. No stranger to danger, he may have relished the perilous situations in which he inevitably found himself. As an avowed United Irishman, he was always liable to arrest and worse in the late 1790s, but there was always the possibility of discovery by his supposed colleagues – his hitherto unsuspecting United Irish friends. MacNally well knew that the offices of Dublin Castle were famously insecure – he once claimed that the United Irishmen had penetrated the Irish Post Office – and he therefore understood that the chance of being unmasked as an informer was always high.[22] Was this part of the thrill?

This is not to suggest that MacNally was reckless in his behaviour, deliberately courting danger. On the contrary, he took every precaution to shield his identity and protect his activities. He burned all communications from the Castle[23] and he rarely used a courier. He adopted the initials 'JW' as his signature, almost never employed any kind of salutation, sometimes disguised his handwriting[24] and always referred to himself as 'my friend', 'our friend' or simply MacNally. It would have been difficult to deduce that MacNally was himself the author of those letters which were delivered to Dublin Castle from 1795 on. And, of course, the very fact that he operated entirely undetected for nearly twenty-five years shows that whatever secret excitement he derived from his dangerous work must have been restrained by cold calculation and tempered by the need for self-preservation.[25]

Lastly, in terms of motivation, in the light of what we know of MacNally's later career as a paid informer, does a scrutiny of his creative writing during the 1780s offer any hint of what was to come or hold any clue as to his motivation for his subsequent betrayal of his associates and clients? In his brief discussion of MacNally, W.E.H. Lecky concluded that he was 'a strangely composite character' in whom were combined 'singularity and melancholy'.[26] The literary or theatrical tone to Lecky's description is apt, for MacNally can be read as a character in a novel or as an actor in a play as well as a figure on the historical stage. On several occasions, he referred to 'the character I assume' and 'the part I have taken', and it was vital for him to play his public role as agitator to perfection.[27] He would have been delighted at the way he was frequently denounced to Dublin Castle, for it offered proof that he was staying in character. The shock and disbelief that greeted the disclosure of his long-standing private deception can only be understood by reference to the complete success of MacNally's long-running public performance.

It is, however, MacNally's secret role over the years that concerns us: was this prefigured in his theatrical or prose writings? Given that so many of MacNally's popular works for the theatre – *Robin Hood*, *Retaliation* and *Fashionable Levities* – all involve some measure of deception, deceit and disguise, it is tempting to see in them ominous signposts to his future career in subterfuge. A recurrent theme in his plays is that no-one-is-who-or-what-they-seem-to-be. And yet, the temptation to read MacNally's plays (with one exception) as indicators of his future duplicitous role ought to be resisted: so very many plays at that time (and since) have hinged on disguise or deception that no conclusions can be drawn. The possible exception to this statement is MacNally's *Tristram Shandy: A Sentimental, Shandean Bagatelle*, a work which, with his prose work *Sentimental Excursions to Windsor and other places*, is possibly worth further consideration.

Leonard MacNally was much taken with Laurence Sterne's novel, or anti-novel, *Tristram Shandy* and by Sterne's other prose writings. He adapted *Tristram Shandy* for the London stage and he published a parody on Sterne's *Sentimental Journey* (1768). Just as Sterne was consciously subversive of all literary conventions, perhaps MacNally relished flouting other codes of conduct by informing on his companions and clients? To do so by writing would surely have added to the enjoyment. After one interminable digression in *Tristram Shandy*, the narrator confesses: 'But this is neither here nor there – why do I mention it? – Ask my pen – it governs me – I govern not it.'[28] MacNally, ever prolix, might have agreed.

In his note recommending MacNally for a pension of £300 per annum, Edward Cooke commented that he was 'not much trusted but I believe [he] has been useful'.[29] Too much should not be made of Cooke's apparent faint praise for MacNally's services: 'useful' carried a much higher approval rating in the eighteenth century than it does today.

MacNally's clandestine services to government lay in a variety of areas. We have already noted his practice of divulging the defences of his clients to the prosecution and his propensity for lengthy depictions of the public mood in the late 1790s has also been cited: little more needs to be said on these points.

MacNally had excellent contacts with some of the leading Catholic activists and through them he could keep the Castle informed on their thinking and plans. His earliest letters date from February–March 1795, a time when Catholic hopes of full emancipation had been dashed by the abrupt recall of the lord lieutenant, Earl Fitzwilliam. Dublin Castle and London were most anxious to learn how Irish Catholics would react to this crushing setback and Mac-Nally duly obliged. He reported how the members of the Catholic Committee had put together a delegation to plead their case before George III in London; how this delegation had returned from England 'discontented, disappointed and disgusted'; and how Henry Grattan had assured the Catholics that, notwithstanding this reversal, he would bring forward a Catholic Bill when the Irish Parliament reconvened.[30] MacNally's letters on this topic ended up, after several copyings, in William Pitt's post-bag, an indication, surely, of the value attached to them. Again, some years later, MacNally described in detail the reaction of Catholic lay leaders to the proposed union with Great Britain. After the union, too, he supplied the Castle with intelligence on the Catholic question: at least two chief secretaries, Sir Arthur Wellesley in 1807 and William Wellesley Pole in 1811, received communications from JW on this perennial issue.[31]

It was, however, MacNally's constant information on the plans and activities of the United Irishmen which most impressed Dublin Castle (and which today elicits a whistle of appreciation from historians). On the face of it, JW was ideally placed to supply vital intelligence. As a senior member of the United Irishmen – though never one involved in military activity – he was in constant contact with leading figures within the revolutionary movement and he was privy to some of their secrets. Moving easily within their social circle, MacNally was in a position to report on the absences (or arrivals) of key players, on journeys which they had undertaken, on the gossip which inevitably was circulating among them and on their personal rivalries. Dublin Castle presumably found such 'low-grade' information valuable in attempting to build a picture of the nature and extent of the threat that confronted it.

Crucially in the eyes of Dublin Castle, MacNally was on intimate terms with James Tandy, son of James Napper Tandy. Tandy *fils* was no revolutionary but his father, a long-time radical, was very active in the conspiracy, having fled Ireland in 1795. Throughout this period, and for some years after the rebellion, Napper Tandy kept in touch with his son who, for his part, saw no harm in showing his father's letters to another long-time radical and James's own confidential friend, Leonard MacNally, who in his turn passed on their contents to Dubin Castle. On the face of it, then, it would appear that MacNally played a major role in the Castle's 'secret war', particularly in the years before the rebellion. Camden and Cooke in Dublin, and Pelham and Portland in London, all accepted him as an 'authority' on the United Irish conspirators and their letters have numerous references to information provided by MacNally, a.k.a. 'JW' or 'my friend' or 'our friend'.[32]

And yet, can we accept without question their estimation of his worth? MacNally's prime sources – the letters of Napper Tandy – are undoubtedly interesting, but their author was emphatically not the leading conspirator that the Castle believed him to be. By the mid-1790s, after his flight from Ireland, his star had waned considerably. He was poorly informed on French intentions and lacking any detailed knowledge of affairs in Ireland; Tandy succeeded only in sowing confusion and spreading disinformation among the United Irishmen – and in misleading Dublin Castle. Napper Tandy was, in short, impossible. Eventually, after the rebellion, even Dublin Castle came to see that he was not the threat they had once imagined.

Furthermore, it should be noted that while Tandy's highly suspect information (transmitted via MacNally) was eagerly accepted by Dublin Castle, significant intelligence also provided by MacNally was sometimes ignored. For example, from an early date MacNally was aware of the abilities and determination of Theobald Wolfe Tone and in September 1795 he claimed that he would not be surprised to hear of his being shortly at Paris.[33]

Again, it was MacNally who broke the news to the Castle that Tone had, in fact, been in Paris for some time and that he had played a key role in organising the French invasion of Ireland and that his early memoranda on Ireland constituted 'the ground work of all subsequent negotiations' between the French and the United Irishmen.[34] MacNally also revealed that Tone had been 'actually on board one of the ships on that expedition [to Bantry Bay]'.[35] Notwithstanding such reports, no particular attention was paid to Tone: Dublin Castle remained firm in its belief that Napper Tandy was central to the conspiracy and that Tone was not. As a result, the Castle seriously underestimated Tone's role in the revolutionary decade.

Lastly, in measuring MacNally's real contribution to the intelligence wars of the 1790s, we should note that, contrary to received wisdom, the Directory of the United Irishmen did, in fact, manage to keep its plans quite confidential. MacNally was not a member of that inner circle of United

Irishmen charged with organising a military structure and preparing for a French expedition, and his attempts to penetrate this group, by and large, came to nothing. He frequently admitted that he came up against a 'secrecy almost inpenetrable' in his quest for information. A more modest assessment of MacNally's contribution to the 'secret' war of the 1790s, and perhaps of the effects of his treachery, would therefore appear to be in order.

MacNally died on 13 February 1820. As the informer JW, he had once unblushingly declared that it was 'very probable' that the famously anti-revolutionary Catholic archbishop of Dublin, John Thomas Troy, was 'up' – i.e. a sworn and secret United Irishman; he had claimed several times that the local Dominican priests, his neighbours in Dominic Street, were the principal agents for disseminating sedition and disaffection; he had revealed the plans of Catholic activists for more than twenty years; and he had been a professed Protestant all his life: but on his deathbed, MacNally sent for a Catholic priest. A final betrayal?

PROFESSOR PAUL BEW

William Ewart Gladstone

William Ewart Gladstone (1809–98) is the heroic figure of English liberalism. In particular, with respect to the Irish question, he is believed to have overcome British and Protestant prejudice by his advocacy of a home rule solution. Gladstone, many believe, advocated a peaceful compromise which would have worked if it had been applied, as he wanted, in 1886. More than that, the Tory refusal to countenance his scheme led to violence, Irish separation from the United Kingdom and a further epoch of discord in Anglo-Irish relations. J.L. Hammond concluded his *Gladstone and the Irish Nation* with the words: 'If the view taken in these pages has any truth in it, Gladstone was at once a great politician and a great prophet, a great Englishman and a great European, a great Minister of State and a great Minister of Justice.'[1]

In the 1970s, there was a decided historiographical reaction against this pious tone. In his Raleigh lecture 'Gladstone and Ireland' at the British Academy in 1977, John Vincent noted acidly: 'When all is said and weighed, it comes to no great sum.'[2] However, following the publication of Colin Mathew's superb edition of the Gladstone diaries – in particular the material covering the period 1881–86 – in 1990, the pendulum has swung back in Gladstone's favour. It is again increasingly commonplace to assert that Gladstone's policies embodied a morally serious attempt at 'historic compromise', which, if not rejected by lesser men, would have averted much violence by opening up a better era in Anglo-Irish relations.

Naturally, Gladstone has long been admired by Irish nationalists, in particular as the first British prime minister to see the essential justice of the Irish nationalist cause – even to the point of splitting his own Liberal Party on the issue and ushering in twenty years of Tory electoral hegemony. Gladstone's conversion to home rule was the first of a long historic engagement with Ireland, an engagement carefully recommended by many nationalists. The Irish MP J.G. Swift MacNeill records:

> I remember that one occasion, during a division in a crowded lobby on a frivolous amendment in committee to the Home Rule Bill of 1893, Mr Gladstone sat down to write a hurried note at a table at which several persons, including myself, were writing. He said: 'This kind of thing would have broken Daniel O'Connell's heart.' The observation was addressed to no one in particular, and no one ventured to reply. Then Mr Gladstone repeated the remark to me, addressing me by name. 'No, Sir,' I replied, 'O'Connell would have been a proud and happy man if he were here with you and the Liberal Party, working for the restoration of the Irish parliament.'[3]

But what was Gladstone's real relationship with O'Connell? Gladstone, then a young, rather priggish high-Tory, first spent a day with Daniel O'Connell on 10 July 1834, when they both sat on the parliamentary select committee on political corruption. O'Connell seems to have made a deep but hardly favourable impression. Certainly, Gladstone was available to support any Orange partisan attack on O'Connell's world and belief system.[4] In June 1835, Gladstone attended at Exeter Hall to hear the Belfast Protestant firebrand preacher the Rev. Henry Cooke denounce the Catholic theology being taught at Maynooth. In 1835 also, Gladstone denounced the policy of the Whigs with reference to the Church of Ireland (an attempt to transfer the payment of Irish tithes from the tenant to the landlord and to appropriate an element of tithes for educational purposes) and expressed his belief that 'if it should be removed that they would not long be able to resist the Repeal of the Union'.[5] Gladstone, throughout the 1830s, maintained these Tory Protestant views. He defended the Anglican establishment in his book *The State in Its Relations with the Church*; and although by 1845 his views had softened, he felt it necessary to resign over the Maynooth grant of 1845. In 1872, Lord Lyveden wrote to Gladstone that, in his political youth, he had been a stout Orange Tory: Gladstone replied that he did not recognise that description. It is always an important moment in a political career when one's reinvention is so complete that one's youthful indiscretions cease to be embarrassing and become instead invisible.

How did Gladstone see the famine of 1846–50, in which a million Irish died? He certainly did not see it as reflecting badly on the Irish Protestant clergy, accused by others of mercenary opportunism. In 1847–8, Gladstone claimed that the 'Irish Protestant clergy came to the Roman Catholic poor in their time of famine like ministering angels of light; and that their own bounty … out of their own strengthened resources was most liberal'.[6] In 1877, Gladstone discussed the famine – 'painful and mournful to the highest degree' – with a Dublin audience. It was, he said, by a severe 'dispensation of providence' in the 1840s that 'instead of eight millions of a population you now have less than five and a half millions'. Furthermore, in Gladstone's view, 'the sufferings have been suffered – the ties have been snapped – the ocean has been crossed'.[7] The important thing now, he stressed, was to concentrate on the improvement of Irish prosperity within the United Kingdom. The famine then, for Gladstone, was a painful chapter but a closed one – hardly the view, for example, of Irish America.

In 1853, Gladstone, as chancellor of the exchequer, significantly increased the tax burden of Ireland. His tone was light: 'He could not see that it was a part of the rights of man that the Irishman should be able to make himself drunk more cheaply than the inhabitant of Great Britain.'[8] It later became a conventional wisdom for many British liberals and conservatives that Gladstone's 1853 budget, given that Ireland was only just recovering from the famine, was a disaster.

In 1867, the Fenian rising took place in Ireland – proof of the existence of a genuine mass movement of disaffected nationalists in the country. Gladstone's response was a supple one: he tended to support early release of Fenian prisoners. Above all, he insisted on the need for Irish Church reform and Irish land reform. Gladstone had voted against Irish Church disestablishment in 1856; but in 1867, he now claimed that the Irish Church represented an injustice of which he had long been aware. Even his daughter Mary felt that there was inconsistency here and later reproached her father on the point. His reply was instructive: 'He said that was quite different. Irish Church rotten, but nobody thought about it, dearth of political energy before Palmerston's death, if Palmerston had lived, Irish Church might not have been disestablished for years'.[9] It was, of course, the perfect issue to bind liberals together[10] following the tactical defeats on electoral reform inflicted on them by Disraeli in 1866–7. As was often the case with Gladstone, self-proclaimed, long-term intellectual convictions turned out to be strikingly compatible with short-term tactical advantage. While Disraeli was still in office, Gladstone pushed motions on disestablishment through the Commons in 1868. Gladstone's opponents stressed the dangerous nature of this radicalism and tried to insist that the issue was not a mere Irish clerical issue. Lord Redesdale declared:

> It is the Church of a minority. Granted, but are the endowments which have belonged to it for centuries, to be disregarded because they belong to minorities? The land of the United Kingdom belongs to a minority smaller in proportion than that of the Churchmen of Ireland. Houses belong to a minority. All property belongs to a minority. The argument, if insisted on as sound, is destructive to the rights of property.[11]

Regardless, Gladstone built up a coalition of liberal Anglicans, Catholics and British nonconformists which swept all before it (outside Orange Lancashire) in the general election. As Thomas MacKnight pointed out: 'The country had been appealed to on the question by Gladstone's opponents, and it returned him with a majority of 112 to support Irish disestablishment. The fact could not be gainsaid.'[12] For the British nonconformists it was a remarkable example of a successful displacement of their complaints against the Church of England; for Irish Catholics (and even Irish nonconformists) the issue was more substantive – a major source of irritation was removed. Gladstone's passionate Anglicanism – 'he can not endure coarse creeds and Irish Catholicism is unquestionably a coarse creed' – was, in effect, turned against the Irish Protestant establishment. Precisely because the prime minister was perceived to be so sound theologically, his logical critique of the Irish Church's position was rendered all the more formidable; precisely because Disraeli had produced insufficient public evidence of deep religious conviction, he was less able to defend the Irish Church with effect.[13] Gladstone's May 1867 speech on the subject in the House of Commons was regarded as a classic: 'No speech ever made here shows more completely the triumph of the statesman over the natural bias of theological propaganda and social prepossession.'[14] Gladstone argued that a state Church is properly the Church either of the majority of a nation or, if there be no such unity of faith among an absolute majority, then even of the majority of the poorest class of the nation. There was only one special purpose for which the religious endowments of Ireland were devoted – they were devoted to the Protestants of Ireland, who were well able to pay for their own teachers and teaching. Significantly, Gladstone refused to consider notions of concurrent endowment (providing state cash for a number of denominations) favoured by some Whigs and at least one liberal Irish Catholic, Bishop Moriarty of Kerry, who feared that simple disestablishment would intensify sectarian animosity within Ireland. The Church of Ireland lost some £16 million, though £10 million was returned. One remarkable aspect of the settlement was the decision to make available the 'balance' for nonreligious causes: the relief of poverty, agricultural improvement and higher education.[15]

In 1870, Gladstone pushed through his first major Land Act – designed, above all, to protect small farmers from unjust and arbitrary evictions. It was to prove ineffectual in the great crisis of 1879–80 but its very failure then determined there would be a further serious attempt at land reform. Even in 1881, Gladstone was not unsympathetic to Irish landlords: 'The greatest credit is due to the Irish landlords for not exacting all that they are by law entitled to exact.'[16] But this was just the point – stronger legislation was now required. In 1873, Gladstone also attempted to reform Irish higher education but fell foul of the Catholic hierarchy who had supported his efforts on disestablishment and land reform. Sour and disappointed on this score, Gladstone left office in 1874.

In 1874, Gladstone also published his *Vaticanism: An Answer to Replies and Proofs*, arguing that Catholicism was incompatible with loyalty to the state. The former premier included a passage attacking the illiberal evolution of the Catholic Church in Ireland.[17] Gladstone was widely perceived to be acting out of a kind of spite – a delayed revenge for Cardinal Cullen's sabotaging of higher educational legislation.[18] It is but fair to add that Catholic authoritarianism had been troubling the liberal leader for quite some time.

The *Freeman's Journal* reflected mainstream Irish Catholic opinion in its response to Gladstone, which verged on disbelief: Gladstone, it said, had adopted the language of the 'No Popery' zealots. 'And what a falling off is here?' The *Freeman* continued by employing a language of mounting anger:

> There was a time when Mr Gladstone's name was a loved and honoured name to the people of Ireland. Mistaken policy created between him and them a wide gulf. There were those who entertained hopes that it might be bridged over. He has himself made

it yawn to such a width as to sever him from the Irish heart and confidence forever. Many things can be forgiven, but amongst them is not the act of the man who places his hand to the juggernaut of English fanaticism.[19]

Even the Ulster liberals, who had a well-deserved reputation for Gladstone worship, were shocked. The *Northern Whig* editorialised: 'Does anybody seriously question the loyalty of our Roman Catholic fellow countryman, whether in England or Ireland?'[20] The attempt to launch a new liberal Catholic movement in 1875 – the great O'Connell centenary celebrations of that year – was easily broken up by supporters of the Fenians or home rulers. But it was Gladstone himself who, more than any single individual, destroyed the prospects of such politics in the mid-1870s.

In the 1870s, Gladstone was slow to see the significance of the emergence of the Buttite home rule movement – incredibly telling the home rule MP, the much acclaimed John Martin, that he (Gladstone) was more popular in Ireland. He continued to believe in the Irish viability of his metropolitan liberalism, though he was prepared to consider that the social (if not the political) path of development of Irish society might differ from the rest of the UK.

It is clear, however, that Gladstone now rejected the notion of an English model for development. Large-scale capitalist tenant-farming agriculture was the reality of English life. 'I am for one … not very anxious that small proprietors should be greatly multiplied in England,' but 'I attach a great importance to it in Ireland.' In Ireland, insecurity in the land was almost a norm:

You have had in this country – unfortunately too much warranted by history – a very sharp division between the interests of the cultivator and the capitalist, or proprietary. The best cure for this is that in a good and appreciable number of instances, the same man shall be cultivator and proprietor.

This willingness to contemplate a specifically Irish path of development – peasant proprietorship – should be noted, even if, as Gladstone admitted, he could not spell out precisely how it might be achieved.

From 1879 to 1882, Irish life was considered by the Land League movement as threatened social revolution. Gladstone's evolution towards home rule in the period from 1880 and 1885 is often treated as a journey of hypocrisy and self-deception. In fact, it is a consistent and tolerably logical progression. At first, he fantasised about the strength of support for his brand of liberalism in Ireland. Gladstone supported the mass internment of Parnellites in 1881, though it is clear from his marginalia on the cabinet papers that he was always, at least, a little sceptical of the working of the policy of repression. As late as 1882, he was prepared (unsuccessfully) to offer the chief secretaryship to an Ulster liberal, J.L. Porter, but thereafter he ceased to believe in the independent validity of Irish liberalism.

If there is a deceit, it lies in Gladstone's refusal to accept that he had struck a bargain, still less a Kilmainham Treaty, with Parnell in 1882. Here, he was hiding from himself the awful truth that his policy was conceding ground not just to Irish democratic sentiment, but also to Ireland's men of violence. This is the root of his awful treatment of W.E. Forster, his late Irish chief secretary: Gladstone refused to even mark Forster's death with a kind word, because Forster, above all public men, insisted on the awful truth of the concession to violence which Gladstone would rather repress.

It is important to register the nature of Gladstone's style of argumentation in favour of home rule and its impact. For Gladstone, the idea of the union of Great Britain and Ireland became an idea which, in its conception and execution, was absolutely bad. Home rule, the logical antidote, on the other hand, was absolutely good. It was a moral imperviousness which infuriated his opponents; it was also based on some rather bad history. To understand Gladstone's retrospective history of the Irish question, it is necessary to look first at Gladstone's view of Edmund Burke and, in particular, his view of that statesman's politics in the 1790s, both with respect to Ireland and France. Gladstone was an admirer of Burke but on a curiously selective and contingent basis. Gladstone felt that Burke's passion against the French revolution was exaggerated and the counter-revolutionary wars had drained Britain's exchequer. But despite this 'distaste', he told Matthew Arnold – the editor of Burke's Irish writings – that he greatly admired Burke's Irish workings.

There are two ironies here. In the first place, it is impossible to separate Burke's Irish writings of the 1790s from his view of the French revolution. Burke became an even more open advocate of Catholic emancipation in Ireland, because he believed it would make Catholic Ireland a loyal ally of England in its death struggle against atheistic Jacobinism. He feared that failure to deliver reform in Ireland would drive Irish Catholics into the arms of the French revolution. The 'half-citizens', he intoned, would become the full Jacobin.

Gladstone registered Burke's sympathy for Catholic Ireland; he does not register the context which gave it its full meaning. Ironically also, Gladstone's view of Burke owed much to Lord Acton, who, in turn, owed much to Thomas MacKnight's fine three-volume study. Thomas MacKnight, the editor of the Belfast *Northern Whig*, was perhaps the leading intellectual opponent of Gladstone's conversion to home rule. Gladstone was uneasy about this, personally reproaching MacKnight that he had forgotten 'your Burke'.

Gladstone told MacKnight that Burke was an opponent of the union. Even Irish nationalists wondered if Gladstone could possibly be right about that. J.G. Swift MacNeill

> ventured to approach him and to ask him how this was, since Edmund Burke died in 1797, and the proposal of a union had not even been broached as a government measure till the autumn of 1798. 'Oh,' said Gladstone, 'do you remember what Dr Laurence said?' Mr Gladstone asked me to accompany him into the library of the House of Commons, and, mounting on a library ladder, without reference to a catalogue, he brought down a volume of parliamentary reports, with a debate on the union proposals of 30 January 1799.[21]

In fact, of course, we can never know what Burke's attitude to the union might have been had he lived to see 1800. Thomas MacKnight was inclined to believe that Burke would have opposed a union without Catholic emancipation but supported a union which granted it. It is a view supported by many serious scholars today. What we do know, however, is that while many self-conscious followers of Burke (French, Laurence and Grattan) opposed the union, others, such as William Cusack Smith and J.W. Croker, supported it. We also know that Cusack Smith, a member of the inner Burke circle, developed a style of argumentation for the union which greatly impressed Pitt and Castlereagh. We also know that Protestant ascendancy supporters of the union, such as Patrick Duigenan, detected in Pitt's style of argumentation for the union the nefarious influence of Burke. By this, Duigenan meant that Pitt's sympathy for the Catholics of Ireland was a direct product of Edmund Burke's persuasion. Of course, despite the expectations raised by Pitt and Castlereagh, the union did not lead to Catholic emancipation until 1829. Those senior politicians and churchmen around the king who persuaded the monarch to block Pitt's scheme of Catholic emancipation effectively damaged the viability of the union project from the start.

The key theme in the case for the union was the idea that it would create 'one people' throughout the United Kingdom. The dreadful murderous horrors of 1798 were to be forgotten; Irish and English, Catholic and Protestant were now to consider themselves a unified body under the set of laws. In 1795, Burke had said that one could not speak as a good Englishman without speaking as a good Irishman and vice versa; in the union debates, Pitt repeated the phrase. A shared and common path of development was much preferable to Anglo-Irish conflict and sectarian rage – both working to the advantage of the common enemy, France.

The Ulster Presbyterians were, in the end, the one Irish group for whom the 'one people' concept had worked: the circumstances of the nineteenth century – economic growth and progressive political democratisation – had allowed them a full and natural identification with the imagined community of the United Kingdom. In his volume *Ireland from 1798–1898*, O'Connor Morris listed as one of the two principal benefits of the union that 'Presbyterian Ireland, hostile in 1791–98, has become devotedly attached to England.'[22] But consider here Gladstone's interpretation of the issues at stake. In October 1885, he told Lord Derby:

> He [Gladstone] thought the question one which must be studied seriously. He had been reading old debates upon it, minding Pitt's speech on proposing it to Parliament, and he was not satisfied with the argument in its favour. He had come to the conclusion that the union was a mistake and that no adequate justification had been shown for taking away the national life of Ireland … though Pitt had been persuaded into it by the King, who believed it would act as a check on the Catholics.[23]

This last judgement is a complete misreading of the concept of the union which animated Pitt: he was not motivated by an anti-Catholic agenda, handed to him by the king, but a pro-Catholic agenda, inherited from Burke. He was blocked by the king and his allies. This is an inherent part of the fatal ambiguity of the union conception. But there is no place for ambiguity in Gladstone's version of the Irish past: it is a simple matter of black and white. It is little wonder that his opponents became so exasperated.

In March 1893, Gladstone told the Belfast Chamber of Commerce – largely liberal-unionist in political composition – that instead of opposing his Irish policies, they ought to return to the anti-British establishment connections of their ancestors in the Belfast of the 1780s. Time travel backwards in time has never been a solution for a major political problem. Gladstone may have, on reflection, come to accept this rhetorical advice would not seriously impinge on the problem. On 3 May 1893 – bizarrely, in the course of a debate on mining legislation – he addressed again the Ulster problem. A discussion about the importance of respecting local conditions in the mining industry led Gladstone to apply the point to Irish politics. He claimed that in 1886 he had signalled a willingness to 'exempt' north-east Ulster from the operation of a home rule scheme. Further, he claimed that he had the support of the leadership of the Irish nationalist party for such a proposal. Gladstone's 1893 remarks attracted some attention at the time. Parnellites pointed out that this vindicated their hostility to Gladstone, who was clearly willing to accept some form of partition. Unionists, on the other hand, publicly distrusted the apparent offer and disputed whether there was sincerity behind it – though we have Edward Carson's word that there was some serious discussion behind the scenes. Reading these remarks more than a century later, it is, however, hard not to be struck by their significance. If Gladstone genuinely believed that Irish political unity was an imperative of a new settlement, that would be logical enough – but if he did not (and it is clear that he did not), then his performance on the issue is considerably less impressive. It is not too much to say that he bears a considerable responsibility for the way in which the partition question dogged Irish politics for the next hundred years – precisely, until the Downing Street Declaration of 1993, when the British government finally won the national leadership to accept the democratic legitimacy of partition in the way in which Gladstone claimed to have done in 1886, but rather cordially threw away. In short, Gladstone threw away the enormous prestige he had attained as the first British prime minister to concede the democratic case for Irish nationalist self-government; instead, despite his remarks in 1893, he was a prestigious sponsor of Irish nationalism's dismissive attitude towards the Ulster unionist case. If a British prime minister felt it right to urge liberal unionists simply to return to their allegiances of the late eighteenth century, why should Irish nationalists behave any differently?

It is true that, in April 1886, Gladstone had offered to consider special arrangements for Ulster but these were never defined. In part, of course, this was due to the opposition's correct assessment that a split Liberal Party could never pass home rule anyway. But even so, Gladstone closed down the whole subject of special provision with an evident show of relief in June 1886, only to return to it in such eccentric style in 1893. It is conventional to say in Gladstone's defence that, had his policies been accepted in 1886, much subsequent violence and sectarian turmoil in Ireland would have been averted. It would be more accurate to say that Gladstone's strategic approach in the 1880s was an important determinant of subsequent disastrous intractabilities and rigidities.

By way of conclusion, it is necessary to turn to two fascinating comments from Sir Edward Carson, the great leader of Irish unionism. In 1922, Sir Charles Biron was startled when Carson told him: '"Well, looking back at politics, I think we made a great mistake in not accepting Mr Gladstone's first Home Rule Bill". I looked at him with amazement.' Biron added: 'But there was no doubt about his sincerity.' On 6 November 1933, Carson wrote to the historian Sir John Marriott: 'I have never had the slightest doubt that it would have been impossible to have made any lasting settlement in Ireland after the GOM [Gladstone]

had adopted the home rule policy.' These differing assess-
ments are seen as evidence of Carson's conflicted political
soul – and they are – but they also convey a kind of truth
about Gladstone's conversion to home rule: necessary, just
and disastrous – all at the same time.

DR ROSEMARY CULLEN OWENS

'The Machine Will Work without Them':
Kevin O'Higgins and the Jury Bills of 1924 and 1927

'A s far as the political rights and constitutional status of women were concerned the New Irish State of 1922 was all that might be desired. Suffrage was universal, no public office was barred to women and there were cast-iron guarantees that none would be.'[1] So stated Maurice Manning in a seminal series of Thomas Davis Lectures on the position of women in Irish society, broadcast in 1975 to commemorate International Women's Year. This situation had not come about accidentally. In 1913, Constance Markievicz had referred to the 'three great movements' then going on in Ireland – the national movement, the women's movement and the industrial movement – 'all fighting the same fight, for the extension of human liberty'.[2] It can be argued that the confluence of women's involvement in these three movements, allied to the equality provisions of the 1916 Proclamation, contributed to this 1922 status.

Markievicz had told the Students National Literary Society in 1909 that 'A free Ireland with no Sex Disabilities in her Constitution should be the motto of all Nationalist Women.'[3] Differences over the following years between nationalist women and suffragists centred not on the principle of female suffrage, but on the propriety of Irish women seeking the vote from an English government. Nationalist women argued that 'the women of Irish Ireland have the franchise',[4] believing equality would follow automatically on political independence. A core group of feminists argued, however, that whatever type of government emerged in Ireland, 'there can be no free nation without free women'.[5]

Constitutional political leaders had not favoured the idea of female suffrage, John Dillon claiming that it 'would be the ruin of our western civilisation ... destroy[ing] the home, challenging the headship of man, laid down by God'.[6] However, when a British government bill in 1918 granted the vote to Irish women over thirty years with certain property qualifications (at the same time extending the vote to men of twenty-one years), there was a change of attitude within political parties on the issue of female involvement. With a general election pending, two notable things occurred: women now found themselves much in demand as speakers on party platforms, and the type of poster formerly published by the Irish Parliamentary Party which read 'Public admitted – ladies excluded' disappeared.[7] Sinn Féin also sought the support of the new women voters, asking Irish women to 'vote as Mrs. Pearse will vote', promising that 'as in the past, so in the future the womenfolk of the Gael shall have high place in the Councils of a freed Gaelic nation'.[8] Promises, promises!

Adult suffrage had been included in the 1916 proclamation and, in the spirit of that proclamation, the Irish Free State constitution of 1922 granted equal voting rights to all citizens of twenty-one years. However, until the provisions of the proposed constitution became law, only women aged thirty and over could vote. Younger women would not be eligible to vote on the Anglo-Irish Treaty and constitution. During the acrimonious treaty debates of the second Dáil that year, the issue of women's suffrage received heated discussion. Both pro- and anti-treaty sides claimed the support of the majority of Irish women, yet it would appear that, as in 1918 when John Redmond's party had feared the effect of a new female electorate, now the pro-treaty side feared the extension of full adult suffrage. The vociferous anti-treaty reactions of many nationalist women, including the majority of Cumann na mBan, did little to reassure them in this regard. In particular, the role of republican women during the civil war was viewed by Free State supporters as unwomanly, turning them into 'unlovely, destructive minded, arid begetters of violence'.[9] Diarmaid Ferriter has remarked that the chauvinism that would emerge in the new state may in part have been a reaction to the politics of female republicanism during that era.[10] P.S. O'Hegarty wrote in 1924 that during the civil war

> Dublin was full of hysterical women [who] became practically unsexed, their mother's milk blackened to make gunpowder, their minds working on nothing save hate and blood … The Suffragettes used to tell us that with women in political power there would be no more war. We know that with women in political power there would be no more peace.[11]

But were women in political power? From the perspective of a newly born state which endorsed in its constitution the equality of rights and opportunities of all citizens, it may indeed have appeared so. Yet, as Manning has pointed out: 'The new regime quickly discarded the radical rhetoric and revolutionary flourishes of the 1916–21 period and settled into a conservative and respectable state.'[12] Its high emphasis on social caution would become particularly evident in its attitude towards women.

Enter stage right – Kevin O'Higgins! Born in 1892, O'Higgins was one of fifteen children of Dr Thomas Higgins and Anne Sullivan of Stradbally, County Laois.[13] A member of the Volunteers, and later Sinn Féin, he was imprisoned in 1918 for anti-British army recruitment and pro-Sinn Féin oratory. Released from gaol in October 1918, he was elected Sinn Féin MP for Laois-Offaly following the December 1918 general election.[14] During the first Dáil, O'Higgins was appointed assistant minister to William T. Cosgrave, Minister for Local Government. During the years 1920–7, O'Higgins played a key role in government, holding the portfolios of Economic Affairs, Home Affairs, Justice and External Affairs. Strongly pro-treaty, O'Higgins was a tough Minister for Justice during the civil war, responsible for the execution of over seventy republican prisoners.[15] He also established An Garda Siochana in 1923. Thirty-two years old when he introduced the first Juries Bill in 1924, thirty-five when the second was introduced in 1927, I would not suggest that O'Higgins disliked all women. He was, after all, married with a young family. He is also reputed to have been in love with Lady Hazel Lavery about this time.[16] Whatever about his relationships with women in his private life, my concern here is with his relationship with and attitude towards women in public life and the impact of those views on subsequent generations of Irish women.

Indicative of O'Higgins's character is his description of himself and his political colleagues as being probably 'the most conservative-minded revolutionaries that ever put through a successful revolution'.[17] When asked by Labour party leader Thomas Johnson in the Dáil whether he believed giving women the vote had been a success, O'Higgins replied, 'I would not like to pronounce an opinion on it in public.'[18] During the civil war, O'Higgins referred to anti-treaty republican women as 'hysterical young women who ought to be playing five fingered exercises or helping their mothers with the brasses'.[19] So perhaps it is not surprising that just two years after the Constitution of 1922, it was O'Higgins who made the first move to restrict the public role of Irish women.

In a departure from British government legislation of 1919 (which had granted women the right to sit on juries), O'Higgins introduced in 1924 a bill which would exempt women from jury service on application. He told the Dáil that the purpose of the act was 'to get rid of the unwilling woman juror', arguing that:

> In this country the number of women who desire to serve on juries is very small, and in practice the insertion of women's names in the Jury Book leads to nothing but trouble; the women do not turn up, or they get themselves excused, or they are objected to.[20]

In response, Labour leader Tom Johnson argued that the proposed bill sought to undo what women had attained only within the last three or four years, pointing to Article 3 of the Constitution which stated that 'Any person, without distinction of sex, shall be a citizen and shall ... enjoy the privileges and be subject to the obligations of such citizenship.'[21] Referring to what he termed Johnson's 'abstract principles about the equality of the sexes', O'Higgins stated, 'we do not propose to drag unwilling women into jury boxes in response to the claims of a certain number of their advanced sisters'.[22] Acknowledging that there were a number of women who were indignant at this proposal, he declared, 'It is open to the advanced ladies to convert their less advanced sisters.'[23] O'Higgins had his supporters in the Dáil. Attorney General Hugh Kennedy stated that:

> We know that there are a great number [of women] who are simply frightened out of their lives at the idea of going on juries in a civil or, still worse, in a criminal matter … It would relieve the courts from having cases for trial held up, and having exhibitions of nerves and what, I suppose, the Minister might call temperament.[24]

Deputy Wolfe went even further, arguing that:

> I do not think it has ever been sufficiently demonstrated that the majority of women were ever in favour of possessing the vote … there has never been a referendum on the subject … and we have never known whether the majority of them wanted to be on the same terms as men or not … I think there is no doubt that a very large number of the women look forward to serving on juries with the utmost dread, and a very large number of them are quite unfitted for it … To insist that every woman, because she has a vote – in many cases against her will – should be compelled to serve on juries is, I think, an outrageous thing.[25]

Deputy Duggan, while agreeing with Johnson's argument on equality in theory, commented that:

> we all know that in practice there is no equality of the sexes, and there never will be. We also know that

the normal woman will have no desire or anxiety to serve on a jury, and she never will serve on a jury if she can avoid it.[26]

O'Higgins concluded the debate, arguing that his provision of exemption on request 'met the case of sensitive nervous women with a positive reluctance and a distaste for this service'.[27]

Women's groups were alarmed at the proposal to introduce exemption purely on the grounds of sex, the Irish Women's Citizens Association arguing that to allow women to evade the duties and responsibilities of citizenship was 'unfair to the men citizens and derogatory to the women'.[28] In a letter to *The Irish Times*, the Women's Independent Association denounced this 'retrograde step' which they feared 'would open the door a little wider to the forces of reaction'.[29] Their fears were justified: 1925 saw the introduction of the Civil Service Regulation (Amendment) Act aimed at restricting women from entering higher-ranking civil service posts, and in 1927 a further Juries Bill proposed to exempt women completely from jury service.

Outlining this new Juries Bill to the Dáil in February 1927, O'Higgins explained its intent was to exempt women as they had been exempted until 1919 'when the British Parliament made them liable equally with men'.[30] He pointed out that 'Up to 1919 the woman juror had no existence in fact or in law.'[31] Based on the low number of women jurors, his arguments centred on the need for financial savings and administrative efficiency. While accepting that those women who had served on juries had 'rendered reasonably good service, probably as good service as men', he argued that the fact that the majority of women were reluctant to serve meant it was not necessary to compel them.[32] During debate on the issue, O'Higgins's personal views were made quite clear. He recognised that in Dublin there existed what he described as a small minority of women willing to do jury service, and he accepted that many of this minority were outstanding examples of women's capacity to take their place in public life and render useful service. But, he asked: 'Are they the normal or the exception?'[33] O'Higgins argued that 'It is the normal and natural function of women to have children. It still is the normal and natural function of women to have charge of households.'[34]

Dismissing those who objected to the proposed bill as 'self-appointed spokeswomen, not representative of the vast majority of women in the state', he argued that such groups were trying to force unwilling women into jury service because they saw the bill as a slight on their sex.[35] In this regard, he commented, 'it seems to me that that is almost as if a vegetarian, speaking on behalf of the human race ... were to demand that legislation should be passed prohibiting the use of meat'.[36]

He did not quarrel with the view of individual women 'who yearn for jury service' but he did deny such a woman the 'right to speak or write as if she were appointed to express the views of her sex in the State when we have the best of reason for knowing that those are not the views of the majority of women in the State'.[37] Obviously *he* felt qualified to express the view of the female sex! O'Higgins also referred to the unpleasant cases that often came before a court – cases of indecent assault, rape and sodomy, cases he noted that 'one would not like to discuss with the feminine members of one's own family'.[38] This point he made not solely in respect of women jurors, but also in regard to female court stenographers, whom he banned from working in the Central Criminal Court and Circuit Courts through-out the country for this reason. Tom Johnson pointed out that while difficult cases undoubtedly arose, 'in most of those cases there is either a woman in the dock or a woman in the witness box'.[39] Major Cooper reinforced this argu-ment when he stated that the basis underlying trial by jury was to be tried by one's peers. A number of deputies also pointed to the anomaly of women barristers being present in court while women could not serve as jurors. Professor Magennis argued that women were being barred because they were women and for no other reason. It was not pro-posed to exclude men who did not like jury service. Regard-ing woman's 'supposed superior delicacy of soul', he argued that a married woman who has seen a great deal of life is often better suited in some cases than a young man, yet 'the younger man is to be selected and the capable woman ex-cluded'.[40] Wondering if the next provision would be to ex-clude women from membership of the Dáil, Magennis asked:

> Do women pay rates and taxes? Is not a woman as much concerned as any ordinary citizen in the right finding of correct verdicts by juries? If it could be shown that women were hysterical in the jury box, or they had given good grounds in consultation in the jury room for the belief that they were incompetent or prejudiced, a case might be made, but that case was not made here. The Minister wants to reserve for one class and for one section of the community a certain civic right by the exclusion of another sec-tion.[41]

In response to these arguments, O'Higgins again cited the economic and administrative advantages against women jurors, commenting that 'we can get enough of jurors without them'.[42] He also alluded to difficulties regarding courthouse accommodation, with 'certain obvious embarrassments when the accommodation has to be shared by both men and women'.[43] In response to the argument that many men did not like jury service, O'Higgins argued that men would not be glad to be released from this obligation:

> Men have not that shrinking from the duty, that reluctance to go into the box and face the ordeal of sitting for perhaps four, five or six days trying a man for his life that the normal woman has. A few words in a Constitution do not wipe out the difference between the sexes, either physical or mental or temperamental or emotional … The vast majority of the women citizen of this country … dislike this work … intensely, and would be grateful to the government that would relieve them from it. We can afford to relieve them from it. There is not the necessity of putting this unpleasant duty on the women section of the country's citizenship.[44]

Speaking at the committee-stage discussion of the bill some days later, O'Higgins argued that it was no use pretending that the question of women jurors did not present very much greater difficulties than jury service for men. Citing the administrative expense and time taken up with vetting various grounds for exemption made by women, he declared that:

> The position of the normal male citizen eligible for jury service is essentially different from the position of the woman citizen. A man can be absent for a day, or a couple of days, from his household, as a rule, without any very serious consequences accruing to

anybody. He can lunch out, and it does not follow that the other members of his household have to do without their lunch.[45]

O'Higgins argued for a distinction between equality and identity, stating that there could be equality of status without identity of function and that his bill was not an infringement of the principle of equality of status. Objecting to the measure, Tom Johnson argued that 'It seeks at one fell blow to substitute male citizens for citizens. It wipes out with one swing of the axe all that has been achieved in the direction of equalisation of citizenship between the sexes.'[46]

Johnson suggested that the next step perhaps would be to include the word 'male' in a new franchise bill, commenting that no doubt the minister would find a good excuse for saying that the Constitution could be amended to this effect. Captain Redmond pointed out that women's desire to serve on juries or not was one question; their eligibility to act in this regard was another question, commenting:

> Even if it were to cost the State extra, the great principle of equality of status is there; the great principle as recognised by law in this country. Women have at present the same advantages as men. I believe that in this respect they should have the disadvantages.[47]

Pointing out that as taxpayers women contributed to the upkeep of the state, he argued:

> I hope the House will not take this retrograde step ... [which would] mean that we shall be the only country in the world which has given women anything in the nature of equal status and has gone back upon that position.[48]

Responding to O'Higgins's somewhat disparaging comment about a 'few words in the Constitution', Professor Magennis pointed out that both he and Tom Johnson had had a large share in introducing those few words regarding equality into Article 3. He also noted that every member of the Dáil had been aware of the 1919 Sex Disqualification Removal Act and knew therefore that the phrase 'shall enjoy the privileges and be subject to the obligations of such citizenship' included women citizens. Magennis declared, 'The fact is this, the Minister autocratically desires to interpret Article 3 of the Constitution as if the words ran – "jury service is an obligation of male citizenship".'[49]

In the Seanad, O'Higgins argued that Article 3 meant that while the obligations of citizenship created by law may be constitutionally imposed on every citizen, it does not mean that a government is constitutionally bound to impose an absolutely equal burden of citizenship on all its citizens.[50] Commenting that 'A very small minority of women feel a yearning for jury service,' O'Higgins cited advice from the attorney general indicating that Article 3 'does not mean that the Government is bound to weigh out in grammes the burden of citizenship and distribute that equally over all citizens regardless of sex'.[51]

Accepting the competency and desirability of women serving on juries, Sir James Craig agreed with O'Higgins that 'between the ages of, say twenty and forty, the majority of women are performing more signal services to the State than if they were serving on juries, by performing the functions of motherhood and in looking after their homes'.[52]

He did allow, however, that 'Where these functions are denied to women from any cause I think it is quite desirable that these women should be allowed to perform the State

functions, which I think their other sisters are fairly de-
barred from carrying out.'[53] Craig went on to argue that:

> A great deal has been talked about the equality of
> women with men, the greater part of which is rub-
> bish. If the women are the equal of men why are they
> not carrying sacks on their backs down on the quays,
> why are they not following the plough? Women are
> not the equal of men; they are far better. They are
> able to perform functions that men can never per-
> form, and therefore it is rubbish to talk about equal-
> ity. If women wish to remain at home and look after
> their homes, their husbands, and their children, they
> should not be compelled to serve as jurors.[54]

In reply to O'Higgins's argument that the majority of
women did not wish to serve on juries, Tom Johnson argued that even if it were true that 99 per cent of women
might like to be relieved of this duty, so might 99 per cent
of men.[55] Arguing that no one, man or woman, is eager to
serve on a jury, Professor Magennis noted that it was not
proposed to exclude men who did not like such service,
asking:

> Does the Minister ask us to believe that woman is
> less than man – a distinct and separate species? ...
> Surely, a Government that has been so meticulous in
> its Civil Service Regulations Act as to introduce sex,
> sex, sex repeatedly in its various clauses is alive to its
> own operations, as separating men from women
> within the law, and while assigning certain duties to
> one, removes them from the other? ... it is not
> because women do not like service he is exempting
> them but because it is women who are in question.[56]

In the Seanad debate on the bill, O'Higgins pointed out that while the 1919 Act had made women liable to jury service on a parity with men:

> We were [then] not sending our representatives to the British Parliament and we had no special responsibility for the provision of the Sex Disqualification Removal Act. I doubt if such an Act would be passed by the Oireachtas of this State. I think we take the line that it was proper to confer on women citizens all the privileges of citizenship and such of the duties of citizenship as we thought it reasonable to impose upon them.[57]

He doubted if a majority of deputies would favour the proposal that women be made liable for jury service on terms of complete equality with men, commenting, 'That particular provision was never effective here. Nobody wanted it and everyone seemed to be in a conspiracy to render it inoperative.'[58] Pointing out that by allowing potential women jurors to apply for exemption under the terms of the Jury Bill of 1924 'we did something to mitigate the farce', O'Higgins argued that 'we still had this situation that large numbers of women, either through carelessness, ignorance of the law or from one cause or another, did not avail of the opportunities of getting their names taken off the register'.[59]

By this stage, a number of amendments to the bill were under discussion. O'Higgins explained the three options available to the House: complete parity for women; complete exemption for women; or a provision that would allow qualified women to volunteer their names to be entered on the register. Personally, he was least enthusiastic about the third option. Accepting that there was discontent about it, he argued there would be discontent about any of the options, asking:

> Does anybody suggest that there would not be the most acute discontent if one were to take compulsory service for women and administer that on terms of complete parity with men? There would of course. I think that under this middle line you will have, at any rate, the least sense of grievance, since the only grievance it leaves the advanced propagandist women – if I may refer to them in that term without any desire to be offensive – is that the Government refuses to dragoon their unwilling sisters into jury service, but they themselves have no grievance.[60]

Accepting that the third option did not meet with the approval of the various women's organisations in the capital, the minister argued that one occasionally has to take steps in legislation and administration with regard to which there is an absence of unanimity, stating his belief that 'This is the soundest and the sanest proposal. It is certainly one that reduces the administrative difficulties to a minimum.'[61]

Arguing that the majority of male voters – and indeed female voters – would be against women jurors, that in fact the issue was a minority demand from a very small majority of the electorate, O'Higgins argued against the proposal that all qualified women should be eligible for jury service: 'People who advocate that are thinking in terms of the Terenure tram and Green Street Courthouse, or the Dalkey train and Green Street Courthouse, and are not envisaging the rural districts at all.'[62] He cited the example of a widow in Belmullet, who, if liable to compulsory jury service and called to serve, would have 'to yoke her horse and car and drive to Castlebar; she then has to hang around the town of Castlebar for a week or so while the Circuit Court is sitting, on the off-chance of being required for jury service'.[63] It was his belief that it is a much greater hardship on the woman to undertake that journey and that work than it is on the man. Responding to what he called the very small number of women in Dublin who wanted him to impose compulsory jury service on women throughout the state, he declared, 'I will not do it … until I have much greater evidence than I have yet received that that is the demand of a substantial proportion of the electorate.'[64] Interestingly, later in the debate he revealed that 40 per cent of those who hold jury qualifications in Dublin were women.[65]

Commenting on the belief of some that the principle of co-equality was at stake with regard to this particular provision, O'Higgins argued:

It is not, of course. It is no stigma, no slight on the women citizens of this State to say that all things considered, we are prepared to exempt them, at the same time leaving open the door to such of them as notify the county registrar that they are available for jury service and have no reluctance to serve.[66]

This was, of course, a shift from his original intent. He appealed to senators that:

We are supposed to be a democratic State. We drew a democratic Constitution and we say that all power and all authority in Ireland, legislative, executive and judicial, is derived from the people. Now, I have not yet got so blasé and cynical that I repeat that Article with my tongue in my cheek, but I brand this as essentially a minority demand, as a minority demand whether you take the electorate as a whole or whether you take one or other sex of the electorate.[67]

During this debate, O'Higgins displayed some verbal dexterity with figures that would no doubt earn admiration from his political successors. Claiming at one point that he doubted 'very much if 25 per cent of the electorate or 25 per cent of either sex of the electorate would favour compulsory jury service for women on terms of complete parity with male citizens', he noted, 'I may be told that it exists elsewhere with excellent results, but I think the excellence of the results may be over-estimated on the same basis as the length of the horns of Connaught cows.'[68] Later in the same debate he argued:

I do not believe that 20 per cent of the electorate as a whole [or] 20 per cent of the women electorate want compulsory jury service for women, and in face of that, lest … I trample on that great principle of co-equality, I am to write into this Bill a provision for compulsory jury service for women. Where is our reverence for democracy? What becomes of the provision that all authority, legislative, executive and judicial, is derived from the people, if we are to do a thing which we know … that not 15 per cent of the electorate would wish or approve of?[69]

With his hand – metaphorically at least – on his heart he solemnly declared:

We find ourselves frequently in the position of preventing people getting something which they pretend they want, and which would not be good for them … In this matter I am really the champion of the women in the State, but I never expect to get any gratitude for that.[70]

In this regard he was correct, his arguments serving only to fuel women's opposition to his proposal. O'Higgins had argued that women had resorted to every possible device to avoid jury service, actually stating that the attorney general very frequently ordered them to stand by in criminal cases. This latter point had been made in a forceful letter to the *Voice of Labour* by Hanna Sheehy Skeffington, who challenged O'Higgins's assertion that few women had shown interest in jury service, stating:

> For over three years, practically no woman has been chosen by the State to serve on criminal cases, women being ordered en masse … to 'stand aside' when they answered their name in court. Mr. O'Higgins was asked during the debate (and by a deputation of women who interviewed him) to produce figures showing how many women answered their names when called for service. He replied that no such figures were available, knowing full well already that it is the court practice not to allow women to serve, because to use his own words, 'women in certain cases are loathe to convict!'. There is no record available, in fact, no note being taken of the numbers of women challenged by either State or prisoners, and Mr. O'Higgins's statement, therefore, is based on a deliberate misrepresentation.[71]

In the Dáil, Magennis had also referred to 'the persistent practice of ordering women, who attend in court to serve as jurors, to stand aside', pointing out that 'there is not one record of a woman juror being fined for absence'.[72] Senator Fanning noted that in his experience of serving on mixed juries he had never met any 'who took more pains to get at the facts of the case, or who followed the case with more attention and more scrupulous care than women jurors'.[73] Senator Sir Edward Biggar argued that it was in the best interest of the state that all citizens be encouraged to take an interest in the government of the state and administration of the law, asking, 'How are you to do this if you are going to reduce the status of women to a plane lower than that of men?'[74]

Women's groups protested forcefully against the bill, arguing both for women's rights and the benefits of having women on juries. The Irish Women's Citizens' and Local Government Association, the National Council of Women and the National University Women Graduates' Association canvassed Dáil and Seanad members in opposition to both the Civil Service Regulation (Amendment) Bill and the 1927 Jury Bill. The issue of mixed juries particularly in cases involving children and young girls was raised by many. The Irish Women Workers Union argued that as both sexes were likely to stand in the dock as offenders 'it is just and right that the question of their guilt should be submitted to juries consisting of both men and women'.[75] A number of the women who actively opposed the 1927 Jury Bill had been active in establishing a Watching the Courts committee in 1914 to report on cases involving injustice to women, particularly cases of marital violence, indecent assault on children and the seduction of young girls. Reports of the committee's findings were reported quite frankly in the *Irish Citizen*, with lenient sentencing, early release of those convicted and judicial attitudes being strongly challenged and criticised.[76]

Within the houses of the Oireachteas, the main female opposition to the Jury Bills and the 1925 Civil Service Bill occurred in the Seanad, particularly from Jenny Wyse Power and Eileen Costello. Speaking on the Civil Service Bill, Wyse Power had pointed to the injustice of 'this sex discrimination' being made by a male Executive Council and by practically a male Dáil, with no consultation of any kind with any representative women on the subject, regretting that such a bill had come from 'the men who were associated in the fight [for freedom] with women when sex and money were not considerations'.[77] The only female Dáil deputy at this time – Margaret Collins O'Driscoll – at no time challenged government legislation. On the contrary, she endorsed women's maternal and domestic role when she told the Dáil in 1925 that 'In the days of my youth it was regarded as a qualification for matrimony that a woman should be able to make her husband's shirts.'[78]

The 1927 Juries Bill received the most forceful criticism in the Seanad, not least from women senators. For Senator Costello, the ideal position was that of complete equality granted in 1919, arguing that the intervening eight years was too short a period to judge women and that 'if women are to take their part as citizens, these duties should be put upon them and enforced, because that is the only way they can be educated into good citizenship'.[79] In response to an earlier argument made against women by Senator O'Farrell that the presence of women jurors 'distracts the minds of other jurors … particularly since the advent of short skirts', Jenny Wyse Power ridiculed this and the related proposal that the age limit for women jurors be raised to over twenty-five years, pointing out that very few younger women possessed the necessary rateable qualification.[80] She argued that should the bill become law, 'the civic spirit that is developing in women will be arrested', noting that developments over the previous five years had seen male political leaders utilising women to achieve their objective. Such activity had promoted women's civic spirit, thrusting them more into public life, but 'the suggestion that there shall be only male jurors in the future cuts at the very root of this development of the awakening of the civic spirit'.[81] She deplored the minister's attitude because he was 'doing such an injustice to what is really a necessary asset to every State, the co-operation of its men and women'.[82]

Consistently, however, in both Dáil and Seanad, the government saw no contradiction in taking away from women rights which they already enjoyed under the Constitution. Inside and outside parliament, women who demanded the right to jury service became increasingly categorised as 'abnormal', with 'normal' women being defined as those who accepted their primary role was within the home. Newspapers of the day asserted that 'real women' or 'ladies' had no desire to serve on juries, to be wrenched from the bosom of their families, from their cherished household duties, from the preparation of their husbands' dinners.[83] Those who fought against the bill were described in the press as 'nothing more than feminists who wanted women to imitate men'.[84] An editorial in the *Kilkenny People* quoted in the *Irish Independent* declared that 'The women of the Free State are not to be judged by their loud-voiced, self-constituted advocates, who are eternally spouting and writing to the newspapers and marching in processions.'[85]

Valiulis has highlighted two important implications of the debate surrounding the issue of female jury service. Citing Senator Jenny Wyse Power, who pointed out that a woman who volunteered for jury service but subsequently had to seek exemption on valid grounds could become the subject of taunts and jibes, Valiulis notes, 'This was an obvious deterrent to women who might otherwise have chosen to put their names forward. Women's organisations saw the amendment as an attempt to divide women, to classify them into acceptable and non-acceptable, normal and abnormal.'[86]

Regarding negative press coverage of the issue, Valiulis argues that perhaps the most damaging charge made against women who wanted to participate in the political life of the state was that 'they were dismissed as unfulfilled and envious, women who supposedly had not fulfilled their "natural" role as mother and wife and allegedly were jealous of those who had'.[87]

In debate about various suggested amendments to the bill, O'Higgins had said, 'So long as I get what I want I am not over-particular as to the form in which I get it.'[88] As a result of the women's campaign and strong opposition in the Seanad, the government accepted an amendment to the bill which, although exempting women as a class from jury service, allowed individual women to have their names included on jury lists on application. Male ratepayers would be automatically called for jury service; women ratepayers would be eligible but had to volunteer. Outlining the amendment in the Dáil in May 1927, O'Higgins commented, 'The change that has been effected … is rather one of form than of substance. But from the point of view of form it is considered an improvement on the Bill.'[89] Regarding the nature of the change, he was correct. The change was of form, rather than substance. His legacy to the women of Ireland lasted almost fifty years, a legacy that resulted in what Mary Robinson described as 'an almost total exclusion of women from jury service'.[90] Robinson's examination of Department of Justice statistics regarding the number of applications from women to have their names inserted on the jurors lists between 1963 and 1973 reveal that a total of nine women in the entire country – four in Dublin – applied during that period to have their names inserted in the jury list. Of these, five women were called for jury service, two of whom were challenged in court, resulting in a total of three women serving on a jury during that ten-year period.[91] As a result of O'Higgins's legislation, the assessment of criminality over almost five decades had been practically an entirely male assessment. Examining the broader significance of this, Robinson notes that:

> Down the years the assessment of criminality has been an entirely male assessment. It is men alone who have decided on guilt in cases of rape, drunken driving causing death, murder, etc. The male jury has been addressed by male barristers, both for the State and for the particular defendant, and after the verdict the sentence has been imposed by a male Judge.[92]

Similarly, in regard to civil juries, Robinson queried the significance of purely male assessment in cases where damages or compensation is sought by a widow following the death of her husband, asking, 'Is this male determination of compensation in civil cases and guilt in criminal cases a possible distortion which should have given rise to concern?'[93] Rosaleen Mills, a feminist activist from the 1940s, later recalled the outrage of her female colleagues that young girls charged with infanticide or prostitution were judged by twelve men.[94] The extent to which the idea of non-woman juries had become entrenched during the decades following the 1927 Act can be assessed by an article written by Mills in 1955 in which she stated that 'Many Irishwomen are probably unaware that in the Republic women do not serve on juries.'[95]

Following a challenge in 1975 to the constitutionality of the jury system as discriminatory both on the grounds of sex and property, the Supreme Court upheld the claim on both grounds.[96] I wonder did Mr O'Higgins turn in his grave at this development, particularly in light of the judges' comments. Mr Justice Walsh in his judgement noted that:

> The provision made in the Act of 1927, is undisguis-edly discriminatory on the grounds of sex only ... it does not seek to justify the discrimination on the basis of any social function. It simply lumps together half of the members of the adult population, most of whom have only one thing in common, namely, their sex.[97]

In the view of Mr Justice Henchy:

> it is incompatible with the necessary diffusion of rights and duties in a modern democratic society that important public decisions, such as voting, or jury verdicts involving life or liberty, should be made by male citizens only ... Juries recruited in that way fall short of minimum constitutional standards no less than would juries recruited entirely from female citi-zens.[98]

Game, set and match to the women of Ireland – after half a century!

Following the attainment of votes for women over thirty years, a 1919 *Irish Citizen* editorial had outlined a list of further equality measures sought by feminists:

We want equal pay for equal work, equal marriage laws, the abolition of legal disabilities, the right of women to enter the hitherto banned learned professions, women jurors and justices, in short, the complete abolition of various taboos and barriers – social, economic and political – that still impede women's progress.[99]

Eleven years later, Helena Molony, reviewing the position of women and labour in Irish society, pointed out that 'Women since [James Connolly's] day, have got that once-coveted right to vote, but they still have their inferior status, their lower pay for equal work, their exclusion from juries and certain branches of the civil service.'[100]

Dr Margaret MacCurtain has noted that while the illiberal legislation of the post-civil war decades has often been explained by reference to the value system of a tradition-minded rural-oriented society, 'Rarely, if at all, is allusion made to the total exclusion of women from public life and from responsibility for public morality.'[101] Indeed, the 1924 and 1927 Juries Acts and the 1925 Civil Service Act did not take place in isolation. Rather, they were introduced against a backdrop of social restrictions affecting women which focused on censorship and control implemented during the first fifteen years of the Irish Free State, culminating in the 1934 Criminal Law (Amendment) Act, the 1935 Conditions of Employment Act and the 1937 Constitution.[102] For many women who had been active within labour, nationalist and feminist movements between 1912 and 1922, the state that emerged from the mid-1920s became a travesty of what they had expected. Independence quickly saw the silencing of radicalism. Mary Clancy has pointed out that 'throughout the 1920s and 1930s, the equality enjoyed by Irish women in 1922, as guaranteed in Article 3 of the Free

State Constitution, was steadily eroded'.[103] In particular, Kevin O'Higgins – and later Eamonn de Valera – was responsible for a series of restrictive legislative measures that indicated clearly to feminists that 'the struggle for women's equality in the Free State was far from over'.[104] The implications of this legislation would impinge on Irish women until the 1970s.

Kevin O'Higgins was assassinated on 10 July 1927. Perhaps it is fitting – bearing in mind that we *are* speaking ill of the dead – that I leave the last words on him to a woman. Writing after his murder, Hanna Sheehy Skeffington felt no regret over O'Higgins, commenting that, unlike Michael Collins, O'Higgins had no kindly personal traits. Rather, she considered him to be 'Mussolini in miniature, ruthless, unrelenting, arid, reactionary and self-righteous'.[105] Certainly, the women of Ireland had no reason for fond remembrance.

PROFESSOR TERENCE DOLAN

St Richard of Dundalk

Chancellor of Oxford and, later, Archbishop of Armagh were very elevated positions for a man who had modestly started life in Dundalk, County Louth, around the year 1300. At that time in his life he was called Richard Rauf. It would take a very special type of personality to be born in Dundalk, then a remote, backward town, and become a star preacher, academic and ecclesiastic in Oxford, London, Paris and Avignon, to associate with the most powerful scholars and bishops of the age, let alone popes and kings, and to die at sixty years of age at the papal curia in Avignon. From there his remains were returned ten years later to be reburied in the Church of St Nicholas, Dundalk. There has been no trace of his tomb for centuries in that church, which is now administered by the Church of Ireland.[1]

It is significant that nowadays the Anglican communion is more devoted to FitzRalph than the Roman Catholic. Indeed, some recognised him as a proto-Protestant because of his highly critical comments on the Church and its members, both clerical and lay, especially on the mendicant orders. The Church of Ireland Church of St Nicholas contains a chapel dedicated to St Richard of Dundalk. As we shall see, some very controversial people gave him the title 'Saint' – so controversial that he was never formally canonised. Popes were understandably wary of heretics, especially those who said that the papacy was a farce, confession a fraud and transubstantiation a confidence trick. The heretic John Wyclif, who died in 1384, said this and it was he who dubbed FitzRalph a saint. Nowadays, his saintly title is maintained only by local, popular acclaim but we shall investigate his life and career to see if this title is unmerited or unearned.

His family name was Rauf. The Raufs were a fairly well-off Dundalk family, one of whose sons was called Dick, Dick Rauf. This was obviously not good enough for an ambitious young man and so, by 1325, he had changed his name to Ricardus FitzRadulphus – in English, Richard FitzRalph – to sound more high class.

One of the richest and most powerful men in Oxford at that time was the aristocratic Richard de Bury, a graduate of Merton College, who was Bishop of Durham from 1333 until his death in 1345. A multi-millionaire by today's standards, he entertained lavishly and gathered around him some of the most distinguished scholars of the age, whom he liked to set disputing about various issues every day after dinner. Medieval meals were enormous and we can imagine them trying to discuss earnest topics such as the Freedom of the Will and Predestination after a huge banquet, if they could talk at all at that stage.

These were most desirable soirées for young men on the make. Among this group was our Richard FitzRalph, who had come to Oxford around 1315 to study at Balliol College. He became a fellow of the college and took his Doctorate in Theology in 1331. Bury was not his only, nor indeed his most powerful, patron. He had also got to know another very powerful, extremely wealthy bishop, John Grandisson, Bishop of Exeter from 1328 to 1369. One of the ways to make money at that time was to get a benefice, an ecclesiastical living which would furnish a 'bénéfice', a French word for profit. Grandisson's father had excellent connections and he had petitioned the pope to allow his son to possess several ecclesiastical offices and the funds and property that went with them. The young Grandisson was only fourteen at the time, an early start to a rich future. At the age of twenty he became Archdeacon of Nottingham. Such shameless wangling, through family connections, must have dazzled FitzRalph, who only began to take a serious interest in pursuing a relationship with Grandisson after he became Bishop of Exeter. FitzRalph had no time for losers. So close did he come to the bishop's family that he took time off from his studies in Oxford to become private tutor to Bishop Grandisson's nephew, John de Northwode, whom he took to study at the Sorbonne in Paris.

Things were going very well for FitzRalph. But he recognised that *the* place to be was Avignon, which had been the seat of the Roman curia since the reign of Pope Clement V, who died in 1314. For a young, ambitious ecclesiatic it was essential to be acknowledged by the pope himself. Besides, FitzRalph liked being around the big players, so much so that he spent a total of thirteen years at Avignon, in the course of this and three other visits (1334–5, 1337–44, 1349–51, 1357–60). Most of this time he should have been working with his fellow clerics and for his parishioners in England and Ireland. A major issue at the time concerned the Beatific Visions, the belief that the Blessed saw God face to face after death. The controversy about this belief arose from disagreement over the time of seeing God – at the time of death or at the time of the resurrection of all the bodies of all humanity at an indeterminate date in the future. Somehow or other FitzRalph contrived to have himself consulted by no less than Pope John XXII (1316–34) and his succcessor, Pope Benedict XII, who reigned from 1334 to 1342, on this issue. Maybe it was because Grandisson had earlier written to the pope asking for 'a prebend or similar appointment for his nephew, John de Northwode, and for his master, Richard FitzRalph, a distinguished Doctor of the Sacred Page who at present – shame it is to say – holds no benefice'.[2] FitzRalph certainly had a powerful friend in Grandisson, who in May 1331 generously gave his Irish friend a salary and promised to get him a benefice.

About this time, too, Grandisson sought permission from John XXII to make FitzRalph a canon. So now he was Canon FitzRalph, but greater things were to come. He had not abandoned his connection with Oxford and at the age of thirty-two or thereabouts he was elected Chancellor of Oxford, a truly spectacular rise to fame and power. But things did not go well. From all accounts, the former Richard Rauf had a mercurial personality, rather like his hero Thomas Becket (murdered in 1170), friend and enemy of Henry II, about whom Grandisson, another of his heroes, had written a book. Indeed, FitzRalph's first sermon to an Avignon audience in July 1335 was on St Thomas of Canterbury.

During FitzRalph's period of office, a number of masters and students decamped from Oxford to the Lincolnshire town of Stamford, in a move which became notorious as the Stamford Schism. We have come to think that Oxford and Cambridge have been major centres of learning almost since their foundation, but their eminence only became fixed in the fourteenth century. Other towns had what we might call third-level institutions, known as studia. Stamford had one of these.

Oxford at that time was a very violent place. Students regularly got drunk and fought in the streets. A major cause of rioting was the feuding between northern and southern students. The northerners decided to withdraw. It is interesting to speculate on why the withdrawal took place during FitzRalph's watch. He was authoritarian and inflexible with the students and this was unwise in view of the delicacy of the situation. Rather than pacifying the students, he made things worse by his high-handed treatment of them. He was clearly very vexed by what had happened and in that hot-headed way of his he wagered his head that the secession would be over in six months. It wasn't and lasted nearly three years. Somebody wrote a poem in 1333 saying that the chancellor should make good the bet and surrender his head. The poem is in Latin and in its first line it reminds FitzRalph of his original name by addressing him as 'Fy-Rauf Fecunda'. His adoption of the splendidly sounding FitzRalph had made him a figure of fun in some quarters. Why he should have been called 'Fecund' is a mystery. It's an odd description to use of a celibate priest. Maybe his celibacy was *á la carte*. I have no evidence for suggesting that, but I am using a device FitzRalph himself liked to use, innuendo.

Thanks to the intervention of King Edward III, the schism ended in 1335 and Stamford was suppressed. It does not seem to have done FitzRalph much harm, though. Possibly it was felt that he had exacerbated the situation so much that the king had to intervene and disabuse unhappy Oxford students of the wisdom of decamping and setting up a university elsewhere. It could be said that FitzRalph brought matters to a head which politically, for Oxford, was a good thing.

After his term of office as chancellor came to an end, he needed a job and it seems that Grandisson and another great figure, Thomas Bradwardine, later Archbishop of Canterbury, whom Geoffrey Chaucer mentions in *The Nun's Priest's Tale*, helped to make him Dean of Lichfield in 1335. He held this post till 1346, though he spent the greater part of that time, 1337–44, back in Avignon, as an absentee. On his return to Avignon he described himself in what has become known as his Sermon Diary as a devoted preacher (*predicator devotus*), a self-preening title which seems to conflict with his perennial absenteeism. It also conflicts with what he says himself on this matter when, speaking as Dean of Lichfield, he castigated those clerical dignitaries who spend all their time in Avignon on clerical junkets.

On his appointment as dean, he set to work straight away and, like a modern developer, demolished some houses to extend and refurbish his main residence, just close to his own residence at Brewood[3] – a neighbour from hell, as we might say now. While Dean of Lichfield, FitzRalph fell out with the Cathedral Chapter because of his imperious treatment of the canons and of one in particular. In a lordly manner, the dean insisted that this man should say Mass in the cathedral every day and, just to make sure that this man did so, he bound him under oath to carry out his instruction. Priests should stay and do their jobs, he insisted. It was most irregular for a legal contract like this to be drawn up to make sure the cathedral clergy behave.

Naturally, this did not go down well with the community and the incident is twice recorded in the cathedral records. Even to this day, the area around Cavan and Louth is famous for the tightfistedness of the locals. FitzRalph, a Louthman, seems to fit into the same pattern. He, too, was mean in the matter of hospitality to his fellow clerics in Lichfield. He insisted that he was obliged to entertain them on only two occasions in the year, according to the letter, not the spirit, of the law – on the feast of the patron saint of the diocese, St Chad, and on the feast of the Assumption. He got the Cathedral Chapter to make a formal agreement to this effect. Such meanness was insensitive and it also disclosed another feature of his personality. He was a literalist and very litigious.

His canons were unhappy with him on several other issues concerning money. It seems that he was not so literal about his own obligations over diocesan funds. For no good reason, he fired the deans' proctor at the curia (the person who acted on his behalf) and the deans gave FitzRalph the money to take to Avignon to pay this man, Robert de Thresk,[4] the sum he was owed. Thresk later wrote to the canons complaining that he had not been paid. What, one wonders, did the dean do with the money? Later in life, he castigated the parishioners of Dundalk for not paying the tithe money that they owed to the diocese. He rarely did what he preached at others to do.

He might not have been generous to his fellow ecclesiastics who had to run his cathedral while he was away, but he was very generous to his three nephews. He facilitated their paths to study in Oxford and arranged appointments for them in Avignon, Ossory and Oxford. The Latin word 'nepos' means nephew and this, I suggest, is a classic case of nepotism on FitzRalph's part – hypocrisy, too. For example, in an address he gave to leading clergy of his diocese in 1352, he castigated them for nepotism and alleged, further, that their so-called nephews and nieces were really their own offspring for whom they pillaged the Church.

He was obsessively conscious of status and carefully designated himself by his official titles right up to the time when he could proudly call himself Ricardus Radulphi Archiepiscopus Armacanus Hybernie Primas – Richard FitzRalph, Archbishop of Armagh, Primate of Ireland. Before that, he formally described himself as Dean Richard (Ricardus Decanus) and he could hardly wait to call himself Richard, Archbishop-elect of Armagh, before achieving the highest title itself.[5] He was also very concerned about the symbols of office, particularly in the matter of his primatial cross, which symbolised his status as head of the Church in Ireland. He insisted that his cross should be carried before him, not just in his own diocese of Armagh, but also in that of Dublin, where the archbishops jealously guarded their sole right to have their primatial crosses carried before them. On one of his visits to Avignon (1349–51), early in his tenure of the archbishopric of Armagh, he asked the pope to give him the right to have his cross carried before him wherever he happened to be in Ireland. At that time, Armagh was a desperately poor, dysfunctional diocese which needed its leader to be there constantly. FitzRalph, though, seems to have been more troubled by the trappings of his office than by his duties as pastor. It was left to no less a person than King Edward III to tell FitzRalph to go home to Ireland to look after his diocese.

To be fair, though, to FitzRalph, the issue over which diocese had primacy, Armagh or Dublin, was quite a long-running one. A predecessor, Archbishop Jorz of Armagh, in 1313 tried to have his cross borne before him when he came to Dublin to attend a parliament but some members of the staff of Archbishop of Dublin John Lech (1311–13) sallied forth and violently disrupted Archbishop Jorz's procession. Jorz had to put away his cross. Matters came to a head, though, in FitzRalph's time and a compromise was reached whereby Dublin was titled the primatial see of Ireland and Armagh the primatial see of All Ireland, on the pattern adopted for the Church in England, with the Archbishop of Canterbury being Primate of All England and the Archbishop of York, Primate of England.

FitzRalph was, from the first, determined to exhibit the dignity of his office. It is recorded that he was consecrated Archbishop of Armagh in July 1346 in Exeter Cathedral, the seat of his great benefactor and friend John Grandisson. After his consecration,[6] the former Richard Rauf of Dundalk rode in state around the city of Exeter dressed in the same white vestments that important ecclesiastics would wear on such occasions in the papal court in Avignon. What the citizens of Exeter, which was regarded as what we now call 'culchie' territory, made of this extravagant, costly grandeur one can only guess. The phrase 'beggar on horseback' comes to mind.

FitzRalph was in no rush to get back to Ireland. He seems to have devoted the time before his homecoming to trying to sort out the primacy question. He returned to his archdiocese before Easter 1348. Soon after his arrival, he spent a fortnight giving sermons in the eastern, Anglo-Norman part of his diocese, visiting, among other places, Mansfieldtown, Ardee and, of course, Drogheda in his native County Louth. The next year he went to Dublin to register his primatial claims. He became so heated over the issue that, in a fit of temper, he excommunicated all those who opposed his primacy. Such shenanigans began to annoy Edward III, who had hoped the new archbishop would be active in bringing peace to Ireland and harmony between the natives and the settlers. But FitzRalph had his own priorities, especially his dignity.

He manipulated facts to suit his own agenda. He argued against the friars concerning the rule of absolute poverty, *paupertas absoluta*. He arraigned the friars for their deception and deviance from this rule of life, conveniently choosing to ignore the fact that only one mendicant order, the Franciscans, were committed to practising absolute poverty. The Augustinians, Carmelites and Dominicans were not bound by this rule. Such was his determination to rid the Church of friars that he used every rhetorical means, true or false, to denigrate his opponents. Ungratefully and ungraciously, he was particularly enraged at the Franciscans, the order whose close familiarity he had enjoyed as a child since they were the only religious order at that time in his native Dundalk, a fact he warmly acknowledged in a sermon on St Francis delivered in October 1349.[7] Here, too, he noted that some of his relations had joined the order. Eaten bread is soon forgotten.

The high point of FitzRalph's final trip to Avignon took place on 8 November 1357. On that day he delivered his most famous diatribe against the friars, especially the Franciscans, the order which he had spent the past ten years excoriating for their venality, delinquency and hypocrisy. It was a tour de force. On this momentous occasion, the pope, Innocent VI, was present and the curia of cardinals, at that time twenty in all, much fewer than today. The text of the speech survives in over seventy manuscripts. After the invention of printing, it was published many times. It was delivered in Latin but in order to give it greater currency in England it was translated into English in the 1390s by John Trevisa. John Foxe (1516–83), the notorious hater of Catholics, summarised it, with copious annotations, in his controversial *Book of Martyrs*, published in English in 1563, and said some very complimentary things about its author. FitzRalph's great address has become known as the *Defensio Curatorum*, meaning the Defense of the Secular Clergy (against the mendicant orders). It did untold damage to the image and reputation of friars.[8]

In this address he seeks to demonstrate that the friars, though ordained, do not have the same rights of ministry as secular priests. He is particularly vexed at the way friars admininister the sacrament of penance in confession. They give light penances, he alleges, in order to attract gifts from naïve, wealthy parishioners, who may later consider burying their loved ones in cemeteries attached to friaries rather than in the parish graveyards, which meant a great loss of income to the secular clergy running the parishes. Like vultures, he says, the friars sniff out bodies and chase after grieving families to bury their loved ones. They love administering Extreme Unction, the last rites, because that brings in lots of money.

FitzRalph's main authority for his denial of the rights of friars to hear confession is a document which issued from the Fourth Lateran Council of 1215. It begins with the ambiguous phrase 'Let everyone of either sex' (*Omnis utriusque sexus*) go to confession to their own priest at least once a year and then at Easter or thereabouts, a rule known as the Easter Duty. FitzRalph said that friars were not priests at all in the accepted sense of the word, a ludicrously wrong-headed claim, since the mendicant orders were sanctioned by papal authority. Understandably, the friars were furious at such preposterous statements and fought back over many decades, sometimes ingeniously. FitzRalph died in 1360 and twenty years later a Dominican friar, Richard Helmslay, said in public that the Lateran Council canon *Omnis Utriusque Sexus* applied only to people who were literally 'utriusque sexus', of either sex, that is, bisexuals or homosexuals – indeed, hermaphrodites.[9] Other than this type of person, no one else need go to confession. We can only imagine what consternation that caused, in all quarters.

FitzRalph's address to the pope and cardinals contains a string of allegations and hearsay, as well as what he proffers as stronger evidence. For instance, he tells a moving story of a father whom he met at the entrance to his lodgings. This man said that he had a son of thirteen and the friars had taken him into their order and he had difficulty in communicating with him. It's a rather tabloid story.

He is especially exercised about the way the Franciscans claim to be living a life of absolute poverty, based on the life of Christ and his apostles. Apart from the fact that, according to him, the hypocritical friars lead rich, consumerist lives, there is also a theological objection to poverty. He denies that Christ lived in this way because poverty is bad and Christ would not espouse badness. This leads FitzRalph to make the outrageous claim that poverty is an effect of sin: if you are poor, he says, it's because you have committed some dreadful act. Therefore, you deserve to be poor. You should work for your possessions. He likes the Old Testament Proverb 14:20: 'The poor man shall be hateful even to his neighbour.' Nobody wants to be poor. They are lazy and should go out to work. It was Thatcherism before Thatcher.

He is not above making allegations about friars and women, especially queens and socialites, above all beautiful ones. He inveigles the pope and the rest of the audience into imagining what the friars and the ladies who were making their confessions to them got up to in their private chambers and then says, 'but I won't go any further into such matters', just like a tabloid journalist. It is a slur, but a very reckless one to make on FitzRalph's part, because the sole royal confessors in England from the reign of Henry III to the fall of Richard II were Dominicans, and the queens had a preference for Franciscan confessors. Confession was always tricky at that time. It was administered in dark, discreet parts of churches. There were no confessional boxes till the sixteenth century, when they were invented in Milan by the local bishop, later St Charles Borromeo (1538–84), nephew of Pope Pius IV, formerly Cardinal de Medici, to protect penitents from allegedly predatory confessors. In FitzRalph's time, because there were no confessional boxes, the risk of scandal was ever present. That is why both Geoffrey Chaucer and his great contemporary William Langland, in his poem *Piers Plowman*, say such critical things about the administration of the Sacrament of Penance.

FitzRalph continually uses scripture to back up his negative views about mendicancy. Sometimes he forces a quotation into a most unlikely interpretation. For instance, 'Lead us not into temptation' from the Lord's Prayer (Matt. 19:21) is interpreted to mean that becoming a mendicant friar leads to temptation. Therefore, studying to be a friar disobeys a central instruction of the Our Father. What he says is sheer nonsense, of course, but it sows the seeds of doubt in the minds of gullible parishioners.

Although he is at the most international court in Christendom, in Avignon, he refers pointedly to the immorality and crime committed in his own archdiocese of Armagh, which could have done without bad publicity at that time. It did not need negative exposure like this:

> I think I must have about two thousand subjects in my diocese of Armagh. Murders, arson, robberies are committed there. The criminals are brought to court and sentenced, which brings with it the sentence of excommunication, and yet only about forty come to me or the special priests responsible for absolving such sins. Why so? Because they are absolved, or are said to be absolved, by friars.

The friars are undermining not only the morality of his parishioners, with their soft penances, but his authority and, most important of all, his income.

The numerical calculations in these famous remarks about Armagh may not be accurate. FitzRalph is prone to exaggeration. He claims that the friars are buying up all the books in Oxford so that his own students can't study properly. He also claims that in his day there were thirty thousand students at Oxford and that that number had reduced to six thousand because of the friars. Parents were terrified to send their sons to Oxford because the friars would entice them to become friars. Instead, the wary parents made their sons become farmers. Recent research shows that there were only about one thousand six hundred students in Oxford at that time and maybe about two hundred and fifty friars.[10] Added to all his other blemishes, FitzRalph is bad at sums, dangerously so. But that does not stop him from using an extraordinary statistic to support his calumnies against the mendicants.

FitzRalph ends his address with the biblical quotation on which it is based and which he inserts throughout its course – 'Judge not according to appearance; but judge just judgement' (John 7:24). I think this sums up the major flaw in his approach. He is judgemental about what the friars appear to be doing. So often in the address he uses hearsay terms such as 'it appears', 'it is said' and so forth. He does not practise what he preaches, neither is he candid about his real agenda. He says that he did not want to abolish the friars, but few believed him. After his death, a poem which featured him, using his eponymous name of Armachan (abbreviated from Armachanus, Archbishop of Armagh), says this about him and the friars:

> With and O and and I, one says full stille
> Armachan destroy ham, if it is goddes wille[11]

The next year, Edward III showed his displeasure at FitzRalph's wild attack. He began to support the friars.

FitzRalph died in 1360. After his death his words still resonated and had some remarkable effects, sometimes, perhaps, disastrously. The longest portrait in the General Prologue to Geoffrey Chaucer's *Canterbury Tales* is that of the friar who is described as associating with the rich, especially rich women, despising the poor, giving easy penances and so forth (lines 210–11, 215–19, 221–4, 243–7). All these allegations had been made thirty or so years before by Richard FitzRalph. In an age when writers rarely, if ever, acknowledged sources or influences, it would have been unlikely if Chaucer had cited FitzRalph. So it is a conjecture on my part that FitzRalph put these ideas into Chaucer's head. The archbishop had been a celebrated preacher in London, Chaucer's home town, for a number of years. He had delivered anti-mendicant sermons in various locations in the city, including the most prominent of all, St Paul's Cross, in 1356–7, when Chaucer was about sixteen. The young poet may have been there or heard about it. Suffice it to say that anti-fraternal sentiments were current all over Europe at that time, but the most famous critic of the friars, who publicly claimed to be speaking on behalf of all secular clergy, was the man from Dundalk, a man who had associations with King Edward III and the court to which Chaucer was himself attached by marriage.

One unintended consequence of FitzRalph's and Chaucer's anti-mendicancy should be mentioned. Chaucer, the most famous and celebrated poet in England, disappeared in 1400 or thereabouts. His death is recorded on a tomb in Westminster Abbey as 25 October 1400. This is probably wrong because the tomb itself dates from 1556, one and a half centuries after the event took place. So what happened to Geoffrey Chaucer? After the assassination of Richard II, the new king, Henry IV, who had usurped the throne from the rightful king, Richard, a major patron of Chaucer's, began a series of witch-hunts against supporters of the old regime. Henry and his chief henchman, the sinister Archbishop Arundel of Canterbury, needed pretexts. What better than to examine alleged miscreants to see if they had made any anti-clerical remarks? The friars were very powerful – confessors to kings and queens – and it follows that criticism of the friars could be interpreted as criticism of the spiritual advisors to the monarch and his wife. If Chaucer was murdered, as Terry Jones and I believe,[12] a factor in the process which led to his sudden disappearance and death could well have been the anti-mendicant sentiments against the royal confessors which he publicly voiced in his writings – sentiments which the huge prestige of FitzRalph had helped to authenticate and disseminate during Chaucer's youth. Moreover, allegations that Chaucer was a secret Wycliffite or Lollard, each heretical labels, were strengthened by the fact that Wyclif acknowledged FitzRalph as a major influence on his thinking and kept referring to him as 'St Richard'. Such connections probably cost FitzRalph his cardinalship and Chaucer his life. Mud sticks. Chaucer had not expected to die so soon, as is obvious from the fact that one of his last recorded acts was to take out a new tenancy on his dwelling.

With all the bad things, one good thing that FitzRalph originated may concern the late President Richard Nixon. In his increasingly frantic attacks on the friars, FitzRalph developed an explosive theory which has come to be known as the theory of Dominion and Grace. It means that if you are in an important, responsible office and if you are held to be delinquent by your peers, you can be removed from that office – in other words, impeachment. Lack of grace means removal from dominion or lordship. FitzRalph began the long career of this process by claiming that the friars were not behaving as their founders wished, especially the Franciscans, and deserved to be thrown out of the Church's ministry – the law of unintended consequences, from Richard FitzRalph to Richard Nixon.

St Richard is a saint only in his native Dundalk. Plans to make him a cardinal and even to canonise him all failed. He became too associated in people's minds with the forces that resulted in the Reformation. The heretic Wyclif, as we have seen, founder of the heretical sect known as the Lollards, frequently called him a saint and espoused his theory of Dominion and Grace. A couplet, said to have been devised by local people, went the rounds:

> Many a man I see, and many a mile I walk,
> But never saw I holier man than Richard of Dun-
> dalk.

I think his holiness was compromised by the behaviour I have discussed and the picture of him that emerges from our investigation of his extraordinary career.

Born in a remote town in a poverty-stricken, strife-torn diocese, educated by Franciscans, whom he later turned on with vicious ferocity, he sought out important patrons in England who aided his sensational rise to fame and power. By nature mercurial and energetic, he lectured and preached in Ireland, England and France. He died in Avignon after having lost a major case against the mendicant orders. He was made a saint by popular acclamation because it helps to have a saint's body in a church. It brings in tourists, pilgrims and money. It's very good for business. But he was never formally canonised. Even so, a later archbishop, by the name of Dowdall, a relation of the Raufs, in 1545 declared that his memory would be celebrated in the diocese every year on 27 June. FitzRalph consorted with the rich, criticised the poor for being poor, got jobs for his family, upset King Edward III, infuriated the scholars and students of Oxford and led the international campaign against the friars, which was a little later taken up by Chaucer in *The Canterbury Tales* and William Langland in *Piers Plowman* in England.

Famously vain, headstrong, opportunistic, venal, snobbish, hypocritical and unpredictable, Richard Rauf of Dundalk, dean, chancellor and archbishop, merits our admiration for virtually everything but holiness. He was a star but not a saint.

RUTH DUDLEY EDWARDS

Mrs Markievicz[1]

O n a trip down memory lane in 1996 during a speech at the Rotunda in Dublin, Gerry Adams spoke of

> when Countess Markievicz, a champion of the poor, a socialist, a feminist, a nationalist and a republican died, permission for her lying in state in the City Hall or the Mansion House was refused by the state. Her remains were brought here to the Rotunda where over 100,000 people filed by her coffin to pay their last respects.[2]

That was Markievicz the outlaw, victim of the wicked Free State, inspiration for a modern IRA that was still killing, maiming, torturing, intimidating, robbing and smuggling for Ireland. The Markievicz of a government minister, Seamus Brennan, in 2003, was a peace-processor. Unveiling a statue to her in Sligo he spoke of

> a woman of great vision who knew that when the fighting was over, and the first steps to freedom won, that guns and weapons should be set aside and work should begin on constructing the political, economic and social framework within which Ireland could grow and prosper as an independent nation.[3]

Now those involved in the peace process must follow her example: 'In doing so, they will be fulfilling the wishes of the Irish people, north and south, who voted resoundingly for a new beginning.'

There are a few problems there. The Constance Markievicz of whom I am speaking ill had nothing peaceable about her. She was a self-indulgent, bloodthirsty show-off who brainwashed children into believing they must die for Ireland, who killed without pity and who – defying the vote of the Irish people in June 1922 to accept the Treaty – continued to murder during the civil war. Craving excitement and the limelight, she adopted causes she barely understood because she was mesmerised by charismatic male leaders.

Although she gave up a life of material comfort when she espoused revolution, Markievicz was a snob with a bogus title. Physically brave to the point of recklessness, she lacked the moral courage to admit her failure of nerve when faced with the prospect of execution. Beautiful and flamboyant, Constance Markievicz was all style and no substance. Along with other uncompromising green harpies of her generation (among whom my grandmother, Bridget Dudley Edwards, deserves a mention),[4] she became a role model for generations of women who mistook pitilessness and intransigence for principle.

The Protestant Constance Georgina – athletic and bohemian daughter of Sir Henry Gore-Booth of Lissadell in Sligo – was thirty when, in Paris at the turn of the century, she fell in love with an artistic Catholic Polish widower, Casimir Dunin Markievicz, who owned land in the Ukraine. To avoid being disowned by her prosperous family, she said he was 'a hereditary nobleman – i.e. the son of a Count whose family has been on a certain property for seven generations'.[5]

Constance's brother Josslyn asked the British Ambassador to Russia to make enquiries: the resulting report said that 'he takes the title of Count Dunin Markievicz without right in that Poland has never had a Count of that name ... He may have been able to buy this title at the Vatican, or to obtain it in Austria.' He had not. Stanislaus, Markievicz's son by his first marriage, in the 1930s left a sealed letter to be opened after his death which read, 'My father was not a count.'[6]

So Constance knew she had no right to the title of Countess. 'Given Constance's disregard for titles and snobbery, such concerns were of little interest to her,' says Joe McGowan. He quotes her letter to Josslyn in 1911 after King George V's visit: 'Even if I were not a nationalist I should object to kings' visits for they but bring out the worst qualities in people: all sorts of snobbery is developed in people ... everyone using every means to get himself noticed.'

Mr McGowan is unduly kind. This was rank hypocrisy from a woman who should have called herself Mrs Markievicz but instead was always known in Dublin as 'the Countess' or 'Madame' – which is how she appears even in Dáil debates.

Constance wasn't the first phony show-off. There was the egregious Maud Gonne, Mrs John MacBride, who also liked to be called 'Madame'. Tom Clarke's widow, Kathleen, observed the ladies' snobbery at first hand:

> In the early days of our imprisonment, when we were out for exercise, Madame Markievicz and Madame

MacBride walked up and down the exercise yard together, discussing their mutual friends and acquaintances, and disputing as to which of them had the highest social status. Madame Markievicz claimed that she was far above Madame MacBride; she belonged to the inner circle of the Vice-Regal Lodge set, while Madame MacBride was only on the fringe of it. I sometimes listened to them, quite amused; I was outside their social circle, and had nothing in common with them socially. Madame Markievicz took pains to make me aware of the social gulf between us; it didn't worry me.[7]

Incidentally, irritating though Constance was, when I read again the beyond-mawkish prologue to Maud Gonne's memoirs, I briefly wondered why I had chosen Mrs Markievicz over Mrs McBride as the person of whom to speak ill:

I was returning from Mayo triumphant. I had stopped a famine and saved many lives by making the people share my own belief that courage and will are unconquerable and, where allied to the mysterious forces of the land, can accomplish anything. Had I not seen death and despair recede! That afternoon, at the Wishing Well in Ballina, where the girls of the town had led me while waiting for the train, I had seen the fish which they said none of our generation had seen; it had darted across the clear water which bubbles up unceasingly at the foot of a green mound where legend says a queen lies buried. I had wished the wish of all our hearts – a Free Republic, but had refused to tell for it is unlucky to tell wishes. I had been seen off at the station by a cheering crowd and a band; the Town Council had presented me an address and a spinning wheel painted green and gold.

Tired but glowing I looked out of the window of the train at the dark bog land where now only the tiny lakes gleamed in the fading light. Then I saw a tall, beautiful woman with dark hair blown on the wind and I knew it was Cathleen Ni Houlihan. She was crossing the bog towards the hills, springing from stone to stone over the treacherous surface, and the little white stones shone, marking a path behind her, then faded into the darkness. I heard a voice say: 'You are one of the little stones on which the feet of the Queen have rested on her way to Freedom.' The sadness of night took hold of me and I cried; it seemed so lonely just to be one of those little stones left behind on the path.

Being old now and not triumphant I know the blessedness of having been 'one of those little stones' on the path to Freedom.[8]

It is women I'm being rough about here, but of course it was men who created the female images of Ireland – Dark Rosaleen, Mother Ireland, the Shan Van Vocht and Cathleen Ni Houlihan herself – who whinged, supplicated or goaded as the mood took them, until they drove their menfolk to valiant deliverance or bloody vengeance as appropriate. In 1902, Maud Gonne appeared in Yeats's play *Cathleen Ni Houlihan* as the Old Woman seducing the boy about to be married into abandoning all to retrieve the old whinger's four green fields. 'It is a hard service they take that help me,' she warned:

Many that are red-cheeked will be pale-cheeked; many that have been free to walk the hills and the bogs and the rushes will be sent to walk hard streets in far countries … many a child will be born and there will be no father at its christening to give it a name.

Maud declaimed her climactic speech to the audience rather than to the cast – causing the journalist Stephen Gwynn to ask himself if such plays should be produced, unless one was prepared for people to go out to shoot and be shot.

Maud Gonne was enjoying plenty of limelight at the beginning of the twentieth century. Constance was bored. She had never had much interest in her daughter, Maeve, born in 1901. Despatched to Sligo as a baby, Maeve was retrieved for a while but went to her grandparents permanently when she was seven. 'Well, that's over,' Maeve said bitterly one year when Constance paid her customary short visit. 'She won't think of me for another year.'

(Mind you, Maud Gonne – always the reliable eejit – disagreed with those who thought Constance a bad mother. 'Constance loved children and it was a great sacrifice when she sent Maeve to be brought up by her mother because life's evolution had made things too strenuous for the child at home. I have heard people criticise Con for this and speak of her as a neglectful mother. Nothing could be falser than that, but she was so unselfish she sacrificed everything for Ireland.')

'What do I want?' Constance enquired of her diary in 1905. 'I don't know … I feel the want. Women are made to adore and sacrifice themselves and I as a woman demand as a right that Nature should provide me with something to live for, something to die for.'

She was growing weary of Dublin artistic circles. Already a keen suffragette, she found another cause in 1908 when she arrived at Maud Gonne's Inghinidhe na hÉireann one night after a Castle function in train, velvet cloak and diamonds in her hair. Soon she was *inter alia* gardening correspondent for *Bean na hÉireann*:

> It is a very unpleasant work killing slugs and snails but let us not be daunted. A good Nationalist should look upon slugs in the garden in much the same way as she looks on the English in Ireland and only regret that she cannot crush the Nation's enemies with the same ease that she can the garden's, with just one tread of her fairy foot.

Like the English Maud, when the half-English Constance decided to become an Irish nationalist, she turned violently against her own kind.

She stayed keen on women's suffrage and violent protests but the suffragette movement lacked uniforms and guns. Finding Sinn Féin tame and respectable, the woman Casimir called 'my floating landmine' founded Fianna Éireann, a republican youth movement, to implement Maud Gonne's proposal that young people be trained to fight for Ireland. In a fetching uniform, Constance helped teach boys to drill, march, scout, shoot, whistle rebel tunes at police, push soldiers into the gutter and learn that 'giving one's life for Ireland' was the noblest option. She found it all great fun and it offered many opportunities for incendiary speeches, even if as a speaker she showed more enthusiasm than skill. 'Her passionate speeches always appeared to be strained and rarely had any sense in them,' wrote Sean O'Casey, 'and they always threatened to soar into a still-born scream.'[9]

Then she found socialism and fell for James Larkin: 'a Titan who might have been moulded by Michelangelo or Rodin'. Listening to him,

> I realised that I was in the presence of something that I had never come across before, some great primeval force, rather than a man. A tornado, a storm-driven wave, the rush into life of spring and the blasting breath of autumn, all seemed to emanate from the power that spoke.

She became the Red Countess, never happier than in her role as Madame patronising her poor, notably in the soup kitchens that in 1913 Larkin's intransigence had consigned them to. Then, as Maud Gonne had done before her, she took up with James Connolly. As Sean O'Casey put it:

> She wanted to be in everything and to be everywhere. She rushed into Arthur Griffith's arms, near knocking the man down; she dunced [sic] in the Republicanism of the Irish Brotherhood; she stormed into the Gaelic League, but quickly slid out again, for the learning of Irish was too much like work; she bounded into the Volunteers one night, and into the Citizen Army the next. Then she pounced on Connolly and dazzled his eyes with her flashy enthusiasm.

So, Constance became a member of the Citizen Army. 'She made herself a uniform of dark green,' wrote Sean O'Faolain:

> high-collared to the chin, glinting with brass buttons, caught about her middle by leather belt, and she wore a wide-awake hat whose leaf was pinned up on one side by the flaming badge of the Red Hand – the insignia of Larkin's union: on her left breast was an immense Tara brooch of beaten silver intended to catch a bratta swung over the shoulder con brio. There were deep pockets high and low; she wore high knee-boots; sometimes a holster was held to her side by the leather belt.

When before 1916 she posed for a formal photograph in full regalia, she looked lovely. As a member of the Citizen Army put it: 'My God, she was it.' There was yet another uniform when Constance merged Inghinidhe na hÉireann with Cumann na mBan, a militant women's republican organisation supporting Irish Volunteers. It was in that uniform that she would later address the Dáil.

She had no qualms about urging armed rebellion. In 1911, her 'Fianna' column in the separatist paper *Irish Freedom* told its young readers that 'the history of the world proves that there is but one road to freedom, and that is the red road to war': freedom attained by 'oratory, logic or votes' was merely 'a more secure form of slavery'. During the war, shrill, bloodthirsty and silly, Constance wanted the fighting to go on until the British empire was smashed: 'The Germans are winning the war, me boys' was added to the Citizen Army's repertoire.

The rebellion in 1916 offered another marvellous opportunity for Constance to show off.[10] Take her performance in

St Stephen's Green, where she liked to give the impression that she, rather than Michael Mallin, was in charge. Resplendent in her Citizen Army uniform, she marched up and down, gun on shoulder, in full view of the Shelbourne Hotel, causing a sensation among guests and the arriving British troops. The head porter thought that 'the Countess took unfair advantage of her sex'.

Did Mrs Markievicz shoot unarmed Constable Lahiff dead in St Stephen's Green and scream, 'I shot him, I shot him'? We don't know. The evidence is inconclusive. But it certainly would have been in character: she was very anxious to kill. In Sean O'Faolain's words:

> Watching from the shelter of some kind of erection in the Green she saw a khaki uniform in the window of the University Club. It was, actually, an Irishman, Dr de Burgh Daly, watching the movements below him from the window of the reading room. The page-boy from the lower floor was also watching and saw the woman raise her rifle and fire. She missed.

Mrs Markievicz had a terrific time, particularly enjoying ostentatiously shooting snipers and threatening to murder Eoin MacNeill for his temerity in trying to stop a revolution he believed to be immoral. There was even an epiphany in the College of Surgeons when she saw Roman Catholics praying. As later recounted by a friend:

> now, face to face with death, she was deeply impressed by the reality of spiritual things to these men and women among whom she had lived. As she shared their prayers there came to her a vision of the Unseen, which wrought such a change in her

that from that moment to her, too, the things that are seen became temporal and the things that are unseen, eternal.

When she surrendered, Constance lost her composure briefly: 'We dreamed of an Irish Republic, and thought we had a fighting chance.' Then she broke down and sobbed, kissing her pistol before handing it over. (I don't go in for psychobabble or I might be tempted to speak of phallic symbols.)

Her court martial was theatrical. The court president, Brigadier-General Blackadder, was so nervous of her that he got out his revolver and put it on the table in front of him. In the formal record of the trial she is said to have stated: 'I went out to fight for Ireland and it doesn't matter what happens to me. I did what I thought was right and I stand by it.' That was untrue. Elsie Mahaffey reported in her diary that 'All her "dash" and "go" left her … she utterly broke down, cried and sobbed and tried to incite pity in General Blackadder; it was a terrible scene – the gaunt wreck of a once lovely lady.'[11]

This was later elaborated on by William Wylie,[12] the prosecutor, in a private memoir written for his daughter more than thirty years later:

'I am only a woman, you cannot shoot a woman, you must not shoot a woman.' She never stopped moaning the whole time she was in the Court room … We were all slightly disgusted. She had been preaching rebellion to a lot of silly boys, death and glory, die for your country etc., and yet she was literally crawling. I won't say any more, it revolts me still.

Yet she claimed to have said in jail: 'I wish you had the decency to shoot me.' Her death sentence was commuted 'solely and only on account of her sex'.

In prison, Constance asked for instruction: it was off with the old Protestant and on with the new Roman Catholic cloak. So powerful had been her mystical experience in the College of Surgeons that she had little need of the priest's services: 'I can't understand Countess Markievicz at all,' Father McMahon told Hanna Sheehy Skeffington after one session. 'She wants to be received into the Church, but she won't attend to me when I try to explain Transubstantiation and other doctrines. She just says, "Please don't trouble to explain. I tell you I believe all the Church teaches."'

When Constance was released from prison in June 1917, she was greeted by a delirious Dublin crowd. 'Lamp posts were decorated with tricolours and cheering small boys,' recounted Diana Norman, one of her hagiographers:

> work had been abandoned for a triumphal procession, which was led by a pipe band, followed by marchers representing all Con's organisations, followed by a car driven by a uniformed Volunteer with Con standing up in it so that the people could see her.

Why did she receive a welcome greater than any other prisoners? In the view of Frank Sherwin, who knew her in the 1920s and found her naïve, tiresome, ineffectual, deluded, high-handed and unfair and ungenerous in her treatment of him, the worship of Constance (which persists to this day) was an indicator of the Irish inferiority complex that has caused it to have so many popular leaders from the ascendancy.[13]

She was back in jail in 1918, this time with Maud Gonne MacBride and Kathleen Clarke. While Mrs Clarke found Mrs MacBride gentle and courteous, Mrs Markievicz was very trying.

> It appeared to worry her that such an insignificant little person as myself was put in prison with her. Again and again she said to me, 'Why on earth did they arrest such a quiet, insignificant person as you are?' I told her the only information I could give her was what was on my charge sheet, which was exactly the same as hers. If she wanted some information on the matter, she could send her query to the British government. That did not stop her. She kept on referring to it constantly, until one day, my patience being exhausted, I said that she seemed to forget that when important people like her were in prison, somebody had to carry on, even insignificant nobodies like myself, and that anyhow I was not here as a result of going on platforms and making speeches asking for arrest.

When news came that Markievicz had been elected to Parliament:

> I was delighted to hear it; at last, I thought, women are going to get recognition. Madame got so excited she went yelling and dancing all over the place. Before leaving us the Governor said, 'And what about little Mrs Clarke?' He made the remark to me, but Madame heard it; she rushed over and flung her arms around me and said, 'Never mind, Kathleen, I'll see you get elected when I get out.' Her air of patronage made me feel like hitting her, but with the Governor and Matron present I had to control my rage.

As Minister of Labour, Constance specialised in making brutal speeches about ostracising the police. During the Anglo-Irish War, as later during the civil war, she was as enthusiastic a killer as ever. Sir Ormonde Winter, Deputy Chief of Police and Director of British Intelligence in Ireland from 1920–22, described her as 'hard, unrepentant, but loquacious' and proudly 'claiming to have killed eight British soldiers and hoping she would be the reason for the death of many more'.

Mind you, compared to some of the harpies she was positively mild. In response to a question from the prison matron as to why she stayed unfriendly while the Mesdames had been responsive, Kathleen Clarke said: 'I am Irish, purely Irish, and as such, knowing my country's history, how can I be other than hostile to my country's only enemy, England?' Though the prison staff were kind:

> I cannot forget what you represent. The other two ladies are different in this way, that they are of English descent, born in Ireland, and they belong to what we call there the Ascendancy, or English element. They have many English relatives and friends, whom they think highly of. They have identified themselves with our struggle for freedom from the conviction that our cause is a just cause, and they have worked and suffered with us in that cause, but naturally they cannot feel the same hostility to England as I do.

Kathleen was a distinguished example of the MOPE (Most Oppressed People Ever) republican tendency. 'I have no knowledge of the English in their own country,' she explained to her well-meaning interlocutor. 'I only know the history of the English in my country, and if there is anything worse in the world than that, I do not know it.'

Still, Constance was equally tunnel-visioned. To her stepson Stanislaus – who had been sent off to the Ukraine in 1915 as surplus to requirements, had endured five years in the Imperial Marine Guard and had been held hostage by Bolsheviks for two years – she wrote in 1923:

> You know I've had a pretty stiff time of it, about three years and a half, and some of it was awful. I did what I could to help you and I think that some of the people whom I got to intercede for you may have been a little help ... Jim Larkin ... promised to try and get certain Bolshie friends of his to try and get you set free ... You rail against the Bolshies. I know little about them, but one thing I do know is that our people suffered far worse from the English.

Most of the women elected to the Dáil in 1921 were there because of their relationship to high-profile dead men: Kathleen Clarke (husband and brother); Margaret Pearse (two sons); Kate O'Callaghan (husband shot by Black and Tans); Mary McSwiney (brother Terence who died on hunger strike). The exceptions were the militant Dr Ada English and Constance Markievicz, though the latter made much use of her friendship with James Connolly. To a harpy, they were bitter irreconcilables. Their contributions to the Treaty debates were much worse than I had remembered.[14]

What a crew! Here is Mrs Kate O'Callaghan:

> Lest anybody should afterwards question my right to stand here and criticise and condemn this Treaty, I

want it to be understood here and now that I have the clearest right in the world. I paid a big price for that Treaty and for my right to stand here … When it was found that the women Deputies of An Dáil were not open to canvass, the matter was dismissed with the remark: 'Oh, naturally, these women are very bitter.' Well, now, I protest against that. No woman in this Dáil is going to give her vote merely because she is warped by a deep personal loss. The women of Ireland so far have not appeared much on the political stage. That does not mean that they have no deep convictions about Ireland's status and freedom. It was the mother of the Pearses who made them what they were. The sister of Terence MacSwiney influenced her brother, and is now carrying on his life's work. Deputy Mrs. Clarke, the widow of Tom Clarke, was bred in the Fenian household of her uncle, John Daly of Limerick. The women of An Dáil are women of character, and they will vote for principle, not for expediency.

And Mary McSwiney:

We have heard a great deal about war tonight and the horrors of war. You men that talk need not talk to us about war. It is the women who suffer, it is the women who suffer the most of the hardships that war brings. You can go out in the excitement of the fight and it brings its own honour and its own glory. We have to sit at home and work in more humble ways, we have to endure the agony, the sunshines, the torture of misery and the privations which war brings, the horror of nightly visitations to our houses and their consequences.

Speaking Ill of the Dead

Mrs Kathleen Clarke:

> I heard big, strong, military men say here they would vote for this Treaty, which necessarily means taking an Oath of Allegiance, and I tell those men there is not power enough to force me, nor eloquence enough to influence me in the whole British Empire into taking that Oath, though I am only a frail scrap of humanity.

Poor Mrs Pearse, brokenhearted, dim and in thrall to de Valera, made a variation on what she called her 'Pat and Willie' speech:

> It has been said here on several occasions that Pádraig Pearse would have accepted this Treaty. I deny it. As his mother I deny it, and on his account I will not accept it. Neither would his brother Willie accept it, because his brother was part and parcel of him. I am proud to say to-day that Pádraig Pearse was a follower and a disciple, and a true disciple, of Tom Clarke's. Therefore he could not accept this Treaty.

And after much *ráiméis* and reminiscence, she concluded:

> Remember, the day will come – soon, I hope, Free State or otherwise – when those bones shall be lifted as if they were the bones of saints. We won't let them rattle. No! but we will hold what they upheld, and no matter what anyone says I feel that I and others here have a right to speak in the name of their dead.

No one rattled the bones like Mary McSwiney, whose most staggering contribution was a three-hour speech which reads like *The Vagina Monologues* without the sex.

She [England] has the military. I know that, but she cannot win this battle, for if she exterminates the men, the women will take their places, and, if she exterminates the women, the children are rising fast; and if she exterminates the men, women and children of this generation, the blades of grass, dyed with their blood, will rise, like the dragon's teeth of old, into armed men and the fight will begin in the next generation.

As the brave Deputy Alec McCabe put it, 'She would not leave us even a grasshopper.' He was dismissed by Constance as 'an old woman'.

While Mrs Markievicz stood shoulder to shoulder with Miss McSwiney, whom she congratulated on 'such an eloquent and well-reasoned speech', she was herself particularly outraged by the notion that – in the interests of reconciliation – some means should be found to give southern unionists political representation.

And what do the Southern Unionists stand for? You will all allow they stand for two things. First and foremost as the people who, in Southern Ireland, have been the English garrison against Ireland and the rights of Ireland. But in Ireland they stand for something bigger still and worse, something more malignant; for that class of capitalists who have been more crushing, cruel and grinding on the people of the nation than any class of capitalists of whom I ever read in any other country, while the people were dying on the roadsides. They are the people who have combined together against the workers of Ireland, who have used the English soldiers, the English police, and every institution in the country to ruin the farmer, and more especially the small farmer, and to send the people of Ireland to drift in the emigrant ships and to die of horrible disease or to sink to the bottom of the Atlantic. And these anti-Irish Irishmen are to be given some select way of entering this House, some select privileges – privileges that they have earned by their cruelty to the Irish people and to the working classes of Ireland; and not only that, but they are to be consulted as to how the Upper House is to be constituted. As a Republican who means that the Republic means Government by the consent of the people [hear, hear] I object to any Government of that sort whereby a privileged number of classes established here by British rule are to be given a say – to this small minority of traitors and oppressors – in the form of an Upper Chamber as against all, I might say, modern ideas of common sense, of the people who wish to build up a prosperous, contented nation. But looking as I do for the prosperity of the many, for the happiness and content of the workers, for what I stand, James Connolly's ideal of a Workers' Republic [A Deputy: 'Soviet Republic'] co-operative commonwealth.

Constance's last contribution to the proceedings was this exchange with Michael Collins as she, all the women deputies and the rest of de Valera's supporters followed de Valera out of the House.

MR M. COLLINS: Deserters all! We will now call on the Irish people to rally to us. Deserters all!
MR CEANNT: Up the Republic!
MR M. COLLINS: Deserters all to the Irish nation in

her hour of trial. We will stand by her.
MADAME MARKIEVICZ: Oath breakers and cow-
ards.
MR M. COLLINS: Foreigners – Americans – Eng-
lish.
MADAME MARKIEVICZ: Lloyd Georgeites.

P.S. O'Hegarty said that during the civil war Dublin was

> full of hysterical women. Left to himself, man is
> comparatively harmless. He will always exchange
> smokes and drinks and jokes with his enemy, and he
> will always pity the 'poor devil' and wish that the
> whole business was over … It is woman … with her
> implacability, her bitterness, her hysteria that makes a
> devil of him. The Suffragettes used to tell us that
> with women in power there would be no more war.
> We know that with women in political power there
> would be no more peace.

So one of the achievements of Constance Markievicz and
her merry band of female fanatics was to convince generations of men that women were better kept out of politics.
Why do we honour people like her? There are Markievicz
statues, one a bust located in St Stephen's Green where she
strutted her flamboyant stuff; there are leisure centres; there
are parks. What a role model for Irish children! She was a
snob, a fraud, an exhibitionist, a murderer who neglected
her own child but trained other people's children to kill and
die for Ireland.

She was a beauty, certainly. But, boy, was she terrible!
A sacred cow indeed.

DR PETER HART

Walter Long: Irish Revolutionary

Walter Long was born in 1854 into an ancient landed family in Wiltshire, southern England. Young Walter grew up on an estate of over fifteen thousand acres, at least part of which had been in the family since the fourteenth century. In his youth – as might be expected given his squirearchical origins – he devoted himself to dogs, horses and sport, and this was equally true of his education at Harrow and Christ Church, Oxford, where he did not distinguish himself academically and did not graduate.[1]

Of course, he didn't have to do either since, once his father died in 1875, Walter inherited his house, land and income. His politics came with the estate. Not only his father but also both grandfathers had been Conservative MPs so it was, again, more or less by inherited right that he in turn was elected to the House of Commons in 1880 at the age of twenty-six. Despite his lack of qualifications apart from social position, he was soon a professional politician and he would spend almost the whole of the next forty years as a Member of Parliament, up until his retirement in 1921.[2]

Taken as a whole, Long's political career was undoubtedly a successful one, albeit far from brilliant. He was defeated in several elections and represented a remarkable total of

seven different seats in all: a testament either to his persistence or to an aptitude for wearing out his welcome. His
ministerial career showed a steady progression through the
ranks. He was made a junior minister of Local Government
in 1886, in which department he made his first mark by aid-
ing in the establishment of county councils. When the Tories returned to government in 1895 after the last of
William Gladstone's ministries, he was given his first seat
in cabinet as President of the Board of Agriculture (where
he earned the nickname of 'Muzzler Long' for his crack-
down on rabies). At the culmination of his political life,
during and after the Great War, he held the prestige portfolios of the Colonial Office and the Admiralty, so he was
able to end his career as guardian of the Empire and the
Royal Navy, a true patriot's wet dream.

By 1918, Long's efforts and ambitions had been slowed by
chronic ill health. At the peak of his political powers, however – in 1911 – he came close to leading the Conservative
(or Unionist) Party. Andrew Bonar Law got the job instead,
as a compromise candidate between Long and Austen
Chamberlain (who both agreed to step aside). Illness may
have played a part in his not winning the prize and probably
diminished his overall political impact, but even if his health
hadn't suffered he would likely have remained what he was:
a secondary figure. He has now largely passed from collective political memory and from the pages of history (even
the history of the party he served all his adult life).[3] He
mostly seems to appear now as the target of passing gibes
in other people's biographies.[4]

Walter Long entered politics as a member of the huntin',
shootin' and fishin' 'Country Gentleman Party' and retained
an occasional reputation for rural idiocy, but he was not
merely a backwoodsman *in excelsis*. He was competent, busy

and ambitious but he lacked speaking ability and was never a big draw in the House or at public meetings. A typical comment after one of his speeches (in 1909) was that he 'does not talk well', but, then again, 'a talking squire is like a talking horse' (in other words, it was impressive that he could do it at all).[5]

Nor were his organisational skills equal to his pursuit of power. Long twice tried to create grassroots movements within British Conservatism, to promote both himself and his favourite causes, but neither really succeeded. One of these was the Union Defence League, founded in 1906 to fight any Liberal attempts at devolution in Ireland. It was equally intended to keep wayward party members in line, however, which neither endeared him to colleagues nor interested many party activists.[6]

Instead, what Long *is* primarily remembered for is for being ill-tempered, sycophantic and an inveterate back-room schemer. Edward Carson, the leader of Ulster unionism and a wary ally, said of him that 'the worst of Walter Long is that he never knows what he wants, but is always intriguing to get it'.[7] Austen Chamberlain, the rival who eventually did become leader of the party, wrote that he was 'at the centre of every coterie of grumblers'.[8] One party insider, comparing Chamberlain and Long at the time of their contest, commented:

> It may be said against Austen Chamberlain that he comes from Birmingham, that he is a Liberal Unionist, that he is not allied by family tradition or landed estates with the traditional Conservative Party. On the other hand, Walter Long has none of these disqualifications, but he possesses every other conceivable one.[9]

As Alvin Jackson asks at the end of Long's entry in the new *Dictionary of National Biography*, was he, perhaps, 'the worst leader the Conservatives never had?'

Which brings me to the title of my essay. Walter Long was, of course, neither Irish nor revolutionary, being both very English and very Conservative. He was a true-blue 'country gentleman': an honest-to-goodness 'Tory squire' in breeding and manner, one of the last of an increasingly *ancien régime*. However, few individuals in the twentieth century had greater personal influence over the course of Irish history and even fewer did more to bring about the Irish revolution.

Long's influence on Irish affairs came from his role as *the* self-appointed expert on Ireland within the British Conservative Party – a position he jealously guarded against all comers. This role was not reflected in the portfolios he held as minister. He was appointed Chief Secretary of Ireland – Minister for Ireland, in other words – for nine months in 1905 but only because two other candidates (including Carson) turned it down first. Instead, Long's power derived from his ability to act as a kind of liaison or broker between Irish and British unionism, derived from his close links with Irish unionists, particularly those among the landed élite.[10] He came by this honestly, as his mother, Charlotte Hume, was from an Anglo-Irish family, as was his wife, Dorothy Boyle, the daughter of the Ninth Earl of Cork. His maternal grandfather, William Wentworth Hume-Dick, was MP for Wicklow for many years and a neighbour of the Parnell family (although no friend of Charles).[11]

Nor is there any doubt about his genuine and visceral opposition to home rule, as displayed in angry speeches in parliament. On one occasion he referred to Irish Party MPs as 'whipped hounds', a remark he later regretted, not because it might have given offence but because it might cause political problems.[12]

Long's unionism was not just a matter of upbringing and sentiment, though; he also clearly used it to further his career. When he lost his Liverpool seat in the Liberal landslide of 1906, such was his reputation as a defender of the union (not to mention a friend to unionist job-seekers and lobbyists while Chief Secretary) that he was quickly given a new seat in South Dublin, then still a bastion of Protestant loyalty. With this came a whole new power base as he also became Chairman of the Irish Unionist Alliance and the Ulster Unionist Council, as well as leader of the Irish Unionist Party in parliament.

Long quit most of these jobs over the next few years and returned to an English constituency in order to refocus on British politics and to avoid getting lost in the party shuffle. He wasn't able to gain the leadership, but his time in Ireland and his constant beating of the unionist drum in England inevitably made him a leading figure in the home rule crisis of 1912–14, with the Conservatives and Unionists pitted against the governing Liberals and their Irish Party allies in the greatest constitutional battle of modern UK history.

The Third Home Rule Bill, introduced in 1912, was actually just the largest of a series of confrontations over the basic legitimacy of Liberal government policies. The first of these came with the so-called 'People's Budget' brought down by Chancellor of the Exchequer David Lloyd George in 1909. This raised money for progressive social measures – and for battleships – partly on the backs of the wealthy and landed: another of Walter Long's key constituencies. When the Conservative-dominated House of Lords rejected it, the Liberals called two elections in a row in 1910 and they and the Conservatives fought the issue to a draw in Britain, leaving the balance of power in the hands of the Irish Party, led by John Redmond. The result was the Parliament Act of 1911, which removed the Lords' veto power and paved the way for a home rule bill, which was Redmond's condition for backing Prime Minister Herbert Asquith.

The majority of Conservatives, including Walter Long, were willing to allow the budget and the Parliament Act through knowing that they did not have the public support to fight to the last ditch. But home rule was a different matter. Not only was the union of Britain and Ireland one of the foundations of their party's identity and world view, but also the Irish question allowed them to set their sights on the generally unpopular nationalists and perhaps win an election in defence of the United Kingdom and the Empire.

Long was not quite the most rabid of anti-home rulers, but he was a true believer in the direness of the threat it offered to property, freedom and national security, and he was fiercely determined to keep unionism to a hard line right to the end of the fight. His rhetoric was always uncompromising: for example, he was involved in the British Covenant, whose signatories pledged to support their comrades in Ulster in defiance of the law. He consistently opposed negotiation or compromise and pushed his leader, Bonar Law, not to make any concessions in his talks with Asquith in 1913 and 1914. He was even willing to push the constitutional envelope by asking the king to intervene against the Liberal government.[13]

Most striking of all for a senior Conservative politician – and for a self-proclaimed paragon of law and order – Long not only encouraged the formation of the paramilitary Ulster Volunteer Force in 1913, he may also have actually helped to arm it. Alvin Jackson has uncovered good evidence that he approved and partially financed the Larne gun-running of April 1914, which brought tens of thousands of rifles into the North under the noses of the navy and the secret service.[14] It was only at this point that the UVF became a credible military threat. To put this another way, Walter Long was instrumental in turning an essentially peaceful protest campaign (whatever the rhetoric) into a direct challenge to the right of a liberal democratic state to govern. And he was also instrumental, therefore, in breathing vigorous life into the nationalist response, the Irish Volunteers, which would soon become the primary vehicle for republican rebellion.

Now, it may well be that this was all part of a high-risk bluff designed to force Prime Minister Herbert Asquith to call an election. It's not as if Long actually wanted a civil war. But even if he had been willing to pull back from the brink if the Liberals refused to blink, pushing the crisis that far would likely have given it a momentum beyond any finesse or control. The stakes could not have been higher, for both his party and his country. The formation of paramilitary armies and the willingness of parliamentary parties to defy legal authority indicate the beginnings of a breakdown in British democracy, which might well have been completed if the Great War had not intervened in July 1914.[15]

To recollect the full magnitude of the crisis, it should be recalled that the Larne operation took place just after the so-called Curragh Mutiny among British military officers in Ireland, raising the spectre of the army taking sides between parties in a political dispute. Long was not directly involved in this but he was delighted by it – and his favoured idea of involving the king would have raised further serious questions of military loyalty. It tells us something of the temper of the times, and of the pall of paranoia hanging over British politics, that Long believed he himself had been targeted for arrest and that the 'mutineers' had prevented a kind of Liberal reign of terror.[16] It wasn't true, of course, but it is exactly this sort of mindset that brings down democracies.

Incidentally, if Asquith had caved in and called an election, Long's proposed manifesto would have included not only no home rule but also universal conscription, the restoration of the House of Lords' power and the reimposition of Anglicanism as the state Church of Wales: a very reactionary agenda indeed.[17]

The UK constitution was ultimately saved by German aggression, but Long battled away to the very end to obstruct home rule. The Buckingham Palace Conference was convened under the auspices of King George in 1914, with Irish political leaders invited to attend and discuss the potential ramifications of home rule. 'If we stand firm, there can be no settlement!' Long wrote on 21 July 1914.[18] War brought a party truce soon thereafter and Redmond managed to win one final trick by getting the Home Rule Bill passed rather than dropping it altogether. It was suspended until the war was over, however, so the nationalist victory was symbolic only – and fleeting.

Long and many of his Conservative and Unionist colleagues still managed to get back into power anyway, thanks to the coalition government of national unity formed in 1915. He was thus back on the inside, in the cabinet, when the 1916 Easter Rising took place and was able to take a leading part in the discussions on what to do next. Once the rebellion was quashed, Liberal and Irish Party thoughts turned to the idea of completing the political settlement, to keep nationalist Ireland from reigniting. Then-Minister of Munitions Lloyd George was told to explore the options and, in a remarkable feat of deal making, managed to craft an agreement between Redmond and Carson. A Dublin parliament would be set up as soon as possible but its writ would not run in the six north-eastern counties of present-day Northern Ireland. Two key issues were creatively fudged, however: the permanence of partition and the extent of cabinet backing for the deal as being necessary for the war effort. Such ambiguities were always present when Lloyd George dealt with Irish politicians but both Carson and Redmond went ahead in good faith and sold the deal to their followers as reciprocal sacrifices.

Before the agreement could be implemented, Long – along with the southern unionist peer Lord Landsdowne – seized upon these inevitable grey areas to lead a wrecking campaign from inside the government. Threatening to break up the coalition, they were able to get the proposals amended to make partition permanent. Redmond furiously rejected this and, as Long and Landsdowne had hoped, the deal fell through in July 1916. This was the last real opportunity for a consensual nationalist–unionist compromise and one backed by all the key Irish players. Killing it was probably Walter Long's greatest political performance.

Lloyd George was bitter at the sabotaging of his efforts, but when he seized the premiership from Asquith later that year, with the backing of the Conservatives, he made sure to keep Walter Long on side when making Irish policy. In fact, he eventually delegated a great deal of cabinet responsibility for Ireland to Long, making him the liaison with Dublin Castle as well as chair of the two key Irish committees in cabinet. He was offered the Chief Secretaryship again – not once but twice – but turned it down, preferring to act behind the scenes as a sort of Ireland Czar (as it might be put in current political terms).

As such, Long was instrumental in placing unionist partisans in key positions in the Irish executive, notably Assistant Under Secretary John Taylor and Lord Chancellor James Campbell. He also encouraged an anti-Catholic climate of suspicion there,[19] as when he encouraged the new viceroy, Lord French (appointed in 1918), to replace his Catholic secretary with Eddie Saunderson, the son of the former Irish unionist leader and an equally bigoted Protestant.[20] In part this was due to his genuine (if unwarranted) fear of spies, which he had had even when Chief Secretary in 1905. But there was a whiff of cronyism too, as Taylor had been his private secretary and Saunderson owed his previous position to Long as well. When objections were raised to the latter's appointment, Long replied that 'he is one of the few Protestants who has the full confidence of Roman Catholics of *all* classes'.[21] If this comment was sincere, it reveals a near-complete ignorance of the Irish political scene in 1918.

Long was prone to spreading wild rumours about rebel intentions and German plots in the guise of 'intelligence', in order to push his default policy of 'restoring law and order' – i.e. suppressing the newly popular and republican Sinn Féin and the Irish Volunteers.[22] His great opportunity in this regard came with Germany's western-front offensive of March 1918, which forced the British government to widen its conscription policy to bring in more soldiers. Long was in the forefront of advocating its extension to Ireland, predicting little resistance. Needless to say, most of the authorities on the ground thought otherwise. At the same time, he saw his chance to deal with what he claimed was German-backed subversion. Based on wildly sexed-up intelligence, he convinced the War Cabinet to arrest and deport most of the Sinn Féin leadership in May 1918, including Arthur Griffith and Eamon de Valera (although not, of course, Michael Collins). The case against these men soon fell apart, to the government's great embarrassment, but Long was unapologetic. As he put it: 'better intern a dozen innocent people than leave one active unscrupulous pro-German at large'.[23] The result was great anger at the government, greater popularity for Sinn Féin and no improvement in either manpower or public order. Sinn Féin went on to triumph in the December 1918 general election, despite – or even because of – the absence of its interned leaders, who mostly remained in prison in England well into 1919. Electoral victory was quickly followed by the establishment of Dáil Éireann and the beginnings of the Irish Republican Army's guerrilla campaign.

'Law and order' was always Long's watchword in Irish policy and after the Rising he insisted that the key to any solution was to first crush Irish republicanism. There should be no talking to terrorists – to any republican – and no conciliation in general. If necessary, martial law should be declared. Long may even have been the first to suggest recruiting British ex-soldiers into the Irish police, an idea that would lead to the creation of the Black and Tans.[24]

One of the features of British policy in these years – especially security policy – was that it was rarely referred to cabinet, so individual entrepreneurs were free to make a lot of it up as they went along. And, for the most part, this meant that a pro-unionist and anti-nationalist bias held sway. The Tans were one result of this neglect, incoherence and ideological blindness, the Ulster Special Constabulary another, the unofficial reprisals policy perhaps another as well. Long's rule by committee had a lot to do with this. It was not until his various protégés from Dublin Castle were evicted, and after he retired in early 1921, that Irish policy finally became coherent and practical.

The one reversal in Walter Long's thinking came on the issue of home rule. In 1919, he was put in charge of finding some form of political settlement to fill the void in government policy in Ireland, as all previous initiatives had failed and the 1914 Home Rule Bill was still on the books. The scheme he championed was for parallel home rule, with two parliaments of limited powers to be established in Dublin and Belfast, with Northern Ireland's boundaries to encompass the Ulster-unionist-preferred six counties. No nationalists or northern Catholics were consulted. This became the basis of the Government of Ireland Act in 1920 but the details were poorly thought out, especially where finance was concerned, and the whole concept was totally unacceptable to even 'moderate' nationalists, let alone Sinn Féin. Much has been made of Long's conversion to federalism or local self-government linked to the idea of a wider imperial union. However, he never contemplated making Ireland a full partner in the empire or the United Kingdom, nor would the devolved administration have had any constitutional protection from metropolitan interference. It was thus far too little too late.

Still, the government persisted in pushing the bill through parliament and defended it as their political bottom line until republican resistance finally forced them to offer actual independence in the form of dominion status along Canadian lines, which became the basis for the Anglo-Irish Treaty of December 1921. By that time, Walter Long had retired from politics and government due to illness but he did have some influence on the final outcome, as he insisted that he had promised Ulster unionist leaders that Northern Ireland's boundary would never be changed, regardless of Catholic and nationalist majorities in many areas adjacent to the Free State.[25] This made it much harder to take the wishes of the actual people involved into account in deciding their political futures.

It seems to me that Walter Long's Irish record is one long catalogue of mischief and error. He helped prevent any rational solution of the home rule crisis and he played an active role in bringing Ireland and Britain to the brink of violent confrontation in 1914. This paramilitary assault on government rule and legitimacy laid the foundation for the revolution to come. He sabotaged the repeated attempt at a settlement in 1916, which helped scuttle the Irish Party and nationalist home rule within a united kingdom for good. He then confirmed Sinn Féin's ascendancy by backing conscription and arranging the erroneous 'German Plot' arrests. His 1920 Government of Ireland Act did nothing to fill the resulting political vacuum, thereby feeding the violence that his security policies helped escalate. If chief secretaries or other ministers contemplated an olive branch or two – as in the spring of 1920 – he helped make sure they were never offered. He was even able to ban any contacts with Sinn Féin outright (although Lloyd George still found ways around this). The more Walter Long got his way, the better republican prospects became. In many ways, he was the secret to the IRA's success.

So what made Walter Long such a terrible decision-maker when it came to Ireland? One thread running through his career was an apparent ideological indifference to democracy – to put it mildly. The wishes of the majority of Irish people, or of the majority in parliament, simply did not factor into his thinking, and the democratic elements of the constitution mattered least. He was a man of the shires, of property and of the empire, not of the people.

This would hardly have endeared him to Lloyd George, among others, so why was he accorded such respect and granted such power? One reason was his right-wing constituency in the Conservative Party, based on his dedicated opposition to nationalism and progressivism. Just as importantly, though, he convinced people that he had special insight into Irish problems. One of his favourite preambles to advice or opinions was his declaration that 'I know Ireland'. Whatever followed, however, inevitably showed this belief to be delusional. For example, when Lloyd George introduced the conscription bill in April 1918, Long wrote to him to say:

> Believe me I know Ireland, you scored a greater triumph there than even in the H of C. The Irish will talk, shout, perhaps get up a fight or two, but they know they are beaten and if we sit tight, make no concessions, you will soon have 200 to 300,000 fine fighting Irishmen in the ranks.[26]

Of course, nothing could have been further from the truth. In fact, his contacts and informants in Ireland were almost all right-wing unionists, out of touch with any form of nationalist opinion, not to mention political reality in general. It was these sources who fed him the exaggerated so-called 'intelligence' that led to the 'German Plot' arrests.

Long's policies proceeded from several set principles. The first was that Catholics and nationalists simply could not be trusted, especially not with political power. Thus, they should not only not be granted self-government, they should also be excluded from senior positions in Dublin Castle. This attitude went beyond a conservative dislike of democratic nationalism to profound ethnic bigotry. Long made many statements describing 'the Irish' in derogatory terms, including the always telling animal analogy – in this case 'whipped hounds'. His dislike extended to religion and to the Catholic Church as bogeyman. He did indeed believe that 'Home Rule means Rome Rule' and he blamed the deteriorating situation in 1918 on the Catholic hierarchy's manipulation of a 'superstitious and subservient' population.[27] This also meant an undifferentiated view of nationalists, with no sense that a John Redmond might be preferred over an Eamon de Valera.

The natural corollary to this attitude was that Ireland should as far as possible be governed by and for unionists (and particularly rich, landed unionists). This was his policy as Chief Secretary in 1905 and it remained the case up to the passage of the immensely flawed Government of Ireland Bill in 1920, when he consulted Ulster unionists assiduously while ignoring nationalists altogether.

In fact, it is a striking feature of Walter Long's Irish career that, unlike other decision-makers, whether Conservative, Liberal or Unionist, he never once negotiated in any way with Irish nationalists. He believed that talking implied concessions and where 'the Irish' were concerned:

one thing and one thing alone succeeds, namely, a strong unflinching attitude towards those who are openly disloyal. It is the only form of Government which the Irish understand. They are very quick, and when they see that disloyalty not only goes unpunished but is sometimes even rewarded they naturally do not hesitate to indulge in their own tastes. It is not because they really want to do mischief so much as, like naughty children, they think it is amusing to give way to their inclinations.[28]

If not ignored, then, nationalists should be repressed and government policies should be imposed regardless of majority views. It was for their own good. Militant loyalism, on the other hand, was not only tolerated but encouraged and armed.

Walter Long was not alone in his views or in putting them into practice. Other politicians, civil servants and soldiers played their part in determining the policies and events I have described. Nor did Irish affairs define him entirely, as he played a part in everything from the reorganisation of local government to early campaigns against hoof-and-mouth disease and rabies. He was also a major player in Conservative politics and helped determine its fortunes – although not notably for the better.

It was in Ireland that he made history, however, and I would say he was more than just a policymaker in this respect. Walter Long represents perfectly the unyielding tradition of conservative resistance to including Irish Catholics and Irish nationalism within the British constitution, going back to the Act of Union itself. Inclusion could have happened in two ways. The first option – speaking very broadly – was to bring Catholics into the British governing élite, into its aristocracy, civil service, regiments, clubs, schools, families, parties and cabinets. The second option would have been to accommodate nationalist public opinion by granting it self-government under a genuine federal structure. Long, and others before him and like him, fought against both until nationalists finally moved on and embraced independence. Given the enormous unlikelihood of true integration, this was probably always going to be the ultimate outcome anyway, but Long helped make sure it was accompanied by revolution and mass killing. The obvious comparison with the fate of unionist-ruled Northern Ireland is made all the stronger by Long's involvement in its formation.

To go a bit further, it seems fair to say that this was more than just a matter of mindset, tradition or poor decision-making. Walter Long represented powerful political interests: landlords, the empire, perhaps 'gentlemanly capitalism' in general. Moreover, he arguably stood as a member of an ethnic élite, of a people defined as Protestant, British, imperial and defined as such in relation to other subordinate peoples – of whom 'the Irish' were one. His career should remind us that, to the extent that the struggle for power in Ireland was between ethnic groups, ethnicity did not stop at the Irish Channel. Irish Catholic separatist nationalism could not have existed as it did without British – or English Protestant unionist/imperialist – nationalism.[29] Which, incidentally, would not be a bad description of Walter Long's governing ideology.

Whatever we think of the rights and wrongs of home rule, independence or revolution, I think we can only speak ill of someone who frustrated compromise and conciliation, defied electoral majorities, threatened and aroused armed violence and repressed or ignored democratic dissent. Walter Long did not just fail to solve the Irish Problem: in many ways, he *was* the Irish Problem.

SENATOR MARTIN MANSERGH

Sir Edward Carson and the Last-Ditch Stand
of the Ascendancy

The title of this piece, 'Sir Edward Carson and the Last-Ditch Stand of the Ascendancy', is taken from much-respected historian A.T.Q. Stewart's *The Ulster Crisis: Resistance to Home Rule, 1912–14*, first published in 1967. The exact quotation is: 'The Ascendancy had undeniably chosen Ulster as the ditch they would make their last stand in.' He goes on to make the very valid point that 'religion was the dynamic in Ulster, and not merely a cloak for other motives: historians have sometimes underestimated it, but politicians never'.[1] Indeed, it is not entirely without significance that, ninety years on, the principal leader of the unionist community is the Rev. Ian Paisley, who made his reputation as a radical religious firebrand in the tradition of the Rev. Henry Cooke, but equally saw himself as the successor of Carson.

Much of the religious factor may have been perception. Stewart wrote:

> The Protestants' fears about a Dublin Parliament may have been exaggerated, and the history of Ireland since independence has, on the whole, tended to suggest that

they were, but they did not think so at the time, and it was upon that belief that they acted.

There were, of course, class interests, economic interests and, among Ulster unionists at least, the sense of a sharply differing national identity and ethnic origin.

Despite the title of this series, only a few historical characters are unequivocally and unremittingly bad. I do not claim that Carson belongs to their number. I propose to adopt as the structure for this essay the extraordinary editorial that appeared in *The Irish Times* on 23 October 1935 with the title 'Carson of Duncairn', the day after his death, which has value as a contemporary witness. *The Irish Times* at that time was still primarily the newspaper of the small Protestant and ex-Southern unionist minority, under one of its most famous editors, R.M. Smyllie. I will provide further commentary and try to make it clear where I agree, and indeed where I fundamentally disagree, with what I presume was his assessment.

The editorial was written from the point of view of the community from which Carson had sprung but had left behind, though he returned to it in spirit in his post-1921 political retirement. Events in which Carson had played a large part had left that community out on a limb and consequently its principal newspaper voice could not share the valedictory enthusiasm of the Church of Ireland primate in Armagh, C.F. d'Arcy, who in his funeral oration could laud Carson's role in 'the great struggle for Ulster', recall his face 'lighted up with the fire of patriotism' and hearing 'the thrilling tone of his voice' and praise 'what the great leader did for the land he loved so well'.[2] Which land, one might ask, did the primate mean, Ulster or Ireland?

The Irish Times editorial began on a starkly different note. 'Edward Carson's career was one of the tragedies of Irish history.' The next and extraordinarily shocking sentence – which all of us would strongly disagree with today because we have the benefit of hindsight and access to much greater in-depth knowledge of the unspeakable characters referred to – can only be understood in the context of its time. It read: 'If he had been forty years younger, Lord Carson might have been a British Hitler, or even a Mussolini.' In 1935, there was a section of right-wing opinion in these islands – newspaper proprietor Lord Rothermere, who was, incidentally, the uncle of my aunt, to the fore – who admired strong leaders on the continent, even though they engaged in histrionics and had no compunction about illegality. Although Sir Oswald Mosley, like Eoin O'Duffy, had a certain following, and doubts about the efficacy or viability of democracy in both islands were quite widespread, there is no evidence that Britain at this period would have been susceptible to dictatorship from Carson or anyone else. For a start, it would have had to have lost the First World War.

The second half of the sentence claimed: 'as it is, he has died at the age of eighty-one, after a life crammed with great achievements, and yet strangely barren of great results'. Carson himself might have largely shared that sentiment. He died feeling strongly unfulfilled and a disappointed and disillusioned man, without the sort of paternal pride in Northern Ireland that one might have expected, especially given the homage he received there in the form of the magnificent statue outside the parliament building at Stormont unveiled in his presence in 1933. The editorial went on to claim Carson for the South:

He was a Southern Irishman in every fibre of his being. To the end of his days he preserved a rich Dublin brogue, and in many ways was typical of the South; yet he is being buried in Belfast, and his whole political career was identified with the Province of Ulster.

His father was an architect and civil engineer, involved in building many elegant houses in South Dublin and its suburbs that nowadays sell for large sums of money. He was briefly a member of Dublin Corporation from 1877, sitting as a 'liberal conservative'. While he built a sewer along Marlborough Road at his own expense, the indictment made against conservatives, whether unionist or nationalist, on the corporation by Professor Mary Daly in her study *Dublin: The Deposed Capital* (Cork, 1984) was their resistance to attempts to relieve gross overcrowding and to fund the most basic water and sanitary facilities – which gave pre-1914 Dublin the second highest infant mortality in Europe – because their priority was to keep down the tax burden on ratepayers.

Those who nowadays talk up Ireland under the union tend to forget the appalling social conditions, not to mention the decimation of the population of the island as a result not just of the Famine but also of a laissez-faire British policy with more than a touch of moral vindictiveness (Ireland to this day being unique in Europe in having a much smaller population than 180 years ago, though that may at last be about to correct itself). There was deindustrialisation everywhere except the north-east, and finally the scandalous fact that till about 1900 the Irish periphery was subsidising the metropolitan centre rather than the other way round.

On a more positive note, Carson's uncle, Rev. William Carson, was rector of Ardmayle in Co. Tipperary and the young Edward spent summer holidays at the rectory. According to local historian Peter Meskill, 'he was introduced to hurling by the local lads, and would later organise a hurling team at Trinity College in Dublin', committing a set of rules to paper.[3]

The editorial went on to praise Carson's forensic prowess at the bar and the fact that he figured in nearly every *cause célèbre*. He first came to prominence as a prosecuting ally of Chief Secretary Arthur Balfour at a time of vigorous re-assertion of the Conservative landlord interest in response to the Plan of Campaign. Carson was in Mitchelstown in 1887 when the police fired into the crowd, though not directly a witness of what was dubbed the Mitchelstown Massacre. He became a fearless champion of the ascendancy, to which he was connected through his mother, a Lambert descended from one of Cromwell's generals.

His court duel with his Trinity contemporary Oscar Wilde in 1895 proved the ruin of the genius, when, in the words of Wilde's biographer Richard Ellmann, Carson marched mercilessly through his liaisons.[4] It is not easy to blame Carson for Wilde's imprudence.

Carson's defence of Dr Jameson was less successful. Jameson had organised a raid at the end of 1895 designed to arouse the British population of the Transvaal to rebel against the ruling Boers. It was ineffective, though it is interesting to note that the raid, and indeed the Boer War afterwards, was all about trying to assert the superior rights of British citizens, regardless of where they were in a minority. I have to declare an interest in that I would not be here today but for Dr Jameson, as he saved my grandfather's life when he caught malaria in the bush, my grandfather having emigrated from Ireland at the age of eighteen and become a railway surveyor beginning in New Zealand and Queensland, before being recruited by Cecil Rhodes to work on the projected Cape to Cairo railway. That got as far as Salisbury in 1893, with photos of the opening in family albums.

Another famous legal case in which Carson was the hero was the subject of a very successful play in the 1960s by Terence Rattigan, *The Winslow Boy*, about a naval cadet, Archer-Shee, wrongly accused of stealing, who was the subject of a miscarriage of justice and whom Carson succeeded in vindicating. Carson was eventually made a Lord of Appeal but found it unexciting compared to high politics.

The Irish Times went on to speak of Carson's wholehearted identification with the Unionist Party and credited him with marshalling opinion in north-east Ulster into an organised campaign. He certainly provided the inspiration. Others may, in the strict sense of the word, have been better organisers. The paper continued: 'Edward Carson was the man who, almost single-handed, brought all the well-laid schemes of Asquith and Redmond to naught.'

Great efforts are made nowadays to obscure the truth of that judgement. A whole school of commentators uniting neo-unionists and neo-Redmondites would try to persuade us that it was P. Pearse and the calamity of the 1916 Rising that tragically frustrated the life-work of John Redmond rather than the unionist resistance to home rule. James Craig's remark that he would rather live under the kaiser than John Redmond has been conveniently forgotten.[5] What we never hear from such commentators is the logical follow-through, which even George V conceded in 1930, that unionist resistance to home rule in the era of John Redmond was totally over the top and tragically misguided.[6]

Let us examine the phenomenon, by no means confined to Ireland, of trying to maintain the hegemony of an imperially backed minority faced with the forces of nationalism and democracy.

The ascendancy was always a minority, even within Protestantism. For the best part of three centuries, let us say from 1529 to 1829, though those are not necessarily the exact dates, Anglican conformity was made as far as possible the basis for distributing what became post-1690 a near monopoly of power, wealth and land.

In the late eighteenth century, Protestant Ireland was even tempted to follow the rebellious example of America, but this foundered on the re-emergence of Catholic power vividly highlighted by the 1798 Rebellion. The Act of Union was a *fuite en avant*, a pact oiled by corruption between ruling élites that, had it been fully revealed, would have caused a scandal, even by the standards of the late reign of George III.[7] The union in no way involved the mass of the people of Ireland, and on the contrary was designed to pre-empt them forever from being able to assert majority rights in an island context. The Anglo-Irish élite, in contrast, were deeply attached to and greatly benefited from the British connection.

Most members of the Church of Ireland, and especially its clerical, political and social leaders, had deep reservations about democracy if it meant conceding home rule or subjecting, in many cases, propertied Protestants to Catholic and nationalist majority rule.

As Patrick Buckland concedes at the end of his book on Irish unionism outside of Ulster, regarding its negotiations with the new emerging order in 1922, its spokespersons were not democrats.[8] William Plunket, Archbishop of Dublin, said at the time of the Second Home Rule Bill in April 1893 that the minority opposed to it

> represent the intelligence, the education and the standing of the people much more than the majority … The mere fact that some of the Irish people wish for it ought not surely to be sufficient reason for this concession … very few, even among those who have voted for it, really care for Home Rule.[9]

Bishop of Down and future primate C.F. d'Arcy wrote in 1912 of there never being in the minds of 'Irish Protestants so deep a dread of Roman aggression' (he was probably thinking of the *Ne Temere* decree of 1907, as disastrous in its timing for the Third Home Rule Bill as the revocation of the edict of Nantes in 1685 was for the reign of James II). Though only a quarter of the population, he claimed they were 'by far the most energetic portion of the inhabitants, a fact which politicians may well lay to heart'.[10] Erskine Childers, then a moderate Liberal home ruler, was deeply shocked by the virulence of many Protestant clergy and the forbearance of the Catholic population of the North in the face of that onslaught.[11] James Connolly was indignant at the proposal to leave the home rule minority 'at the mercy of an ignorant majority with the evil record of the Orange party'.[12] Little of the role of the Churches has been properly explored by historians.

Nowadays, in some quarters, the Home Rule Party is extolled as the essence of democracy, in contrast to the republicanism that emerged from 1916. The modern word for home rule is, of course, devolution, now working well in Scotland and Wales and waiting to be restored in Northern Ireland. Arguably, it could and should have represented an historic compromise between unionism and nationalism, home rule taking place within the context of the union, the Act of which would not even have needed to be repealed. Some explaining has to be done as to why that cause, or rather, stopping it, justified civil war if necessary.

Hysteria was whipped up in north-east Ulster. Carson denounced home rule on a platform as 'the most nefarious conspiracy that has ever been hatched against a free people'. Privately, he wrote to Lady Londonderry, 'How I long to see Home Rule defeated – it is I think a passion with me ... I cannot bear the hypocrisy of so-called political toleration.'[13]

The Asquith government was ludicrously described by Carson as 'a revolutionary committee, which has seized upon despotic power by fraud',[14] an allusion among other things to the removal of the absolute veto power of the House of Lords, which he opposed to the end. The Ulster Covenant of 1912 is an absolutely anti-democratic document, which compares very poorly as a foundation document with the 1916 Proclamation. It does not concede so much as an inch of legitimacy to the democratically backed demand for self-government in any other part of Ireland going back to the time of O'Connell. It simply states: 'Home Rule would be disastrous to the material well-being of Ulster as of the whole of Ireland' and speaks baldly of using 'all means which may be found necessary to defeat the present conspiracy to set up a Home Rule Parliament in Ireland'. Lord Chancellor FitzGibbon, too, regarded democracy as a subversive conspiracy.

Many commentators today try to focus on what they regard as the reprehensible militarism of the republicanism that between 1916 and 1921 created this state. Yet prior to 1916, it was the Ulstermen who were proud to be the fighters, the Prussians of Ireland,[15] 'Ulster will fight and Ulster will be right', in contrast to the ineffectual romantic Ireland dead and gone and presumed to be with John O'Leary in the grave. Protestant Churchmen waxed lyrical about making the ultimate sacrifice. Archbishop Bernard of Dublin, preaching at Christmas 1915, referred to home rule and said: 'The way of peace may be through war even for the followers of the prince of peace.' This was quoted in the *Irish Church Quarterly* of April 1916, printed just before the Rising, by W.S. Kerr, who wrote of Ulster: 'We who know her are thrilled by the spectacle of a law-abiding industrious people, preparing through fidelity to principle, to make the ultimate sacrifice and committing their cause to the God of their fathers.'[16] Not too much wrong, then, with unionists sacrificing lives to prevent home rule nor much sign of the war having brought unionists and nationalists together, as fondly imagined by neo-Redmondites today.

The Irish Times of 1935, in contrast, took a thoroughly jaundiced view of the effects of Carson's pre-war actions:

> In the light of subsequent events, however, there can be little doubt that Lord Carson's campaign against Home Rule proved to have been a disservice to the cause to which he was so passionately loyal. When he decided to arm the Ulster Volunteers and when

his lieutenants ran their guns in such a spectacular manner on the Antrim coast, he hardly could have anticipated that his example would be followed very shortly by the political extremists in the South. He had hoped to keep Ireland in the British Empire – indeed within the United Kingdom, and to use force, if necessary, in pursuit of his ideal. The men who took their cue from him in the South were equally determined to remove Ireland from the Empire, and to use their guns against the British authorities. In the event, a wretched compromise was achieved. Ireland ran red with blood for two or three years, the Anglo-Irish treaty was signed, and partition became an accomplished fact. We do not believe that Edward Carson ever desired partition; yet he remains as its supreme architect. He defied the law in the North in order to strengthen the imperial bond; similar methods were employed in the South with precisely opposite aims, and the results are all too apparent today.

As Eoin MacNeill entitled a famous pamphlet, 'The North began'. It was E. Carson, not P. Pearse, who first established a provisional government, making no bones about its illegality.

If he had established it and occupied key buildings in Belfast, what British general would have been ordered to suppress the rising, what gunships would have shelled the city and gutted the public buildings and what firing squad would Carson, Craig, Crawford and other ringleaders have faced? As Roger Casement said at his trial to F.E. Smith, comparing treason: 'The difference between us was that the Unionist champions chose a part they felt would lead to the Woolsack; while I went a road which I knew must lead to the dock.'[17]

In the Irish Convention of 1917–18, he resisted strong pressure from Southern unionists for compromise and acceptance of home rule for the island, being at most prepared to concede as a fig-leaf a Council of Ireland to run some residual joint services, an idea later converted by unionists into a nationalist conspiracy.[18] In a recent article in the *Sunday Independent*, Ruth Dudley Edwards made out that Carson wanted a united Ireland.[19] Yes, that is true, a united Ireland as part of the United Kingdom with no home rule. Needless to say, one need not subscribe to *The Irish Times*'s negative view of the struggle for independence and by implication of the Irish Free State, which was also the title of my father's first book in 1934 at the age of twenty-four, much more positive in tone than *The Irish Times* editorial but written by a young person from the same tradition with a respect and enthusiasm for the pioneering efforts of building a new state.[20]

A similar view was expressed by Dorothy Macardle, author of an immensely valuable sourcebook with a foreword by Eamon de Valera, *The Irish Republic*. She was a teacher at Alexandra College, which, although a unionist educational establishment, kept her job open when she was imprisoned in Mountjoy in 1922. Towards the end of her life – she died in 1958, the Rector of Raheny presiding at her funeral – she, along with others, including my father, contributed with a retrospective piece on Pearse and Connolly to a series of Thomas Davis lectures, published in a volume entitled *The Shaping of Modern Ireland* edited by Conor Cruise O'Brien. She referred to problems in intervening decades as 'passing ills' and concluded:

> Perhaps the existence of the Sovereign Independent
> Republic of Ireland might seem a sufficient – indeed,

a superb reward for all the toil and anxiety and sacrifice, despite its flaws. Defects we have in plenty – and
we are not without being told about them … And
are we not free? And is not a free-born generation
preparing to take the future of the Republic into able
and fruitful hands?[21]

It is argued that Ireland should have waited a generation
and it would all have happened naturally, which is another
way of saying that some other unfortunate country should
have been left to do the independence fighting. Stanley
Baldwin's dictum that there must not be another Ireland in
India[22] shows that those who fought in the independence
struggle did a significant service to humanity.

In 1920, Carson made an unforgivable incendiary speech
which led to Catholic workers and 'rotten Prods' (i.e. trade
union leaders) who were 'the Trojan horse of the IRA'
being driven out of the shipyards. He often expressed the
view that loyal Protestants should not have to work alongside disloyal Sinn Féiners, i.e. Catholics.[23]

He bitterly opposed the Treaty, and the whole notion of
negotiating with terrorists, and claimed in the House of
Lords debate on the Treaty, with false naïvety, that he had
been betrayed by a purely power-seeking Tory Party, rightly
attracting the scorn of the Lord Chancellor, Lord Birken-
head, F.E. Smith. One can, of course, also find many
calmer, more conciliatory and constructive statements by
Carson, but they did little to repair the damage done by the
more incendiary ones.

In later life, apart from a helpful intervention in the dispute
over the Hugh Lane pictures, he acted as a postbox for

disillusioned and unhappy erstwhile loyalist followers in the South, for whom he felt some responsibility. Expressing the view in the late 1920s that a republic would be more honest did not stop him bitterly complaining, in his last speech in the House of Lords on 7 December 1933, to the government as de Valera was dismantling the Treaty:

> Every single promise you have made to the Loyalists in Ireland has been broken, and every pledge as to law and order has been destroyed. Everything that makes life and property safe has gone, and now the last remnant is to be taken away.[24]

It is amazing that little more than a decade later, post-war, wealthy people emigrated from England to Ireland, seeking a safe haven from the 1945 Labour government and a socialist England, what my father used to call 'the retreat from Moscow'. As Garret FitzGerald has pointed out, even Churchill at this period began to warm to Ireland.[25] All of this would be very surprising if independent Ireland was as coldly inhospitable to Protestants as is sometimes made out.

The main lines of *The Irish Times* 1935 editorial stand: that Carson's career was one of the tragedies of Irish history; that his histrionics were destructive, not least of community relations; that he destroyed both Redmond and home rule and that, while not desiring partition, he was the principal architect of it. The gamble of using north-east Ulster to defeat or nullify home rule for the rest of Ireland failed. It is not clear how far he reciprocated the pride in Northern Ireland that unionist Northern Ireland expressed in him.

Unionists in the North, and nearly everyone in the South, are strongly attached to the state to which they respectively belong without always caring too much about the pros and cons of how they arrived at their present constitutional position. If one wishes to be critical, the Ulster resistance to home rule is every bit as debatable as 1916 and the War of Independence, but whatever view one takes of any of these it is not likely to alter very much what we have in both parts of the island today. Political accommodation has to proceed from where we are, post-Good Friday Agreement, rather than from where any of us might wish to be, if we could alter the outcomes of eighty or ninety years ago. Each section of the community must make its own analysis and future choices freely and without coercion.

In my view, Carsonism was a failed attempt, conspiracy even, by reactionary interests exploiting popular sentiment in north-east Ulster to block even a limited form of self-government in Ireland, let alone a national democracy, with a separate Northern Ireland under its own version of home rule becoming the fall-back position. In the short-to-medium term, post-1922, Ulster unionists were insulated from the rest of Ireland and had only a quite large but seemingly impotent minority to contain. Cross-border challenges, political or paramilitary, were easily brushed off. A terrible retribution, to use a Gladstonian phrase, came with the civil rights movement, the collapse of stable majoritarian rule and a bloody and deeply wrong attempt by an armed minority of a minority to achieve at one remove the physical coercion of a million people, little caring whether they stayed or went, which simply compounded the wrongs. Even today, walls are needed to protect communities from each other and the legacy and persistence of division, which now has a proliferation of causes, is not an uplifting sight.

My own view, and I am speaking of the island as a whole, is that the Protestant tradition, including, where applicable, the Ulster British community, belongs with Ireland, that it should not be afraid of minority status, which should matter less and less in a modern pluralist and multicultural society, or of being unable to hold its own in a more accommodating and less farouche way. Within wide legal limits, people's choice of identity is their own. I do not believe in the permanence or even the full coherence of a two-nation dichotomy. Ireland, with or without Northern Ireland participation, now has an exciting future as an advanced European country, with every prospect of enjoying a very high degree of prosperity and excellent quality of life. If a majority in Northern Ireland does not wish to participate, as they are free to do, the loss may be theirs as much as anyone else's, though their choices have unnecessarily penalised nationalists for over two generations, who would mostly much prefer, if their votes mean anything, to be an integral part of an independent Ireland. But the peace process, which has largely removed the physical and political threat, together with the very balanced Good Friday Agreement, opens up many halfway houses, accepting it may be much too soon to contemplate taking any fuller step, with so much bridge-building in all directions needing to be undertaken.

Whatever limited role I may have in public life, I would like to use in part, working with others, to encourage the sense of honour in the island-wide tradition to which my forefathers belonged and to contribute to undoing some of the nefarious legacy of history left behind by Sir Edward Carson, who came from the South.

MARGARET O'CALLAGHAN

Arthur Balfour: Tory Maker of Modern Ireland

At the end of his career of over forty years as a Conservative in politics, in the mid-1920s, Arthur Balfour said, 'Ireland is nothing more than the Ireland that we made.'

Of whom was he speaking and what was 'the Ireland that they had made'? Arthur Balfour, on his father's side, was the grandson of a younger son of a minor North Briton Borders family who, having made his fortune through India, based himself in a new ancestral pile called Whittingehame in East Lothian outside Edinburgh. Arthur Balfour's own father consolidated that wealth by marrying into one of the most distinguished political families in England – the Cecils. The first politically important Cecil, whom Elizabeth I ennobled as Burghley, was indispensable to her in all of her major projects in Ireland and elsewhere. The second distinguished Cecil, Robert, masterminded the Stuart succession to the throne of England and arguably acted as an *agent provocateur* in setting up the Guy Fawkes plot to discredit the Catholics of England and conclude their high expectations under James I of England. He became the first Marquis of Salisbury. The Cecils, by then sometimes also referred to as the Salisburys or the Cranbornes, the title of the heir to the marquisate, then lived in relative obscurity from the mid-seventeenth century to the mid-nineteenth in the magnificent former royal residence Hatfield House, granted to them by Elizabeth I.

Arthur Balfour's formidable mother was born in Hatfield House in Hertfordshire. Her brother Robert Cecil, known as Cranborne before succeeding to the title of Lord Salisbury, was to become prime minister. Under his careful patronage and guidance, her son Arthur Balfour was to become one of the leading Tory politicians of the Victorian and Edwardian period and eventually prime minister in the early twentieth century. Salisbury and Arthur Balfour between them became the glittering centre of a cohort of Cecil family relatives and in-laws, whose reach extended into the higher echelons of the Conservative Party for much of the twentieth century. Dubbed the Hotel Cecil by their enemies, they looked after and promoted one another, certainly from the 1880s to the 1920s, and the family influence is still unextinguished. The expression 'Bob's your uncle' came into the lexicon during Robert Cecil's period as prime minister in the 1890s, the implication being that his nephews, and indeed sons and in-laws, would be cared for.

Arthur Balfour was his uncle's most talented protégé. His father's early death meant that his mother saw her brother as effectively his guardian. Balfour was tall, slim, languid and quite beautiful. He had formidable intellectual capacities and extraordinary personal charm. Unlike most of his generation, the classics were incidental to his education. At Eton and Trinity Cambridge, his interests were literary, scientific and philosophical. Through friendships and the marital choices of his siblings and cousins, he was at the centre of the English Victorian political, literary and scientific intelligentsia, which was – in intellectual style – distinctly Liberal politically. As John Morley later said, everything was either Mill or Gladstone in the 1860s and 1870s. The strange formation known as the Souls linked the Cambridge Apostles to country-house society and metropolitan style, and Arthur Balfour by the early 1880s was at their centre. His closest friends were Gladstone's daughters. His London home at Carlton Terrace was a few doors from that of the Gladstones, and the occupants of both houses lived in friendship and intimacy. May Lyttleton, another of the glittering set, died young and it was said for decades afterwards had been the love of Balfour's life. He never married, though he had some fairly low-powered passions with distinguished women. His dark and rather strange sister Alice kept house for him in his maturity.

Balfour signalled his singularity by spending twenty years of his life in writing *The Defence of Philosophic Doubt*. He later said that writing this book had been important to him, less in terms of what it contained intellectually than in the fact that it provided him with a way of being in the world. Tortuous and intellectually convoluted, it represented his attempt to further develop his Cambridge tutor and in-law Sidgewick's demolition of the tedious self-referential positivism of John Stuart Mill's moral earnestness. Though keeping Liberal company, Balfour was out of sympathy with what he saw as Liberal moral earnestness, and when he entered the House of Commons he signalled this by becoming a loosely affiliated member of what was then known as the Fourth Party, with other talented mavericks such as Lord Randolph Churchill.

He had a minor public profile as a man of letters – even though his major work was yet to appear – but he never made his living as Salisbury had done by working as a journalist. In Balfour's early thirties, Salisbury, as part of Disraeli's government of the late 1870s, brought him to the Congress of

Berlin as his personal secretary. Here Balfour saw realpolitik and statecraft at the highest level and apprenticed himself to his uncle's formidable grasp of Britain's interests in an international context. Salisbury was a passionate English patriot, a formidable reactionary and a genius of international diplomacy. A strange man who failed to recognise cabinet colleagues who had sat beside him for years, Salisbury had wept at the triumph of the North in the American Civil War, correctly discerning that its consequence would eventually be a United States that would successfully challenge the British empire's hegemony in world affairs. In Berlin, Balfour met all of the leading international players of the age. Otto von Bismarck, creator of a united Germany, said to him, 'When I was a young man we all read Walter Scott. We were told he was so very proper.' In the Commons Balfour shadowed Randolph Churchill, whose brilliance and panache made him a possible future Conservative leader. Charles Stewart Parnell entered the Commons at around the same time and, with the old Fenian Joseph Biggar, was gradually making the Irish Party a distasteful and unavoidable reality on the floor of the House.

The Irish Land War was the key political issue of the early 1880s and politicians positioned themselves around it. In 1922 Arthur Balfour, then in his early seventies, said that when he thought of domestic affairs in the House of Commons, which had been so long a central preoccupation of his life, the 'culmination and the decline of that marvellous Parliamentarian phenomenon, the Irish Party under Mr Parnell' preoccupied him. He 'saw its rise and small beginnings'. But the Irish Party was not welcome in parliament in the early 1880s. The Land War presented all kinds of ideological problems for both the Liberal and the Tory parties. Fortunately for the Tories, Disraeli was defeated and Gladstone was left with the task of dealing with it in 1880. W.E. Forster, as Gladstone's chief secretary for Ireland, wanted to introduce a Compensation for Disturbances Bill to deal with the situation on the ground. He could not get it through the House of Lords, where those with lands and estates on both sides of the Irish Sea represented the situation in Ireland as the first phase of Armageddon. Parnell mocked Gladstone, who, unlike most of the other members of the Nationalist Party, he neither liked nor trusted, as 'this masquerading knight errant, this pretended champion of the liberties of every nation, except the Irish nation'.

The Liberals, throwing Forster to the wolves, did a kind of deal with the Irish Party at Kilmainham. They were prepared to undermine the central principles of political economy by agreeing to a rent-setting arbitration system. For the Tories, this was sacrilegious. The ownership of property should be untrammelled. A vital principle had been conceded. Ironically, this was to make most Tories the eventual supporters of a peasant proprietorship in Ireland as an alternative to this infringement of the rights to property.

Salisbury and Gladstone's central preoccupation in the mid-1880s was with the management of what now appeared to be the unavoidable expansion of the franchise. They both hated the idea of it, Salisbury more than Gladstone. Neither had a clear image of how their parties would do with a massively expanded electorate. That expanded electorate was to have highly significant consequences in Ireland. Parnell's holding of the balance of power in 1886 delighted Salisbury and Balfour. As shrewd observers, they recognised that, in order to secure Parnell's support for his government and as a consequence of what he saw to be the unsustainabilities of the Dublin Castle administration, Gladstone would risk everything and propose a home rule measure. The endless subsequent debate on Gladstone's motivation – a passion to 'solve Ireland' or an old man who couldn't wait to get back into office – is in many ways irrelevant.

Gladstone's decision gave Salisbury what he had long been waiting for – a platform for a new politics and an agenda for a spoiling operation in Ireland for the foreseeable future. The instrument of Salisbury's politics was his untested nephew, Arthur Balfour.

Balfour came to Dublin in March 1887 as chief secretary after Sir Michael Hicks-Beach in the Conservative government that had succeeded Gladstone after the defeat of the first Home Rule Bill. Parnell's central aim from 1882 onwards had been to control land agitation and put home rule to the forefront politically. He was affirmed in this goal by the imminent expansion of the franchise. He had played both parties for so-called concessions from 1883 to 1886. Gladstone's administration had not been notably beneficent under the Liberal 'Red Earl' Spencer. Before the Kilmainham Treaty there had been an attempt to indict leading members of the parliamentary party as inciters to agrarian violence in the case of the *Queen versus Parnell* and others of 1880, which was effectively a state trial. Voluntary rent abatements in the light of the economic situation were what most Liberal chief secretaries advocated. That was what had happened on most English estates in the economically hard years of the early 1880s. But as Thomas Henry Burke lamented, as the chief Irish civil servant in Dublin Castle before his murder by the Invincibles, if landlords would not listen to sense then the Castle administration had no choice but to administer the law with the full panoply of process servers, sheriffs, bailiffs and the Royal Irish

Constabulary. The settlement of the Kilmainham Treaty in 1882 was Gladstone's admission that the country could not be held under the ordinary law. The price of rent control through the Land Commission was that Parnell would, through the parliamentary party, assist in controlling his own supporters.

Parnell did this for his own reasons, chief of which was the higher prize of home rule. He had drilled his supporters through the National League to vote and demonstrate their fitness for home rule. It was essential for his purposes that the home-rule movement could demonstrate that they were effectively a polity if not a state in waiting – but 1886 blew his strategy apart in a variety of ways. It tested his supporters' patience in Ireland. It enabled the Conservatives to begin a renewed propaganda war against home rule for Ireland. The Conservative speeches on the 1886 bill represented a catalogue of Irish barbarism, criminality and vice. The secret service was active throughout Spencer's years, and the murky world of Fenian intrigue provided Conservatives with a rich arsenal of examples of Irish criminality. The key aims of the Tory government in 1886 were to consolidate their reputations with the new British electorate by the cry of 'Empire in danger'.

When Balfour arrived in Dublin, the nationalists joked about him. He was 'Pretty Fanny', a butterfly on a wheel, an effete philosophical scribbler. The newspaper *United Ireland* had a field day lampooning him. But Ireland was Balfour's big political opportunity. His task was to change the terms of the debate on Ireland, to stiffen the backs of Dublin administration, to give courage and hope to Irish unionists and to save the union. Within a year he had done well. The Special Commission on Parnellism and Crime, established by Salisbury, was dredging through every police report going back to1879 to demonstrate that Irish nationalism was, and always had been, criminal – in effect, a criminal conspiracy. The Crimes Bill was introduced to demonstrate that the Tories had no intention of continuing with a Liberal relativism. That, at least, was the rhetoric. In fact, the Liberal administration under Spencer had been anything but liberal between 1882 and 1886.

The action which made Balfour's administration notorious in nationalist circles – police firing into a crowd of tenants at Mitchelstown – was not planned, but Balfour was able to avail of it to indicate that the game had changed. The only legal brain he found willing to back him up in his account of what had happened at Mitchelstown was the young Edward Carson, who had been present. Recognising a figure of mettle, Balfour made Carson's career over the following decades.

An ideological scorched-earth policy, with a high leavening of ridicule, were Arthur Balfour's most powerful weapons. He got rid of faint hearts in Dublin Castle, strengthened the police and the law officers and reformulated the categories under which crimes were categorised. He may have had some sympathy for Parnell as the wolves devoured him in 1891, but Parnell's image of the promised land of home rule was effectively a millennial project. Parnell dealt with Balfour on the Land Purchase Bill of 1890, destined to collapse in any case.

For Balfour, the issues were exquisitely simple. Ireland was 'an imperfectly assimilated backward fringe area' in the United Kingdom. It was absurd to countenance the notion that so desolate and disastrous an entity could threaten the empire and the empire's position in the world. In Balfour's own words, the resources of civilisation were not exhausted. He despised what he saw as Gladstone's bleeding heart humbug, possibly correctly. He correctly surmised that with Gladstone out of the way, the Liberals would see sense and drop Ireland, a disastrous platform in British politics for the foreseeable future. In this, as in so much else, he was right. He knew that Parnell was followed everywhere by police and secret service agents and that American Irish Fenian circles were riddled with British state-paid *agents provocateurs*. He found it all distasteful but unavoidable. The daily unfolding of the evidence of the Special Commission on Parnellism and Crime amused him, as the Irish ran in circles endeavouring to prove that they were not criminals. He genuinely believed that Irish nationalism was no more than greed and ignorance and a desire to appropriate the land of others dressed up in sentimental, rhetorical nonsense.

Unlike Randolph Churchill, who had been partly brought up in the Phoenix Park, he didn't have a congenial and attractive Irish unionist circle. He and Salisbury had already disposed of Randolph Churchill's political future in any case. He was prepared to back brave and fearless outsiders such as Carson, but he had no time for cosy Irish unionist chats. He did, however, take seriously his duty of care and loyalty to Irish unionists and recognised that he shared with them a mutuality and commonality of interests and goals, if not always of desires. Most Irish landlords bored him but he was prepared to have the state provide funds to buy them out on favourable terms to end the anomalies in Irish land law that had potentially damaging precedents for land law elsewhere in the United Kingdom and to create a nation of peasant proprietors whose greed would be sated by ownership.

Ireland could be improved once popular delusions were re-moved. When he left Ireland in 1891 Balfour was made pol-itically. He had effectively secured his position as Salisbury's future successor as leader of the now Conservative and Unionist Party. Though he became British prime minister, presided over the Balfour Declaration and occupied the first rank of politics throughout the First World War and the years of Versailles, he himself believed at the end of his life that his work in Ireland had been the most impor-tant of his career.

No Tory high-political decision on Ireland was made from the Parnellism and Crime episode of 1887 right up to the Boundary Commission of 1925 in which he did not play a key role. His formidable intelligence, his strategic brilliance and his cold eye meant that by the end of his career he knew his Ireland intimately. He did differ from Salisbury in certain notable ways. The most significant land-purchase measures in Ireland were made under the chief secretary-ships of his brother Gerald Balfour, who succeeded him, and his close associate, the brilliant and flawed George Wyndham. They both saw themselves as having a duty to shape the mess that was Ireland into a workable part of the United Kingdom. Wyndham, a direct descendant of Lord Edward Fitzgerald, had even deeper intent. Salisbury, how-ever, was on a spoiling operation on Irish nationalism in the 1880s and 1890s; beyond that, Salisbury's interest in a place he instinctively hated did not go. He was at a loss as to why Arthur was poring over the details of a land-pur-chase measure with Gerald in the 1890s. 'I can't understand it,' he wrote. 'Arthur, who has never made a mistake in his life, has made nothing but mistakes for the past weeks.'

But then Salisbury was not Balfour. He had not gone to Ireland as an untested young man with almost proconsular powers. Roger Casement said that he became himself in the context of his work on the Congo. So, too, Balfour became the man he was to be in the context of his years in Ireland. If Salisbury saw Tory policy in Ireland as a way of finding a jingoistic public platform that simultaneously wiped the shadow of Irish nationalism indefinitely from the sun of empire, Balfour himself recognised by the time of the Buckingham Palace Conference on the eve of the First World War that the Tory strategy had been at best a holding operation. By 1914 he was realistic enough to recognise that the British state had changed so much, particularly through Lloyd George's budget and the emasculation of the vital House of Lords, that the best that could be done for the Union was to remain loyal to those who had been loyal to Britain and to him. In this context he always felt that Ulster unionists should opt for trying to get four, not six, counties out of the apparently inevitable home rule settlement.

I often think of Balfour in odd social situations. One of his best lines was that he 'felt positively faint with boredom'. He effected to despise displays of emotion. His favourite author was Jane Austen, as she had been his mother's. He was feline, worldly, cynical; if he had emotions, which he certainly had, they were so well checked that they largely atrophied. He giggled at the antics of William O'Brien and bemusedly agreed to the penultimate phase of Parnell's destruction in which his ally Joseph Chamberlain had certainly had a part. He was both the prototype for and embodiment of a particular version of what it was to be an English gentleman.

On only one occasion do we have a record of him displaying passionate emotion in public, and that is at a meeting of the Conservative Party at the Carlton Club in July 1916. It is an extraordinary episode. After the Rising of 1916 in Dublin and the executions of the rebels, a circle around Lloyd George wanted to concede an immediate and limited form of home rule to twenty-six counties of Ireland. The other six would be ruled from London. At the time of this Carlton Club meeting of the parliamentary Conservative and Unionist Party, Redmond, Devlin and Carson had agreed to this arrangement. The cabinet appeared willing to support it. Balfour, who also backed the proposal in the context of coalition government, thought that all that was required at this point was backbench Tory support. He begged the backbenchers to support the measure for it. Uncharacteristically he pleaded, beseeched and threatened. He spoke in passionate defence of the Irish parliamentary party, who he said would be washed away and replaced by new men, followers of the rebels, if the measure was not granted. A home rule parliament, even for twenty-six counties, would, in Balfour's eyes, have given something real and concrete to Redmond and Dillon, to maintain their ground in a battle with the rebels for control of Irish public opinion.

In dramatically addressing the meeting with vigour and passion, he said that the life's work of the Irish parliamentary party would be wiped out if they were not given a home rule parliament. More extraordinarily, he drew an analogy between the behaviour of himself, the Tory Party leadership and Irish unionists on the eve of the First World War with the behaviour of Roger Casement, whom he mentioned by name. He said that it was the case that he (Balfour) and they (Irish and British unionists before the war), given their unconstitutional behaviour in opposing home rule from 1911 onwards, stood in as treasonable a position as Casement, who was weeks from being hanged for consorting with the king's enemies overseas.

Despite Balfour's entreaties, the mass of Tory backbenchers refused to follow Lloyd George's scheme. Home rule for twenty-six counties of Ireland did not become law in 1916. The Irish parliamentary party was, as Balfour predicted, destroyed in the Sinn Féin victory of 1918. But the divided Ireland that emerged after the vicissitudes of the ending of the First World War, the Anglo-Irish War, the partition of Ireland, the Treaty split and the 1925 Boundary Commission was nonethless partly Balfour's creation. He had been present at or presided over every key high-political decision about its shape from the 1880s to 1916 and had a significant input into British high-political decisions in the crucial years from 1916 to 1925.

SENATOR DAVID NORRIS

Sean MacBride: The Assassin's Cloak

There is something within me that naturally recoils from the notion of speaking ill of the dead. To be *advocatus diaboli* in this fashion seems so absolute and our general title is, of course, a twist on the old Latin dictum *de mortuis nil nisi bonum*, 'of the dead nothing but the good', which is itself a little unbalanced. I do not propose to demonise Sean MacBride, rather to balance the hagiographers by illuminating what I see as some of the more questionable aspects of this complex character. At the time of his death in 1988, I caused something of a stink in Seanad Éireann when I attempted to distance myself from the pious platitudes of some of my colleagues who were intent on celebrating his demise with a fulsome republican tribute.[1]

Virtually all of my contribution was rendered inaudible by what are euphemistically described by the official transcript as 'interruptions'. I had indicated that while naturally one felt sympathy in a human sense towards those bereaved, there could be no concealing the fact that MacBride was a colourful and highly controversial character. I went on to say (although this appears to have been drowned out by the clamour) that the one thing I imagined I shared in common with him was a distaste for the pieties, in some cases quite hypocritical, with which he was being showered.

Let me acknowledge at the start that I do have a bias. I have never greatly warmed to gunmen. Indeed, when I look at the title I chose, 'The Assassin's Cloak', by which I meant not merely his early career and continued association with violent republicanism but more particularly his mean-spirited attempts at character assassination of figures greatly, in my opinion, his moral superior, such as Noel Browne, I feel that perhaps an even more appropriate title would have been 'Sean MacBride: The Shadow of a Gunman'. For it was a shadow that, like the Provisional IRA, never quite went away. Nor do I imagine he would have disliked this sobriquet, for in his posthumously published memoirs he has given us a number of examples of the pleasure he took in toying with guns from his early teens and, more curiously, delivered himself of a number of compliments on his working attire: 'I was reasonably well known in the locality and dressed rather dapperly. I used to wear a yellow waistcoat, not that I especially liked fine clothes, but I was usually dapper on these occasions.' These occasions were in fact ambushes and he details them in a clinical manner that is remarkably free from any sense of compassion or identification with the victim:

> I don't remember the casualty figures. Not many in Mount Street although we wounded quite a number and disabled some of their tenders. Our objective was to get hand grenades into lorries, to disable the soldiers, kill them and destroy the vehicle.

MacBride apparently was not just a natty dresser for occasions of ambush or assassination; he continued his taste for sartorial elegance (for which he again chooses the word 'dapper') when he was engaged in a gunrunning operation in Germany in 1922: 'I was dressed rather dapperly with my carnation and a pair of gloves, not at all in keeping with the surroundings. It made me conspicuous.'

However, he did subsequently discover a distaste for the death penalty as a result of witnessing a series of miscarriages of justice committed both by British military courts and the IRA kangaroo courts.

There are, of course, extenuating circumstances. Principal among these one must include family background, which could, I think, be satisfactorily covered by Dr Garret FitzGerald's elegant phrase about another Irish politician, 'a flawed pedigree'. His mother, Maud Gonne, was something of a rackety gal. She was the daughter of a colonel in the British Army and in fact had no Irish blood whatsoever. She came from a wealthy Anglican background in England and was well acquainted with the county set with whom she attended hunt balls and other festivities in both England and Ireland. Prior to meeting Sean MacBride's father, she had had an extended liaison with French adventurer Lucien Millevoye, by whom she had two children, a boy who died in infancy and Sean MacBride's half-sister Iseult. However, she took a fancy to Ireland, which she had visited when her father was stationed at the Curragh military camp. She converted to Catholicism and became a fiery gun-toting republican. Despite her lack of a single corpuscle of Irish blood, she founded Inghinidhe na hÉireann, the Daughters of Erin, and attended as an official Irish representative to the Irish Race Convention in Paris in 1922. She also passed on to her son a disposition to take a provocatively anti-British line. Nor did she suffer from undue diffidence as an Englishwoman in operating as a judge of the Sinn Féin courts.

Indeed, Maud Gonne's expression of her newfound religion was at the more florid end of the scale, according to her biographer Anthony Jordan:

> Maud, and her son were received in a private audience in the Vatican by Pope Pius the X. The following morning Sean assisted at the Pope's mass, and he and Maud received Holy Communion from the Holy Father. A few years later on the 21st of June 1913, Sean was confirmed by Cardinal Amette, the Archbishop of Paris. This was no ordinary mother and child.

Indeed!

His father, John MacBride, had earned the ire of the poet W.B. Yeats, who was his rival for the love of Maud Gonne, on account of what Yeats considered his drunken boorishness combined with repeated, though unconfirmed, suggestions that he had sexually molested his stepdaughter. Nevertheless, from Yeats's point of view these flaws were glorified out of MacBride's character by the terrible beauty that was 1916. Whatever about prurient speculation, there is no doubt that Maud Gonne vigorously expelled John MacBride from the family home and circle within a few months of the birth of his son and that Sean MacBride had virtually no contact with him until, while still a schoolboy, he had to confront the harrowing circumstance of his father's death. Mercifully, the French order whose school he was attending at that time delivered this blow in as gentle a manner as was possible.

Although W.B. Yeats developed surprisingly paternal feelings for the young Sean MacBride, I have to conclude that the absence of a real father figure and the fact that his mother dragged him around Europe and the British Isles in a series of St Trinian-style republican escapades could not but have had an unsettling effect on the formation of his personality. His early education in France left him with a pronounced French accent that he cultivated to the end of his long life and which caused some derision among his opponents, who suspected that a less vain man might have acquired an accent more in keeping with his passionate identification with Mother Ireland.

Even late in life some of his legal colleagues delighted in stories about his accent. One in particular concerned an outbreak of Tong warfare among the Chinese restaurants of central Dublin. MacBride was appointed counsel in one of these cases and during cross-examination addressed a witness, saying, 'Mr Wong, is it trhue that you rhun a rhestaurant in Rhanelagh?' Mr Wong very naturally replied, 'Woh?' and the judge then instructed MacBride to repeat the question, which he did. 'Mr Wong, is it trhue that you rhun a rhestaurant in Rhanelagh?' to which Mr Wong again replied, 'Woh?' at which point the judge intervened to say wearily, 'He is asking you do you run a chipper in Ranelagh.' This is a light-hearted story but it may also illustrate something about MacBride. I heard a parallel story from an acquaintance who happened to know Henry Kissinger's brother and asked him why he, the brother, had no trace of a German accent whereas Henry sounded as if he had just bounced in from Munich. The brother replied that, 'Unlike Henry, I listen to other people.' MacBride's hearing could also be selective.

Both mother and son involved themselves in the 1916 Rebellion, which was almost universally unpopular in the beginning and only received support due to the callous stupidity of the British in organising a long-drawn-out series of brutal executions. This led to the Sinn Féin victory in the election of 1918. The Dáil then convened and by democratic majority voted to accept the Anglo-Irish Treaty. Sean MacBride was among those who refused to accept the wish of the Irish people and became involved in the occupation of the Four Courts. During the early part of this occupation, his antics were not confined to the Four Courts area and both he and the late Dr C.S. Andrews have left descriptions of his escapades at this period. These included commandeering civilian cars at gunpoint for joy-riding expeditions in the countryside, during one of which he crashed into an army lorry in Nassau Street in a stolen car but managed to abandon the vehicle, hopping out and waving his pistol around his head. Indeed, his reputation as a gunman flourished to such an extent that following the assassination of Kevin O'Higgins he was arrested for the murder, a crime which he could not have committed. He might, in fact, have suffered the ultimate penalty were it not for the integrity of a unionist member of Seanad Éireann, Major Bryan Cooper, who gave evidence that at the time of the assassination he had actually been engaged in conversation with Sean MacBride on the mail boat in the middle of the Irish Sea.

By 1931, MacBride and Peadar O'Donnell combined to form a new republican organisation, political in constitution but with a heavy penetration of IRA personnel, Saor Éire. Characteristically, in his memoirs Sean MacBride suggests that his own involvement in this movement provoked the jealousy of Peadar O'Donnell, who wanted to have the stage to himself and subsequently left MacBride to do all the hard work and eventually be carted off once more to jail. In his speech at the founding of Saor Éire in the Iona Hall in North Great Georges Street, MacBride railed against the British and the privileged classes. He called for 'the dispossession of the aliens from their privileged position in Irish society', apparently quite untroubled by the fact that it would not be unjust to suggest there was a certain whiff of alien privilege about his own background.

This can be illustrated by the fact that even during the Second World War the MacBride ménage at Roebuck House included a chauffeur, cook, parlour maid, kitchen maid, sewing maid and two gardeners, and even MacBride's unpaid resident amanuensis, Louie O'Brien, also herself employed a maid. Perhaps it was this background of which Frank Aiken was thinking when, on 7 November 1947, he referred to MacBride ironically as 'The Kingstown Republican'.

In 1934, a group of Protestant workers from the Shankill Road decided to dip a toe into the republican puddle. A lorryload of them travelled down to take part in the republican rally at Bodenstown in memory of Wolfe Tone, whose ideal it was to reconcile Protestant, Catholic and dissenter. At this stage there were two distinct elements within the republican movement. One had a rather confessional Catholic tinge, while the other veered towards progressive socialist ideas. MacBride belonged to the Catholic wing and was, in effect, one of its principal leaders. When the Protestant workers arrived at Bodenstown, they were ambushed by the Southern republicans, beaten up and expelled from the graveyard. While I have discovered no written authorisation from MacBride for this, there is little doubt that it could not have happened without his consent.

In 1936, Sean MacBride became Chief of Staff of the IRA following the arrest of Moss Twomey. However, the following year he was got rid of and someone regarded as more representative of the Irish people, Sean Russell, later to become an active collaborator with the Nazis, was installed. At this point, MacBride claimed to have accepted the 1937 Constitution and severed his official connection with the IRA.

In 1946, Sean MacBride once more spearheaded a movement to set up a new party, this time to be called Clann na Poblachta. The party's programme included the reunification of Ireland and a vigorous economic and social agenda. In the 1947 general election Clann na Poblachta won ten seats and joined a coalition government with Fine Gael, Labour and Clann na Talmhan.

MacBride's republicanism did not fade with his inclusion in the cabinet. After he got himself made Minister for External Affairs, one of his main objectives was to sever the link with his mother's native country – England. MacBride was, in fact, prepared to remain within the Commonwealth, and indeed to join NATO, but the price of this was the reunification of the country. Interestingly, Mr de Valera, a wily politician and strategist, was forced into a corner by MacBride's manoeuvring and was unable to come out with his real position, which was that remaining as an independent republic within the Commonwealth might constitute a bridge with the Northern unionists. The views of Garret FitzGerald on this matter are also of interest:

> I had been brought up to regard MacBride with deep hostility; a member of the IRA from the Civil War onwards, he had been its Chief of Staff in the mid

30s just after some particularly shocking murders had made a profound impression on me, including one near Ring College when I was in school there. His later conversion to constitutionism had seemed to me ambivalent. My unhappiness was intensified when the Taoiseach announced the Government's intention to declare a Republic. At that time this clearly meant leaving the Commonwealth, for the evolution of which into a body of sovereign, independent states John Costello as Attorney General, with people like my father, Paddy McGilligan and Kevin O'Higgins, had worked so successfully in the years before 1932.

The leader of the British Liberal Party declared that, while it would seem that the purpose of Éire in deciding to become an independent republic was to secure the reunion of Ireland, they had now taken the one step most calculated to defeat that purpose.

Moreover, two days after the declaration of the Irish Republic and the repeal of the External Relations Act, India secured the status of a republic but has remained to this day within the Commonwealth. However, despite whatever doubts one may have about the wisdom of this action, there can be no doubting MacBride's intellectual brilliance in the debate between himself and Mr de Valera in which he forensically dissected de Valera's ambivalence.

The most imaginative appointment of this administration was that of a young, intensely motivated doctor, Noel Browne, to the Department of Health. Noel Browne's family had been devastated by tuberculosis and he made it his principal aim to eradicate this scourge from Irish life.

Dealing with the appointment of Browne, MacBride employed a classic smear tactic, writing that Browne was 'a young man who was or had come from Trinity College and that kind of conservative, Unionist background. I don't think that at that time I knew that he was the son of an RIC man.'

This is classic MacBride, caricaturing Noel Browne, a man from an impoverished TB-ridden peasant family in the West of Ireland, as a member of the Trinity establishment with a conservative unionist background. Moreover, far from being an RIC man, Browne's father was in fact an RSPCA inspector who lost his job when he contracted TB.

In his posthumous memoir, Sean MacBride does everything to claim credit for the fight against TB while simultaneously disassociating himself from responsibility for the Mother and Child débâcle which was to follow and to smear Noel Browne. May I say, from twenty years' practical knowledge of politics in this country, every department in this state is stuffed with good ideas, plans, programmes and proposed legislation which never come to fruition. Whatever else can be said, it is incontrovertibly true that Noel Browne acted upon the proposals and by his individual energy secured their implementation.

Browne then moved on to the provision of maternal services by the state in the notorious Mother and Child Scheme. Once again, in his memoirs MacBride seeks to undermine Noel Browne's responsibility for this, on the grounds that a tentative proposal of this nature already existed in the department. Indeed it did. A watered-down version of such a scheme had been timidly mooted by Mr de Valera but he immediately beat a strategic retreat at the mere suggestion of a belt from an ecclesiastical crozier. Noel Browne rapidly reinstated a fuller version of this with provision for free health care for mothers and their children up to the age of sixteen. This caused some disquiet among the fat cats of the medical profession but most particularly evoked a negative response from within the Roman Catholic hierarchy, who saw here a symptom of creeping communism. They stated that 'the right to provide for the health of children belongs to parents and not to the State.' This theoretical position completely ignored the parlous state of many families in the Ireland of the 1940s.

However, the opposition of the Church was enough to provoke a major crisis. The Taoiseach, John A. Costello, said, 'I am an Irish man second: I am a Catholic first and I accept without qualification in all respects the teaching of the Hierarchy and the Church to which I belong.' During the actual Dáil debate he said, 'I, as a Catholic, obey my Church authorities and will continue to do so.'

In the middle of this crisis, MacBride and Browne met for dinner in the Russell Hotel in November 1950 at MacBride's suggestion. MacBride has left an account of this in which he claims that Noel Browne declared his intention of destroying Clann na Poblachta, bringing down the government, humiliating MacBride and, if possible, replacing him as leader. There were no witnesses to this exchange, although MacBride did make a contemporaneous note. I have read this note. I knew both Sean MacBride and Noel Browne. I am proud to have been able to call Noel Browne a friend of mine for nearly thirty years. He was a man of honour, integrity and compassion. I also knew Sean MacBride, although not terribly well. In my dealings with him, I found him narrow, Machiavellian, cunning and evasive. I do not accept MacBride's version of events as in any sense likely to reflect the truth.

At the reconvened cabinet meeting, Noel Browne asked each member in turn for support. Not one person was prepared to challenge the right of the Roman Catholic hierarchy to dictate policy to the government of Ireland. A day or two later, Sean MacBride precipitated the dismissal of Noel Browne from government. In his memoirs, MacBride claims that Noel Browne had said to him on a number of occasions prior to this, 'If I can really pick a row with the Irish Hierarchy I will be made.' I give this no credence whatsoever. It is difficult to comprehend how MacBride imagined this ecclesiastical kowtowing would assist in his programme for incorporating a million or so uncooperative Protestants into his Workers Republic.

The net result was the collapse of the coalition. By 1957, MacBride, unlike Noel Browne, had become unelectable and withdrew from parliamentary politics while continuing a career at national and international level as a lawyer.

He had already been partly responsible for the European Convention of Human Rights and the establishment of the European Court of Human Rights under the Council of Europe and this is greatly to his credit. It is, however, highly unlikely that MacBride would have welcomed many of the decisions which subsequently emerged from that court, including my own victory on the question of the decriminalisation of homosexual behaviour.

I only knew MacBride in the last ten years of his life. I had been prominent in the struggle for gay liberation since the early 1970s and was one of those responsible for the creation of the International Gay Association. As a result, I was contacted by a Finnish gay group who were under very considerable surveillance pressure and the threat of physical brutality from the Russian police. They sent to me an appeal that this matter should be brought up at a meeting of international jurists in Geneva, where Ireland was to be represented by Sean MacBride. I wrote him a detailed explanatory note and enclosed documentation from the Finnish group requesting that he take an interest in this matter. To my astonishment, the entire parcel was opened, my letter was opened and read and then my letter reinserted in its envelope, the whole thing parcelled up and posted back to me without as much as a single word of acknowledgement. I had not expected such brutal ignorance from a man such as MacBride, but I would have done so had I known of his views on homosexual behaviour which he subsequently expressed in an interview in *The Crane Bag* with Peadar Kirby. When Kirby raised the question of discrimination against gay people, MacBride blithely dismissed it, bracketing homosexuals with heroin addicts, a not entirely flattering companionship.

But there was even worse. I had become passionately concerned at the fate of the great humanitarian and Swedish diplomat Raoul Wallenberg. He had saved a very large number of Hungarian Jews by going, unarmed, onto the cattle trains taking them to Auschwitz, braving the armed might of the Gestapo and issuing them with Swedish passports. He was subsequently captured by the Russians and disappeared into the Soviet Gulag. I raised his fate by formal motion at the 1983 general meeting of Amnesty.

MacBride made every effort to quench my initiative and, to my horror, at the 1984 AGM in Hatch Street, I discovered that he had actually succeeded in deleting every reference to Wallenberg from the record. I subsequently insisted on an amendment to the minutes to include a reference to this situation.

Raoul Wallenberg was one of the greatest heroes of the twentieth century but, tragically, was never adopted by Amnesty as a prisoner of conscience. Why should MacBride take this attitude? Was it to ingratiate himself with his Soviet friends who had conferred upon him the Lenin Prize for Peace or was it that he knew, as I was to discover only later, that Raoul Wallenberg was himself homosexual? Whatever the reason, there was, in my opinion, no excuse. MacBride's homophobia also led him to complete blindness about the situation in Ireland. He told his *Crane Bag* interviewer that, although the Irish were naturally intolerant people (which I question), there was no legal discrimination whatever in the republic. Presumably he thought gay people didn't exist at all, even though I had attempted on numerous occasions to draw his attention to the state of affairs here regarding this oppression.

In conclusion, I have a somewhat quirky grudge against Sean MacBride from the field of Joycean studies. I was friendly with the late Maria Jolas, who published *Finnegans Wake* in episodic form in Paris in the 1930s. She told me that in the aftermath of the Irish state bringing the body of the poet W.B. Yeats back to Ireland by gunboat after the war, Nora Joyce approached the Irish government to see if they would do something similar for her late husband. The matter went to government and Maria told me that, for some reason, Sean MacBride refused to support it and the matter was spiked. Harriet Weaver, a year or two later, wished to find an appropriate resting place for the manuscript of *Finnegans Wake*. She wanted to donate it to the National Library in Dublin. However, according to Maria Jolas, when this was broached with Nora Joyce she absolutely refused to countenance such a plan in the light of MacBride's refusal. Thus one of the most significant manuscripts of the twentieth century was lost forever to Ireland. The outline of this regrettable situation is referred to in Brenda Maddox's biography of Nora Joyce but without specific reference to MacBride's role.

Towards the end of his life, MacBride was given significant honours internationally. He received the Congressional Medal of Honour from America, the Lenin Prize and the Nobel Peace Prize. However, it should be noted that among other recipients of the Nobel Peace Prize around that time were those well-known 'men of peace' Menachem Begin and Henry Kissinger.

Sean MacBride died in January 1988. He was a complex, talented and somewhat sinister personality. He helped to create the machinery for human rights legislation in Europe, opposed nuclear armaments and served the United Nations well in Namibia. He deserves our gratitude for helping to establish Amnesty International but he remains narrow, sectarian and too close for comfort to the armed republican movement. He was a man without self-awareness or a sense of irony. Risteárd Mulcahy summed him up well in a review of his posthumous memoir, saying:

> MacBride emerges as a man of energy with a wide interest in social, economic and political affairs. However, he also emerges from his own writings as a man of unusual vanity, less than charitable to his opponents, happy in the company of world figures, consistent in seeing himself in a favourable light and without providing the necessary evidence to allow historians to take an impartial view of his contributions to recent Irish history.

PATRICK F. WALLACE

An Error of Judgment: Rescuing Adolf Mahr's
Contribution to the National Museum of Ireland[1]

In a way, this is an attempt to emphasise how the 'speaking
ill' process works by reversing the normal approach of
spotlighting questionable aspects of otherwise hitherto
revered historical characters by instead rescuing the positive
contribution of a flawed figure. Someone of whom I believe the good was interred with the bones of Adolf Mahr
(1887–1951), whose atrocious miscalculation and hopeless
political judgment in his embrace of Nazism eventually
wrecked his own life and that of his family. However, as I
hope to show, he also accomplished so much in his twelve
years (1927–39) at the National Museum of Ireland that it
could be said that he was the founder of scientific archaeology in Ireland as well as of a proper museum service.

The main authorities on Mahr and his politics are David
O'Donoghue, whose *Hitler's Irish Voices* was published in
1998, and Gerry Mullins, whose *Dublin Nazi No. 1: The Life
of Adolf Mahr* was published in 2007. It was Mullins who
came upon the Mahr–Bender correspondence at Mills College, Oakland, California. There are additional letters in the
custody of the Mahr family and there are relevant papers
among the former director's files at the National Museum.
The latter, which were brought to my attention by Mullins,

were used in my essay (2004) on Mahr's part in the training of Seán P. Ó Ríordáin, then a young museum assistant who went on to become Ireland's first home-grown modern archaeologist and, arguably, the best practitioner of the subject we have seen.

Apart from Mahr's letters to Bender in Mills College, the other Mahr documents in the director's files at the National Museum and the papers still in the possession of the Mahr family, there are also three manuscript notebook diaries (from 16 September 1927 to 14 February 1931; 15 February 1931 to the end of 1933; and 1 January 1934 to 31 July 1935, respectively) in the museum. These are crammed full of information on accessions, amounts paid, fieldwork, lectures, names of visiting scholars to the museum and some press cuttings of exhibition reviews and relevant social events. Sadly, their successor volumes up to 1939, which must have been compiled, do not survive, at least not in Ireland. The diaries we have are witness to the variety of Mahr's industry on behalf of the museum and the enormity of its scale, especially in building up a network of contacts and supporters. They also show how quickly he set up a modus operandi and stuck with it. Maybe he simply transferred this from a parallel way of doing things in Vienna.

Mahr, an early Celtic specialist at the Natural History and Prehistoric Museum in Vienna, started work as Keeper of Irish Antiquities at the National Museum in September 1927, when he succeeded another German archaeologist, Walther Bremer, who had died after less than a year in the position. Mahr's diaries also include Bremer's dates, including his last admission to the Adelaide Hospital. These appointments of Germans may be seen with parallel positions in the sugar company, the army music school and the fledgling electricity supply service as efforts on the part of the

Free State to seek foreign expertise when needed from places other than the former colonial master. Glances at the pages of the *Proceedings of the Royal Irish Academy* and the *Journal of the Royal Society of Antiquaries of Ireland* for the early and mid 1920s show how provincial and out of touch with mainstream European developments Irish archaeology and museum studies had become, especially after E.C.R. Armstrong's early retirement at the end of 1922. As we shall see, this was all to change with Mahr, who built on Bremer's good start and on the Lithberg report on the museum which had been commissioned by the Department of Education and reported in 1927.

Part I

Mahr and the Nazis

In 1927, Minister Kevin O'Higgins was assassinated and Fianna Fáil came into the Dáil. It was a time of confusion, violence and polarisation at home and abroad. Mahr's diaries, for instance, record the breaking of two panes of glass 'apparently by a rifle bullet' in the museum studio on the night of 11–12 November 1932. Nevertheless, Mahr managed to lunch with the minister shortly after his appointment. Six years later, in 1933, at age forty-six, he was surely mature and content enough in his position and working hard for the overall directorship, which he was to secure the following year, to be interested in events outside the National Museum and the internationalisation of its growing reputation, which he had single-handedly resurrected. But he wasn't.

The year 1933 saw the dissolution of the Dáil, the re-election of Eamon de Valera as President, the dismissal of

Eoin O'Duffy, the growth of the Blueshirts and their proclamation as an unlawful association, the arrest and release of O'Duffy, the formation of the Communist Party of Ireland and a general election in the North. It was the year that Hitler became German Chancellor – and also the year the director of the National Museum of Ireland became a Nazi. Not content with being a mere supporter or being socially involved with the expat community in Dublin, Mahr became *Ortsgruppenleiter*, or head of the Auslandorganisation (AO) in Ireland. In this position he outranked even the minister (ambassador) at the German Legation, becoming, in Mullins's phrase, 'Hitler's top man in Ireland'.

John P. Duggan, in his work *Hempel at the German Legation 1937–1945*, describes Mahr as 'notorious' and relates how 'the Germans … arrogantly rode roughshod over Irish economic sensibilities … blind to the effects of their boorish behaviour', adding that 'by 1934 [Mahr] had worked his way with de Valera's acquiescence to the top museum post', as if, by implication, the President of the Executive Council promoted him because he was a Nazi. Nothing could have been further from the truth, although like any museum director worth his salt, Mahr sought to interest the relevant political leaders in his projects. For example, he enlisted the interest of de Valera in the exhibition of the Bender collection of oriental art and in the tardiness of the OPW in preparing the chosen gallery, as well as using the Special Employment Scheme (from 1934) to assist archaeological excavation programmes in different parts of the country and Seán MacEntee to support the quaternary study project in Irish bogs.

The Irish authorities were not blind to Mahr's activities and did not ignore them. Up to the time of what turned out to be his final departure in August 1939, ostensibly for an archaeological conference in Germany, Dan Bryan and the Special Branch were shadowing his movements, as is evident from army intelligence files. In addition, as early as July 1938, Mahr wrote to Joseph O'Neill, the Secretary (General) of the museum's parent, the Department of Education, offering him his voluntary resignation as leader of the Nazi party in Ireland. In his view, this was not because it had any 'immediate bearing upon my work in the National Museum', but lest anything he had done 'ever could be incompatible with the oath of allegiance which binds a civil servant of this country, a country which has honoured me significantly by entrusting me with the custodianship of its national treasures'. He had 'a perfectly clear conscience', claiming his influence had obtained fifteen 'Humboldt Studentships' for Irish students. He concluded that he had no wish to embarrass the minister or the government at a time when 'an almost apocalyptic foreboding of international disaster' was in his view being deliberately fomented in order to 'psychologically' prepare 'another crusade against the liberty of a great nation'.

Mahr's inclinations were already known to his assistant, Seán P. Ó Ríordáin, in 1933, when, after a visit by him to a school, the teacher (by sheer coincidence father of the archaeologist A.B. Ó Ríordáin, himself director of the National Museum from 1979–88) signed off on a letter to Mahr with 'Heil Hitler' – Seán P. obviously having told him how best to impress his boss! The three surviving Mahr diaries are almost completely free of any political reference, except for 9 July 1934, when on a single line he notes 'O'Duffy (retired)' and adds a tiny imperfect swastika. There was no irony intended in the entry, but can he really have believed O'Duffy was a Nazi? Fascist, yes, but hardly a Nazi. (Incidentally, the *New History of Ireland's Chronology,*

Volume VIII, has O'Duffy resigning from his political positions on 21 September 1934, not 9 July. Perhaps Mahr was talking about O'Duffy's earlier intention to resign or something else altogether.)

The Dublin-born Jew Albert M. Bender, having made his fortune from insurance in San Francisco, used his money to endow museums and bought extensive amounts of oriental art, which he persuaded a reluctant Mahr to acquire for Dublin in honour of his late mother, Augusta. He innocently wrote to Mahr on 5 April 1933: 'These are days of chaos and the reversion of an enlightened nation like Germany to 14th Century barbarism is so atrocious that one loses confidence in the progress of the human race. Such conduct on the part of Germany is turning the hands of the clock backward for four or five hundred years.' This drew a lengthy reply from Mahr on 28 April in which he barely conceals the depth of his feelings and explains his reasons for Germany's then current political position.

Bemoaning the loss of territory and 16 million German inhabitants 'under the terms of the so-called peace treaties which were announced as the final readjustment of the "crimes" committed by the Central powers', Mahr asks Bender to understand that 'we cannot well be expected to swallow contemptible terms in addition to mistreatment'. He also explains how because of 'the Balfour declaration (1916) by which international Jewry was enlisted to support the anti-German cause ... the Germans have a very great grievance against America in the question of the "fourteen points" which were most flagrantly turned into their very opposite without scruples or conscience. But you are not Mr Wilson or Mr Trotsky and I am not Mr Hitler ... ' So Germany's grievance all went back to Versailles and the 'treaties' that were offered 'at the point of the sword after a most inhuman blockade which was carried on for half a year after armistice and which put hundreds of thousands of children and old people etc., etc. to death'. Mahr himself was born in Trent (now Trento) in the then South Tyrol, which became part of northern Italy after the Treaty of Versailles.

Bender recovered from this blast by mid-May 1933 and apologised, conceding that he was 'unconscious of the fact that I was writing to a gentleman of foreign origin'. Mahr replied in early June that he hadn't taken offence, but resumed the rant about 'the cruelty with which the French have tried to annihilate Germany, under the connivance of other nations' and mentions the 'world-wide atrocities propaganda; the political dismemberment on nearly all frontiers' and, again, 'the breach of the fourteen points'. Tellingly, though, and almost contradicting himself, Mahr adds that all these problems have led to 'a frame of mind which is completely different from what Germany once was'. Thus he wasn't entirely blind to the effects of Nazism.

Mahr's long correspondence with Albert Bender and the mutual regard that they evidently had for one another – and not least his relentless beseeching of Bender to bail out his Jewish friend from his days in Vienna, the archaeologist and museum man Dr Alphons Barb – shows that while he was not anti-Semitic, he was nonetheless prepared to turn a blind eye to the reasons for Dr Barb's isolation and discrimination, presumably choosing the overriding Nazi position about German Jews which went back before the First World War. Mahr was not an anti-Semite, as Mullins's biography established, though this was contradicted by Cathal O'Shannon in a foreword to the same book, where Mahr is described as 'undoubtedly a fervent anti-Semite' and 'a virulent anti-Semite', which seems excessive. Nevertheless, it seems astonishing that Mahr could write to Bender in October 1938 that 'recent developments in Austria deprived [Barb] of his career, and recent developments all over Europe preclude any possibility of finding for him a position anywhere in Europe ... ' The arrogance of which John P. Duggan wrote is evident in Mahr's letter to Bender on 10 November 1938, in which he gives Dr Barb's address as in 'Vienna 1, Germany'. This is undoubtedly more a celebration of the Anschluss of March that year than either a mistake or a deliberate insult to the centuries-old status of Austria's metropolis, a former imperial capital. It could also betray an awareness that communications from abroad with Jews were being watched and as such was a way of allaying suspicion. Thankfully, Dr Barb got out of Austria in 1938 and met Mahr in London in 1939. He wrote a letter in favour of Mahr from his then home in Leeds in January 1947, pointing out how Mahr had tried to help several Jews.

Mahr only managed to join the German Foreign Office in 1940. After his arrival in 1939, he spent an initial period working in a Berlin museum and then spent the remaining war years at the Irish desk in the Foreign Office, from where he controlled Germany's radio propaganda broadcast to Ireland from November 1941 to May 1945. By 1944 Mahr was head of the section dealing with political broadcasting to the US, England and Ireland. He had known Reich Foreign Minister Ribbentrop during the latter's time as German Ambassador in London (1936–38) and had attended the 1937 coronation of King George VI with him. According to Dr O'Donoghue, Mahr drew up a fifteen-page document for Ribbentrop which 'was a mixture of Nazi dogma and Mahr's personal vision of a united Ireland which was heavily coloured by his contacts with the Irish republican ethos from 1927 to 1939'. This may be exaggerated in view of his obvious disappointment with Mícheal Ó hÉanaigh (Heaney), a native of Garvagh, Co. Derry, who he placed in foreign museums for training with Seán P. Ó Ríordáin in 1932. Whether Mahr's employment of Ó hÉanaigh, who O'Donoghue says was on the run from 1937, constitutes 'sheltering' is debatable. A solitary reference in a report to Mahr to W.T. Cosgrave's government as 'a junta' hardly constitutes hard evidence for subversion. In any case, Ó hÉanaigh was finally informed of his dismissal by Irish Antiquities Senior Assistant Michael Duignan as late as 1940, when he wrote to him at his home in Derry.

Mahr's broadcasting team held out until early May 1945, after which his attempts to return to Ireland were foiled on a number of fronts, including by Colonel Dan Bryan, Head of Irish Military Intelligence, who had shadowed Mahr in the late 1930s and now, according to Gerry Mullins, urged the government not to help Mahr.

By the end of 1945, James Dillon was taunting the Education Minister, Tom Derrig, about the possibility of Mahr's return to his old position. Mahr was arrested and imprisoned in a British prisoner of war camp at Oldenburg in early 1946, possibly, Mullins suggests, as a British favour to de Valera, though this seems unlikely. His health deteriorated very quickly owing to starvation and exposure, so much so that he nearly died at the hands of the British, who released him to avoid the embarrassment of his dying in their custody. Further implications by Dan Bryan made it impossible for any return to Ireland.

By the end of 1948, following a change of government in Dublin and an unanswered letter to John A. Costello, a sad and doomed Adolf Mahr wrote in German to his wife

Maria about a Christmas Eve letter he had received from Dublin offering him a paltry pension and lump sum in recognition of his service at the National Museum. According to Gerry Mullins, it was Dan Morrissey, a minister in the new coalition government, who objected to his resumption of the Keepership of Irish Antiquities, the directorship being ruled out anyway. Mahr finally conceded 'that I am to some extent to blame for losing my wonderful position'. Reluctant though he was to take the blame for bringing such tragedy upon himself and his family, he admits to an 'error of judgment'. Broken from starvation and imprisonment but fortified by the restoration of family life and the quest for work, he felt let down by the German archaeological establishment ('and for this riff-raff I have, idiot that I am, sacrificed my scientific existence!'), which at least shows that his scientific work in Ireland was undertaken in the greater interest of German archaeology.

His personal appeal to de Valera, a number of letters of support from his former colleagues – some of whom exonerated him from anti-Semitism – and his move to Category II (and later, in 1948, Category III) Nazi status didn't facilitate his much-wanted return to Kildare Street. He was surprised by the silence of his former colleagues at the National Museum and by the inspector of national monuments, who he felt had turned against him. He was convinced his old adversary, Gerhard Bersu, was actively working against his interests. His long-time enmity towards Bersu went back to at least 1933, when, in a letter to then travelling student Seán P. Ó Ríordáin, Mahr warned, 'be careful with Lantier and do not speak about political developments in Germany because he is a great friend of Bersu, Unversagt [Berlin Museum Director], and there is no use your being mixed up with intercontinental quarrels'. In his disappointment, he blamed what he thought were pro-British elements in the Academy in Dublin and, he might have added, the colourful but bitter personalised outbursts of James Dillon in the Dáil. Although clearly not wanted in Dublin, Mahr managed to get a position in a mining history institute in Bonn with his son Gustav as his assistant. This was to be short-lived; he died of heart failure in Bonn in 1951, aged sixty-four.

Explaining the Inexplicable

Adolf Mahr was the architect of his own downfall. He was consumed above all by an ambition which extended far beyond his profession and career. His moves were calculated. One cannot help thinking that his conversion to Protestantism from the Catholicism of his parents and, according to Estyn Evans, his flirtation with Quakerism were also somehow calculated. His Protestantism probably was to set him and his family at a remove from the majority of the Irish population and possibly cut off some of the possibilities of escape in post-war Germany. His mistake was not so much in joining the Nazis, but in becoming so identified with them and by implication with their covert plans in Ireland that his return after the war was rendered impossible. He should have known the risks he was taking, or was he so arrogant, self-consumed and ambitious that he blinded himself to the activities of his associates in the organisation, thinking Germany was invincible? In the attitude one often finds among the citizens of great countries towards those of smaller nations, did he think the Irish and their authorities were stupid or so lost in persisting anti-Britishness that they would overlook his flaunting of their rules and their regard for the status of one of their revered official positions?

It wasn't enough for Mahr to be director of the National Museum and, on his merit, to attain academic and scientific significance in Ireland and beyond. Ireland, it appears, was merely a useful step to something else, not a destination in its own right. His jaundiced support for a distorted cause could only end in disaster, which would have been even greater for him and his family if he and his associates had been victorious. Did he never reflect on why Alphons Barb was being so discriminated against and why he, Mahr, had to tell Bender that Barb, a fellow scholar, along with his wife were prepared to work as domestics, anywhere, just to escape the regime Mahr was championing to the detriment of his own very life?

The principal lesson of Mahr's life for us, his successors in museums and related institutions, must be not to become involved in politics of any kind, but particularly with the obnoxious brand of human association known as National Socialism. The golden rule must surely be not to get into the cage with the tiger, all the more so when the tiger in question is such a vile representative of the species. It is hard to understand why such a settled middle-aged man, well into his forties, would embrace such a movement in a foreign country which was then trying to bed down democracy in an atmosphere of so many undemocratic uniformed groupings. Instead of playing a passive rôle, albeit in a patently redundant movement in which he could have pleaded the conflict his paid official position placed him in to avoid high office, he sought the most conspicuous rôle, one that could be interpreted as subversive to his host country and in conflict with the interests he was employed to uphold. There is in Mahr's attitude and behaviour an implied contempt for the land of his employment and yet, as I shall show, few in that rôle have served that land better.

His reluctance to assimilate, while understandable in someone of mature years, hardly excuses such an obvious identification with an alien community in a land where his official position was to isolate and champion the artefacts and treasures which identify Ireland, and particularly its Celtic past, as different and separate from and yet part of the broader insular and European worlds. Mahr even forbade his children to speak English in the home, insisting on German. Being culturally Protestant, the family attended schools and had friends among smaller circles who, sadly, were divided from the vast majority of their fellow countrymen because of the circumstances of the time.

Mahr's regard for Ireland was deep, but it was that of a scientist for his laboratory. He seems to have had little connection to the population at large or does not seem to have had empathy in any relationship with the government and its attempts to modernise and rebuild the economy after colonial neglect, war and civil and economic strife. His regard wasn't total; rather, did it stem from his realisation that contemporary Ireland preserved craft practices and traditions which had gone unchanged since the later Middle Ages and, in turn, because of their relationship to a preserved ancient landscape and enormous archaeological richness constituted a unique, almost living archaeological laboratory? He was an explorer in paradise, thinking of what he could do to further himself with the academics and scientists of his fatherland and beyond. Had he disengaged more from the pull of the fatherland in all its manifestations and integrated more with the people and values of his adopted land, which in ways he served so well, things might have turned out very differently for him and his family.

Part II

Mahr's Internationalisation of Irish Archaeology

Not content merely to rest on the laurels of the great network of international archaeological and museological contacts Mahr brought with him to Dublin, he actively multiplied those contacts as he tirelessly sought to make the National Museum, its collections and its works better known outside the country. His diaries record a veritable parade of visits from the cream of European scholarship: V.G. Childe (April 1930 and June 1934), E. Estyn Evans, Leonard Woolley, E.T. Leeds, Poul Norlund, D.B. Harden, Robin Flower and A. Kingsley Porter, among others. He personally entertained the famous Austrian expressionist painter Oskar Kokoschka, who himself later fell foul of the Nazis. He made several conference cum study visits to places like London, Berlin, Cambridge and Madrid and was a main mover in the Archaeological Institute of Great Britain and Ireland's conference in Dublin in July 1931, when Mortimer Wheeler of the London Museum and T.D. Kendrick and C.F.C. Hawkes of the British Museum all called to Kildare Street.

Mahr was present at the Congress for Pre- and Protohistory in London in August 1932 and persuaded a number of the delegates, including Danish and Spanish representatives, to come on to Dublin to discuss crannogs. He had expressed an early interest in crannogs which intensified after the visit to the museum of Hugh O'Neil Hencken from 3 to 7 July 1931. This led to Prof. E.A. Hooton announcing a tripartite archaeological, sociological and physical anthropological mission to Ireland in June 1932 (*Irish Times*, 10 June; *Irish*

Times, 21 June; *Irish Press*, 23 November) about the mounting of a scientific examination of racial history. Harvard and Hencken's literally groundbreaking excavation of Ballinderry crannog started on 10 June 1932, with Hencken bringing the newly discovered hanging bowl or lamp from the site to Kildare Street on 29 June, according to Mahr's diaries, an event he also wrote about to Bender. Hencken was back on a second Ballinderry site for a new season from 2 June 1933. By 1934, the Harvard excavations were state funded, along with the work of the Committee for Quarterly Research in Ireland and the Relief of Unemployment Excavations for Archaeological Purposes to give them their official title, the latter being funded to the tune of €3,000 and under the overall direction of Mahr and H.G. Leask. The long 1934 Harvard season in Ireland lasted from 4 June to 23 October. The 1934 finds were shown in a temporary exhibition at Kildare Street from 1 June 1935 (*Irish Press*, 31 May 1935).

Mahr's Vision for Irish Archaeology

The best statement of where the National Museum was and where he brought it in his first four years is provided by Mahr himself in a long typed letter to Albert Bender on 21 August 1932. He talks of how when he reported for duty in the Irish Antiquities division in September 1927, 'I found one small office which I had to share with my assistant. There was no telephone. The lavatory was right across the building, downstairs. Today I have four magnificent offices and two new assistants whom the state sends abroad for 15 months training. When I came there was no preparator [technical assistant?] or preparation room [laboratory space?]. I have now two preparation rooms and the new preparator has been trained by the British Museum laboratory.

There was no library [worth] speaking of, but although it is very little, I have now 38 periodicals running (against 3 in 1927). The museum had <u>never</u> made an excavation; today I have £150 p.a. for field work. A monumental legislation has been issued. The yearly average of acquisitions is 35 times what it was in 1927. We have got a good intelligence service over the country to watch new finds. In short, we are alive, at last … '

He repeats, 'There was no work worth speaking of done within the last 30 years in Irish archaeology and it is my duty to bring the country which pays my salary up to the standard of the other European countries.' This slightly boastful yet proud letter was written before his embrace of Nazism and shows what Ireland lost when that tragic infatuation eventually seems to have led to the dedication of his scientific work to the service of Germany.

This 1932 letter was the one in which he tried to dissuade Bender from donating his oriental collection to the National Museum, trying instead to get Bender to invest his money in turning the museum into a great centre of Celtic studies for which comparative materials might be obtained. Mahr believed Ireland was 'not yet mature' enough for an oriental collection, saying 'we are perhaps 50 [years] behind our time' and that 'we are even worse off than under the English, not only in grants, but also in accommodation'. He tells Bender that the museum's main block of offices, which contained the geology collection, was allocated to the Dáil, and this is where his sincerity, independence and strength as a museum man shine through: 'Nobody protested … the [show] cases were sawn to pieces … no government would have done it with a collection of which I was the Keeper.' It is a sentiment that is entirely believable.

Mahr's 'programme is to link up Irish archaeology, through the median (*recte* medium) of Britain, with European archaeology, and through Europe with the remainder of the world. No British archaeological problem can be solved without Irish evidence and vice versa. I have to represent the British archaeological interests in Ireland to the benefit of Irish archaeology itself. I have to do it from a sound national Irish standpoint without being an Irishman.' Significantly, and this is where my earlier 'laboratory' and 'paradise' similes find documented support, Mahr reckoned the 'real world importance' of Ireland lay in 'its archaeological heritage with its bearing on the formation of European civilisation', adding, 'Irish archaeology is the only thing which can give us a status in European learning'. He clearly had little idea of the significance of Ireland's literary texts (some in the vernacular) for their contributions to law and a myriad of early medieval social and material concerns lost elsewhere, and he was undoubtedly lopsided in his view that archaeology 'can be made the pivot stone by which to raise the whole standard of learned work in the country'.

All this is Mahr before his formal conversion to Nazism, and while this conversion may eventually have contributed to a change in the goal, possibly from the time of his six-month sick leave owing to a breakdown in 1936, when he couldn't even formulate a testimonial for UCC Archaeology Chair candidate Seán P. Ó Ríordáin, his zeal and productivity remained unchanged, as the statistics he parades in his magisterial survey of Irish prehistory in his 1937 presidential address to the Proceedings of the Prehistoric Society show. In the ten years since 1927, the museum filled 800 drawers with acquisitions, a yearly intake forty times greater than before, added to which were the accessions associated with the large-scale systematic excavations which had been going on under the aegis of the Harvard archaeologists since 1934. That the first Harvard site, Ballinderry, was recommended by Mahr suggests how intimately involved he was with this whole operation. 'The fillip which Irish archaeology received from these American excavations was tremendous. It was the first time that large and difficult sites were tackled ... entirely from the aspect of gaining scientific evidence'.

Mahr was obsessed with training a home-grown 'school of archaeologists', and apart from his own museum-specific scheme of training Ó hÉanaigh, Ó Ríordáin and, afterwards, Joseph Raftery, he was glad to record that 'the excellent field technique of the Harvard excavators served as a most valuable training ground'. The success of the Harvard experience in Ireland inspired sufficient public (and possibly political) interest so that the country saw 'fit to undertake its own programme of work, and on a very ambitious scale'. He is referring to the establishment in 1934 of the Relief for Unemployment state-financed scheme by which large sums of money became available for excavation. Mahr did the thankless and time-consuming job of doing the financial returns for these operations.

Thanks to Annika Stephan and Paul Gosling (2004), we have an overview of Mahr's 'contribution to archaeological research and practice' in both Austria and Ireland. This, combined with the as yet unpublished bibliography of his father's publications, recently compiled by Gustav Mahr, shows the enormity of Mahr's scientific output. The twelve years in Dublin were his most productive as a writer. Apart from card-indexing, to which Mahr was addicted right up to the time of his death and which the museum's archives are now the beneficiaries of, Mahr was an indefatigable wielder of the pen. Not only is his broad fountain pen's loose writing all over the museum's topographical files for the period of his stay in Dublin, there are huge caches of his letters, such as those pertaining to the accession of Bender's oriental collection, about which more presently. Thanks to the generosity of Mahr's family, especially Gustav, whom I have visited in Berlin, the museum now possesses each of the drafts of his *Christian Art in Ancient Ireland* album, published for the Eucharistic Congress in 1932, and his presidential address to the Prehistoric Society, published in 1937.

In 1932 alone, fifteen publications bearing his name appeared. The *Christian Art* volume is particularly important, not only for Mahr's text and discussion, but for the wonderful photographs by Michael Kellymore. Volume I, which was presented to the papal legate by President de Valera on his visit to government buildings, is an eighty-plate album with a short introduction completed around Christmas 1931, while Volume II, which appeared in 1941, when it was edited by Joseph Raftery, who also contributed lengthy 'descriptive and chronological notes', contains a further fifty plates and significant chapters by Mahr on the 'pagan background' and the 'early Christian epoch'. Mahr's 1937 presidential address runs to 176 pages and is a major snapshot of Irish prehistory at the time; it takes full account of all the activities that had taken place in the previous decade. According to Stephan and Gosling, 'it contains the first assessment of the chronological and environmental implications of the new technique of pollen analysis then being applied in Ireland by Jessen'. It was probably Mahr who first interested Jessen, who was met by his emissary Seán P. Ó Ríordáin during his study stay in Copenhagen, and probably also Mahr who first recommended the then very young G.F. Mitchell to be Knud Jessen's assistant in

Ireland. Mahr's own publication on the Altartate, Co. Monaghan cauldron was the first to include a pollen diagram (supplied by Jessen) 'to support the relative dating for an archaeological object found in a peat bog'.

According to Stephan and Gosling, Mahr's presidential address was 'the first explicit attempt to apply the tenets of "culture–historical archaeology" to Ireland'. Then at the cutting edge of archaeological thought, Mahr used this framework to, for instance, 'identify (what he named) the Riverford people ethnographically', comparing distributions of such finds to philological evidence for alleged non-Indo-European 'tribes' in Ireland. This may not have won much credence, but 'in terms of the development for archaeological thought in Ireland, it was Mahr's approach that is of lasting relevance.'

Mahr's Training of Museum Staff

Related to this and of even more enduring impact are Mahr's conscious attempts to train Irish archaeologists and museum men. With breaks over a two-year period, he sent Ó hÉanaigh to Britain and Scandinavia and Ó Ríordáin to Britain, Scandinavia, Germany, Switzerland and France. In January 1933, Mahr noted in his diary that Ó Ríordáin was in Hannover and Ó hÉanaigh in Cambridge. Ó hÉanaigh had seniority, reporting first on 1 October 1931. He was dispatched for training on 1 July 1932 and with breaks was back by 1 October 1933. Ó Ríordáin was appointed on 23 December 1931, took up duty on 1 January 1932 and, according to the diaries, was already undergoing his 'apprenticeship' at the British Museum by the 27th of the same month. Ó Ríordáin was back in Kildare Street on 4 June but off on his travels again on 22 September 1932, to return on 2 June 1933. Ó Ríordáin's final return seems to have been on 1 January 1934. There is a summary of Ó Ríordáin's visits to other institutions in the diary for 21 April 1932. Incidentally, Miss Barnes of the museum also received training in the British Museum laboratory in June 1932 and Joseph Raftery, Mahr's collaborator on the second volume of *Christian Art in Ancient Ireland*, started at the museum on 5 October 1934, having worked earlier in that year on Hencken's Poulawack (June–July) and Cahercommaun (July–August) excavations in Co. Clare.

We learn from Mahr's letter to Ó hÉanaigh on 5 October 1932 that the two purposes for supporting his and Ó Ríordáin's extended study tours were to expose them to top-class practices and to get them to form a *corpus* of Irish archaeological specimens in the holdings of the various museums in which they were being trained. 'I want you as well as Mr O'Riordan to share two purposes at the same time; to do your own work and to learn … And to card-index the Irish stuff in the individual institutions so that sooner or later we will have at least something to guide us in the question of how the Irish stuff is scattered'. More than anything, Mahr himself was an inveterate card-indexer and compulsive cuttings hoarder. Nothing, it seemed, was irrelevant to the many compartments of his myriad awarenesses within the broad culture–archaeology–museology spectrum. Even in the period before his death, when he was in a mining history museum, he had already embarked on building up categorised cuttings and references to his breakdown of the subject matter.

Training abroad started for Ó Ríordáin before the end of his first month at work, for according to a typed résumé of his various reports by the last week of January 1932, he was already in London at the British Museum 'under the guidance of the officers of the Department of British and Medieval Antiquities'. There, he worked 'on pre-historic archaeology with special attention to their Irish Bronze Age collections'. During his stay in London '[he] was enabled on [Mahr']s introductions' to examine collections in several other museums as well, while 'Dr Mortimer Wheeler of the London Museum very kindly allowed [him] to attend his weekly lectures on pre-history'. In April he attended the Easter school at the Pitt-Rivers Museum, Dorset, where the lecturers included several well-known authorities and where local museums and field monuments were visited in the afternoons.

That Mahr's interest in Ó Ríordáin was good for his career for the long term is evident in his letter of 30 April 1932, telling him to go to V.G. Childe in Edinburgh: 'I should strongly advise you to join him, even if it be only for a few days … I have reason to believe that afterwards you will be glad to have done it.' Thus, in early May, Ó Ríordáin left for Edinburgh on the advice of Mahr, who arranged that he work with Childe on a hill fort excavation in Scotland: 'This work continued until May 30th after which I was able to spend some days in the National Museum of Scotland and to visit the Royal Scottish Museum'.

Mahr had singled out Childe, who is the only one to write to him as 'My Dear Adolf' (deingetreuer, vgc), as he did after Ó Ríordáin's visit. 'I must congratulate you on your new assistant and thank you for putting him in touch with me. He struck me as remarkably intelligent and well informed … moreover, he is a pleasant companion on a dig'. The Mahr–Childe friendship and its human side is clear from a message in a letter of 30 May: 'Childe sends his love and says to tell you he has done the worst ausgrabung ever seen', but clearly not wishing to be guilty of making a judgment on the work of a senior colleague's friend, Ó Ríordáin quickly adds, 'this of course you need not believe' because 'it was a tangled subject to excavate but I think he managed to clear up the problems well'.

Ó Ríordáin's letters to Mahr show the richness of the network of contacts Mahr commanded in Britain and Europe and the high degree to which he was esteemed by the enduring names of European archaeology – Bøe, Brønsted, Childe, Leeds, Hawkes and Kendrick among them. The young travellers' enthusiasm for Europe, its museums, their collections and their systems of organisation seem to underline the need Mahr perceived in Ireland for such contacts, for the modernisation of the subject and for the very training of new recruits for which he had argued in the Department of Education. By the same token, Ó Ríordáin's and, less obviously in Ó hÉanaigh's case because he was not as committed, need for such training and his zeal for it when exposed to it demonstrate how inadequate and out of touch the degree courses in archaeology offered by RAS MacAlister in Dublin and the Canons, Power and Hynes at Cork and Galway, respectively, must have been. Mahr was the catalyst who enabled Ó Ríordáin to return to Ireland a changed and inspired man from the exciting and productive world of contemporary European archaeology to a country apparently up to then out of touch with such developments.

But it wasn't just Ó Ríordáin. Joseph Raftery, who was to spend a lifetime at the museum, was his protégé, while Michael Duignan, later Professor of Archaeology at

University College, Galway, became close to Mahr in the museum (Mahr notes in his diary in July 1935, 'Duignan helps a lot with fieldwork preparations, especially in connection with the Quarternary Research Committee's work'). William O'Sullivan and G.A. Hayes McCoy were employed by Mahr and H.E. Kilbride Jones and Kevin Danaher were also taken on in different capacities by the museum before Mahr's return to Germany.

Mahr apparently encouraged his trainees to stay aloof from the political developments of the day, particularly on the Continent. Although he did warn Ó Ríordáin not to engage in political discussions with Bersu – and in this he was prophetically correct, because it seems that after the war, Bersu campaigned to prevent his return to Ireland – and to be careful of one or two others, especially in France, he probably didn't welcome over-familiarity, preferring relationships with his trainees to remain on a formal basis. Ó Ríordáin appears to have read this properly by hardly ever becoming familiar enough even to wish the director the Season's Greetings, never writing salutations in languages (including Irish) which Mahr didn't understand and by always speaking well of the more senior foreign colleagues he met through the director's introductions. Ó hÉanaigh was older and more political and in his letters to Mahr showed his anti-Cosgrave, pro-de Valera views, with which he may not have ingratiated himself as much as he thought. His Irish salutations might have hurt Mahr by making him feel inadequate about his inability to use the first official language, while with his 'use' of Danish, Swedish and German he was fooling nobody, least of all his director who, clearly, would have preferred if his reporting energies had gone more into archaeology, collections and museums and less into generalisations, excuses, platitudes and familiarities.

Mahr's Archaeological Fieldwork

Mahr was a regular visitor to excavations around the country. For example, he found time to visit Macalister and Praeger's site at Uisneach, Co. Westmeath in September and Mount Gabriel copper mines in early October 1929 and by New Year's Eve was excavating the Keenoge, Co. Westmeath cist. Sometimes he could barely contain his delight at new discoveries (both in letters to Albert Bender on 10 August 1933 and 14 July 1936 and only slightly less restrained in his 1937 Presidential Address to the Prehistoric Society), as for instance at the discoveries of the sword and hanging bowl at Ballinderry by the Harvard mission. We do not have a clear picture of his competence in or personal desire for this aspect of archaeology. Mahr made the scientific announcement of the discovery of the inscribed sword 'Hiltiprecht' in a German article, mentioning its German name in the title in the journal *Mannaus VI*. Although he had excavated in his earlier career in the Halstatt salt mines in Austria, he seems to have developed more into a museum and desk archaeologist than a field or excavation man. Was it for diplomatic reasons, for example, that he assisted Macalister and Praeger's dig on Friar's Island, Killaloe when he must have known that Macalister's methods were so out of date? Sadly, in a letter of 11 January 1935, Mahr has to convince the Secretary (General) of his department that his membership of the Ancient Monuments Committee of Northern Ireland should be regarded as official rather than private, especially in the matter of expenses. On 23 August 1934, in a letter to Bender, he tells of the government wanting him to excavate to the tune of £3,000 (i.e. the Relief Scheme) and accordingly 'I have to improvise, out of almost nothing, a local "school of archaeology" at a time at which I should have said we are not mature yet. This cannot be said any longer; we now have the "school" and work is going on in nine different sites simultaneously, but the strain it puts on me is hard ... however, it is great [to] think that excavations have been recognised as a state function'.

According to Martin A. Timoney (*in litt.* 23 April 2004), Mahr personally excavated a crannog in Feenagh Lake, near the caves of Kesh, Co. Sligo, from 28 September to 3 October 1928. Lorraine Burke (*in litt.* 12 May 2004) reminds me of Mahr's involvement with the archaeological fallout from the Shannon scheme and with engineering involved in the dredging operations of the Shannon, Erne and Barrow, and particularly of his correspondence with A.B. Killeen, the resident engineer on the Shannon who later became president of the Thomond Archaeological Society. Mahr published a paper on the origins of the crannog in the Proceedings of the International Pre- and Protohistorical Society in 1932, i.e. just before the Harvard mission addressed this subject in Ireland in earnest.

Mahr's diaries make clear the extent of his travels around the country. It was on 17–19 January 1934, for instance, that he made a 'trip to Burren and Killaloe for collar [i.e. Gleninsheen] and river Shannon finds'. His lectures were another way of getting around the country, as on 5 April 1935, when he lectured in Kilrush on 'Recent Antiquarian Finds from Clare and Adjoining Regions', and in Ennis on 'Recent Advances in Irish Archaeology'.

Mahr and the Accession of the Bender Collection

Mahr's accession of the Bender Collection of oriental art for the National Museum may be said to have started with a letter from Albert M. Bender (1866–1941) on 5 December 1931. Bender tells Mahr he was prompted to write to him by Walter Starkie of Trinity College who, apparently, had already spoken to Mahr that summer about Bender's idea of presenting twenty-two Tibetan pictures to the museum in honour of his late mother, Augusta, because 'I remember our family association with that city [Dublin] with deep emotion and gratitude'. Starkie had also spoken to Æ, who encouraged Bender to send the pictures to Dublin despite the interest of the Louvre. Mahr's diaries concede that the Bender Collection would never have been acquired but for Starkie.

Mahr's assistant, Seán P. Ó Ríordáin, brought photographs of the pictures in question to A.J.D. Campbell, Deputy-Keeper of the Victoria and Albert Museum's Indian Section, who, in May 1932, wrote to Mahr, 'such hanging pictures are termed Y'ankn or Kut'an, and are hung in the temples and monasteries of Lamaism both in Tibet and in China (including Mongolia). The subjects represent 13 of the Buddha's disciples.' Mahr had already accepted the donation in a letter of 29 December 1931, by which time the consignment was on its way. According to Mahr's diaries, the museum received consignments of Bender material on 23 April, 8 August, 29, 30 and 31 August as well as on 12 September 1932 and on 25 February and 25 and 27 July 1933. It was the first consignment which arrived on 23 April 1932 that was the subject of the first (temporary) showing of the material on 9 June 1932.

Bender (18 January 1932) was determined from the outset that the pictures go to Dublin, although 'just before shipping a director of one of the great galleries of the world was here and suggested that I present them to his country'. The dealer from whom he bought the pictures told Bender it was the only time in his forty-five years trading that he had come across an entire collection of the paintings of a temple. Mahr showed the pictures temporarily in the museum's Rotunda in the early summer of 1932, but had them removed to temporary storage because of events connected with the Eucharistic Congress. A letter to Bender on 16 March 1932 tells us that the costs of mounting the pictures was high. Bender shipped a late Ming bronze head to Dublin in late March, while in mid-April three Japanese tapestries and three Chinese embroideries were added. The shipper in a separate letter of 16 April explained that the Japanese pieces were tapestry *furoshiki* 'of the so-called thumbnail tapestry', the method of weaving being practically extinct, while the Chinese brocades 'are of a type which is seldom used'. A letter of 26 November 1932 from the Secretary of the Department of Education to the Secretary of External Affairs contains a list which shows that Bender's bequest continued to grow and now also included twenty-four Chinese snuff bottles and forty-one Japanese woodblock prints among other *objects d'art*. By now a decision was made to have a permanent exhibition of the Bender Collection and the letter contained a request to Foreign Affairs that Ireland's diplomatic representatives express the government's best thanks to Mr Bender for his donation to the National Museum. This message was conveyed by Michael MacWhite, Ireland's Envoy Extraordinary and Minister Plenipotentiary, in January 1933.

After inevitable delays and time-consuming consultations, the Bender 'Memorial Room' was finally ready by June 1934. Bender's list of names for invitation to the opening included Walter Starkie and Provost Gwynn of Trinity College, Oliver St John Gogarty and W.B. Yeats and their wives, the Misses Yeats, Æ and the artist Estelle Solomons and her brother. The reception, according to Mahr, was 'grand'

and 'a very great success'. He said to Bender on 26 June 1934, 'your cherished idea of a visible memorial has thus been carried out and the museum may call itself very lucky to have been chosen by you as the favourite shell'.

Despite his initial reluctance and his attempt to deflect Bender's money in another direction, Mahr's accession of the collection and his permanent exhibition of it was a major success. So was the preliminary publication of it in the *Museums Journal* by Ada K. Longfield (later Mrs H.G. Leask), who Bender presented money to in order to purchase a typewriter, so grateful was he for the work she had put into the later stages of the exhibition (according to Mahr's diaries, she worked on the Bender exhibition from December 1933).

The Augusta Bender Memorial Room and its collection were decommissioned, as it were, in 1973 to make way for a Viking and Medieval Dublin exhibition. Happily, plans are now advanced to resurrect a modern version of this exhibition in a gallery in the decorative arts area of our Collins Barracks branch, where it is being curated by my colleague Audrey Whitty, whose devotion to the collection and its donor is commendable. Ms Whitty's *Catalogue* and study will soon do justice to the generosity of Albert M. Bender and the foresight of Adolf Mahr, who conducted such a long and fruitful correspondence with a great Dubliner who deserves to be better known in the city of his birth.

The reason we have such extensive correspondence between Mahr and Bender is that although they seem never to have met, a close friendship developed between them and it may also have been that Mahr, in his self-imposed relative loneliness in Dublin, wanted to have someone to gossip with and sound off to and Bender, a Dubliner at a remove, fulfilled that need. For his part, Bender appears to have been an extremely generous person, had time on his hands, had no family of his own and was very rich. As early as 16 March 1932, Mahr thanks Bender for a gift of 'beautiful fruits [sic]' and tells how his son, then nine years old, was learning a great deal about California. On 2 January 1933, Mahr thanks Bender for a gift to his wife, then in hospital expecting a baby, and six years later, on 3 January 1939, we have a letter from Mrs Mahr herself thanking Bender for a Christmas gift of a fur cape.

Mahr and the Importance of Folklife and a Folklife Museum

One of the stoutest philosophical planks in the platform of Adolf Mahr's beliefs was the importance of a folklife collection and, related to its proper expression, the need for Ireland to have its own folk life museum run on Swedish lines as a branch of the National Museum. His consistently expressed belief in folk life stemmed from a belief in the accumulation of such a collection for its own sake, especially in a country in which farming and other non-urban practices were about to become mechanised. He believed in making such a collection even more strongly because it could be used to better understand archaeologically documented practices of the medieval and later periods in more industrialised countries where such traditions had long since disappeared. A largely non-tillage and grazing economy, coupled with the absence of economic or large-scale industrial development, especially outside the large cities and the north-east, led to the survival of a conservative and largely non-mechanised rural culture which relied to a great extent on locally grown materials and meant that many craft traditions survived unchanged for decades, if not centuries. This was surely the living side of the scientific paradise, in which Mahr must have revelled almost as much as its older, deceased close relative, the archaeological side.

As early as 14 May 1932, two years after the government set up the Irish Folklore Institute, three years before the Irish Folklore Commission was established and a decade before Seán Ó Súilleabháin produced his Swedish-inspired magisterial *A Handbook of Irish Folklore*, Mahr wrote to the Secretary (General) of the Department of Education enclosing a long list of different items from the countryside which he, as Keeper of Irish Antiquities, wanted to hear about 'for the completion of the Irish Folk Collection'. He was really looking for lists of teachers, inspectors, departmental officials and others to whom his list could be circularised. Mahr's so-called *List of Desiderata* announced that items were 'wanted from all parts of Ireland'. A two-page explanatory note appended to the three-page list explained that the museum was 'very anxious … to illustrate the arts and crafts of the rural districts and of the fishing population as these appliances are to-day likely to be replaced by machine-made articles which are turned out by manufacturers'. He adds that 'at the present time of financial stress it is obvious that the museum is not in a position to devote large sums of money to the purpose, but if necessary, the question of purchase will be considered'. Loans and especially donations were especially welcomed. 'Only home-made articles are wanted, *or* objects which have been individually made by a local craftsman or other handy person: The museum is not interested in manufactured articles which have been turned out by hundreds or thousands'. This is, was and should continue to be a blueprint for the collecting policy of our folk life division and, by implication, anticipates problems of deaccessioning by three-quarters of a century.

The *List of Desiderata* is divided into nineteen categories, beneath which are subsets of relevant activities. For example, under category 1 – land reclamation, preparing the ground, tillage, etc. – are separate entries for breast ploughs; steveen; wooden ploughs; mallets for breaking sods; appliances connected with seaweed manure; other appliances for manuring; wooden harrows; old-type shovels; manure forks, etc; drag-stone; sowing sheet (sheenauns); seed-lip for sewing; and rattles, etc. for bird scaring. Apart from the land, the other main categories include turf cutting; domestic animals; cattle; horses; livestock; hay-making; harvesting; hones; preparation of plant food; brewing; fisheries; hunting; transport; the house; light; spinning and weaving; other house techniques; different appliances; charms and cures and pastimes.

Mahr was later to assess (in an apparently unsent minute to the department on the importance of folk culture and of folk research in Ireland) the importance of the Swedish folk culture missions of 1932 and 1934 and the work of von Sydow of Lund and Åke Campbell of Uppsala, among others. 'The various visits resulted in a special exhibition staged in the National Museum of Ireland in 1937 which was declared open by An Taoiseach.' (Was this term current before the commencement of the New Constitution Act on 29 December 1937?) In a live radio relay from the exhibition on 26 May 1938, Mahr uses the phrase 'President of the Executive Council', therefore the minute has to post-date this and the inauguration of the new term for the head of government. The exhibition was later sent to Edinburgh. In his view, 'folk research fills the gap between national archaeology and national history' and that 'it is undeniable that the backbone of European civilisation, the farmer, had practically been forgotten in the framework of the studies of cultural development'. He put it another way elsewhere in the same minute: 'The social element that constitutes the most important continuum by which the archaeological past and the present society are connected in an unbroken succession, <u>the farming community</u>, remained all too long the Cinderella of cultural research.' While praising the establishment of the Folklore Commission and 'enthusiasm for the language', Mahr repeats, 'national self-consciousness implies more than an exalted place for the national language. It requires a proper appreciation of all other forces that have cooperated to form the national character. Now, of these forces, folklore studies can unveil only part. The material culture of a farming community remains practically untouched ... From the Bronze Age up to the time of the Industrial Revolution every cultural movement that has swept over Europe deposited its residue here at the last outpost of Europe on the borders of the ocean. The accumulation of those cultural elements is a unique feature of this country, not matched anywhere else in Europe ... the only surviving Celtic State.'

The accession of a specially made Boyne coracle in 1930 provided an opportunity for Mahr to combine his interest in folk life with his talent for publicity. According to the diaries, a number of trips were undertaken with a photographer, Lewis, including one with J.H. Delargy, when 'a Eoiphone record[ing]' of the maker of the coracle, Michael O'Brien of Oldbridge, was made. Mahr's diary records the cost of the hide at £7.0.4 and the work and transport at £4.12.0. The museum later paid 7/6 to O'Brien for the tools he had used. A film was also made and bought from First National Pathé for £10. This was first screened publicly at the College of Science, Merrion Street, Dublin on 4 July 1930, when the 'original coracle' was on show. One of the reactions was the presentation of a currach from the Rosses in Donegal by the Department of Lands and Fisheries in November, while on 14 February 1932 there was a coracle exhibition in London preceded by the headline Mahr dreamed of in the *Irish Press* of 6 February: 'A Museum for Irish Folklore'. The government appointed Mahr to the Irish Folklore Commission in February 1935, according to his diary.

Mahr and the Popularising of the Museum's Role

The opening of the folk life exhibition by Eamon de Valera occasioned a 'wireless discussion' on Radio Athlone, for which a corrected and colour pencil-marked (by Mahr?) typescript survives, between Åke Campbell (who spoke poor English, according to Bo Almquist after my 2004 lecture on Mahr to the Royal Society of Antiquaries of Ireland) and Mahr (who, despite his excellent written English, upon which I have been so dependent throughout this assessment, also spoke in accented English), which was relayed live from the National Museum on 26 May 1937. Mahr opens by summarising the two Swedish folk life seasons in Ireland and leads Campbell by saying all this cooperation and work with the museum should bear fruit 'as soon as the contemplated Irish Folk Museum in [the] Phoenix Park materialises'. Campbell had similar notes for his study of a Kerry village: 'In Ireland a new world opened up before my eyes ... I fully realised how important the Celtic element is which in many parts of Europe underlies both the Roman and Teutonic strata of culture'.

The possible oversell of the folk museum and of the work of the Swedish mission, which may unintentionally have been condescendingly delivered and in foreign, accented tones, seems to have drawn a backlash, because on the same day as the broadcast Frank Gallagher, Deputy Director of

Broadcasting at the GPO, wrote to Mahr of his desire to 'broadcast a commentary from the section of the museum devoted to the relics of the War of Independence ... sometime late in July or early in August'. Mahr agreed the following day and possibly identified the source of the pressure and possible jealousy that may have caused Gallagher to write by saying, 'the Keeper of this section is Mr Gógan [Westropp had by now retired] and I think it will be easiest for you to get in touch with him directly'. In a concealed but detectable tone of frustration which also sought to put Gallagher in his place, Mahr added, 'Some day National Antiquities should also get a crack of the whip as I have discussed a little while ago with Dr Kiernan' (i.e. Gallagher's boss). T.J. Kiernan wrote to Mahr on 2 March 1939 for permission to relay a programme entitled 'The Harp and Its Music' from the Music Room of the National Museum on the upcoming St Patrick's Day between 6:00 and 6:30 p.m., to which, obviously, Mahr had 'no objection'.

Mahr's diaries inform us that he had done a 'wireless talk', as he called it, as early as 23 February 1931, when he spoke on 'The Aim of a National Collection of Antiquities', which he followed up with 'A Walk through the Irish Antiquities Collection, National Museum, Dublin' on 6 March. He was a pioneering user of radio in the popularisation of museum work, an experience that he would put to use later when he returned to Germany.

Mahr also used film and the print media. He was on the Aran Islands from 20 to 27 September 1932 and from 5 to 15 April 1933 with Robert Flaherty and was very excited, as he told Bender on 10 August 1933, to be with the famous Hollywood film producer during the filming of part of *The Man of Aran* on the Aran Islands when, incidentally, Seán Keating did a charcoal drawing of Aran boatmen on a currach which he, 'John Keating', dedicated to 'Dr Adolf Mahr' and which the Mahr children presented to the National Museum in 2000. Flaherty visited the museum on 12 April 1934, there being a temporary exhibition of stills from his film from 16 April to 7 May, and wrote to Mahr on 3 July 1934 thanking him for various cuttings he had sent and regarding photographs sent to a Mr Ray (could this be Man Ray?) in Chicago which Flaherty wanted for the National Museum. Flaherty reported that 'the picture has proven very successful in its various runs in England. It played 5 weeks at the New Gallery Cinema and was the best run at this particular cinema of any during the last three years; and after the New Gallery run it played at the Marble Arch Pavilion for another 5 weeks'. It is unclear whether Mahr was an historic advisor to Flaherty on the latter's payroll or whether his involvement in *Aran* was deemed museum fieldwork. To be fair, his presence there appears to have taken place after a considerable intake of local folk life material, including, it would appear, of line fishing equipment in 1928 (which, incidentally, I was to use decades later in explaining the use of seemingly mysterious boat-shaped lead weights from Viking Dublin).

Mahr used newspapers to popularise the results of research, including from excavations (a legacy he was to pass on to Seán P. Ó Ríordáin, who seemingly bequeathed it to Liam de Paor and others of that generation). He clearly fed information to journalists that was rehashed, as in a report in the *Irish Press* on 21 August 1933 of the Harvard excavations at Ballinderry and of two smaller excavations by 'Irish archaeologists'. *The Irish Times* of 30 July 1932 carried a report of the Ballinderry excavations with a sketch of the site taken from Dr Hencken's notes. The museum line (courtesy of Mahr) is very evident in these articles, as it is also in a round-up of the year's excavations (1933) in which all the right diplomatic buttons (including recognition of finders and their names and of helpful local teachers, etc.) are pushed, including intriguing reports of a Viking burial in the Ards peninsula and of the Islandbridge, Dublin excavations.

Obviously, press reports of museum and excavation work are more accurate when published as Mahr wrote them himself and published under his name, as was often the case. The *Irish Independent* published a photograph of the cist discovered at Knockast on 7 December 1929 and Mahr followed this up with a lengthy article in the same paper on 29 January 1930, which featured a photo of himself taken by Lafayette. He strayed outside his normal prehistoric realm by writing on medieval wooden carving in the *Irish Press* on 10 August 1932 and, again, under his own name in May 1933 wrote of various collections of artefacts which were in private hands as well as of donations to the museum.

While he used newspapers to the advantage of the museum, Mahr had little respect either for them or some of their reporters. This is clear in a letter to Bender on 2 December 1932 after the opening of the temporary exhibition of Bender's donation, when he describes the *Irish Press* without naming it as 'only the new daily of the Republican Party and has no tradition'. This was because they dared send him a female reporter, whom he did not take seriously: 'no reporter deserves serious treatment'. His superiority and condescension to Ireland also shows through: 'in a little educated country the press is almost the only source of information for a vast majority of people. I was annoyed that a newspaper dared to send me such a poor creature. It will not happen again as I told the head reporter what I thought … ' Earlier, though, on 22 October 1932, he had written to Bender: 'I am not such a complete bookworm as not to understand how badly hit America is; as a matter of fact I am a great newspaper reader, having done quite a lot of journalism myself in the past, and with my friends of Harvard … in the evenings they would come to our house at any hour reading new books and periodicals of the continent', saying that apart from archaeology they also discussed ephemeral and philosophical matters, which was enjoyable because he had 'comparatively little opportunity here for discussing such problems'. Mahr clearly lacked intellectual company in Dublin, or maybe he preferred the company of other foreigners, preferring to stay aloof from the native population, a possible social awkwardness which also led him to increasingly seek out the company of German and Austrian expats, which was to have dire consequences.

Mahr's Dealings with Irish Politicians

A letter to Seán MacEntee of 9 June 1934, in which, incidentally, Mahr asks to be upped to the position of the directorship, and which he was shortly thereafter to achieve on 11 July, according to his diary, reminds the minister of their recent pleasant lunch and their conversation about what Mahr calls the Bog Research Scheme. This was because MacEntee had got his private secretary to phone Mahr about the file on a subject which obviously interested him and which was soon to start under A. Farringdon and Knud Jessen of Copenhagen's Botanic Gardens with G.F. Mitchell as field assistant. Mitchell's first contract was on Ballybetagh Bog in Co. Dublin, where he started on 9 July 1934, three weeks after Joseph Raftery started at Poulawack, Co. Clare.

Mahr also adverts to the question of the Vice-Regal Lodge, which MacEntee asked him to submit a memorandum about. He tells the minister he thought it best in this regard to have his own Secretary (General) hand over his two most recent memos on this subject, the first being the one 'which set the ball rolling; the second outlines the practical proposals'. In February of 1934, writing to Bender, Mahr says the Lodge 'has been given to the museum for extension' and that 'this is a most important event in the whole history of the museum'. The Lodge, he tells him, 'and its wonderful garden, have been earmarked as the future Museum City and to it two thirds of the contents of the present building will be removed with greater or lesser speed, amongst them the Chinese, Japanese, Burmese, and Indian Collections … I will select the best room I can find for the [Augusta Bender] Memorial Room'. Sadly, this was not to happen, especially after the Lodge became the residence of the President after the enactment of the 1937 Constitution. Museum directors came and went after Mahr and dreamed of finding additional space for the collections. It was to be a full sixty years before Collins Barracks was set aside in 1994 for the museum's expansion; it was finally opened to the public by Minister Síle de Valera in 1997.

Mahr had had some contact with Eamon de Valera, most notably in the opening of the first exhibition of the Bender material in 1932 and, later, in 1934, when the Bender Room itself was inaugurated. In notes supplied by Mahr to the President's office for de Valera's speech, we read 'the main duty of a National Museum is to serve as an educational institution for the country itself and to enable the citizens to realise the position of their own country in the universal context, peaceful or otherwise, of races, nations and civilisations, which contribute to the complex phenomenon of world history and development'. The President's staff rewrote the speech and placed the main emphasis of the museum on education. Mahr's notes were extremely complimentary of Bender and mention that there was also a Bender Room in Mills College, all of which was said by the President according to detailed press reports of the time.

Mahr had a number of other contacts with President de Valera that relate to the President writing a cheque to Mahr to enable work on excavations for the relief of the unemployed to carry on. This has been well documented in *Archaeology Ireland* by the late H.E. Kilbride-Jones. Less well known is Mahr's (in my opinion) ill-judged complaint to the President of OPW tardiness in regard to completing the permanent Bender Room, as reported to Bender on 17 June 1934. Incidentally, Mahr's objections to the Ceann Comhairle, Frank Fahy, about moving heavy volumes into the Museum Annexe drew a frosty command to comply from Fahy on 16 August 1934. To Mahr's great credit, he wrote to Fahy the following day, saying, 'I hope that the vivid personal impression which you now got of the awkward state of affairs which exist in the museum will help towards a more sympathetic attitude of the Dáil in all matters intended to relieve the unbearable congestion.' Mahr was not going to be pushed around as some of his successors and (going by his remarks noted earlier about the sawing up of cases) predecessors had allowed themselves to be.

An intriguing memo of 8 February 1938 to the Secretary (General) of the Department of Education refers to the Secretary's previous minute relative to a Department of Finance minute of 20 January about the 'use of the Ireland in its application to territory'. Mahr thundered back, 'Never has the title "National of Museum of Ireland" been questioned in any quarter, never was there any suggestion that we should be called only "National Museum of Saorstat

Eireann", nor was there, so far, any hint ever expressed that our title now might and should read "National Museum of Éire"'. He further explains that 'the Museum in Belfast is a Municipal Institution … is simply a Corporate institution, vaguely felt to serve the whole of British Ulster, but not purporting to be a provincial museum, has greatly helped us.' This situation changed long ago with the development of the Ulster Museum in Belfast, but it is a rare occasion when Mahr's Irish nationalism was clearly in evidence.

The initial loan of the 1916 relics for exhibition (announced in the *Irish Independent* on 8 June 1932) in what was called the Folk Room was meant to be only for the weeks of the Eucharistic Congress and the Tailteann Games. The exhibition was reported in the *Irish Press* on 28 June and the *Irish Times* on 6 July.

An instance of what could be called Mahr's nationalism or possibly his skill at reading the signs lies in a letter of 9 July 1932 from Nellie Gifford-Donnelly, the Honorary Secretary of the 1916 Research Committee, whose patrons were the Mrs Pearse, Ceannt, Clarke, Connolly and Plunkett. This was a letter to thank Mahr for putting on 'The 1916 Relics Loan Exhibition' with 'such unavoidable haste', the whole undertaking being 'successful in arousing public interest in the importance of safeguarding these Relics', a permanent exhibition of them being clearly the aim of the 1916 Club. Ms Gifford-Donnelly clearly wished the collection to be permanently kept in the National Museum. She wrote again on the following day, saying she had had a long interview with President de Valera, who had agreed with her that there should be such a permanent collection and that he would ensure that there would be. By 9 January 1935 there was a formal appeal for relics of 1916 on behalf of the National Museum in the *Irish Press* and on 16 April

1935, according to Mahr's diaries, the Irish National Independence Movement Section of the museum opened. This is the beginning of what museum staff to this day call the Easter Week Collection, now one of the most important and most utilised in the whole institution.

The Keeper of the Art and Industrial Division, M.S. Dudley Westropp, then wrote to the Secretary (General) of Education on behalf of Mahr on 31 July 1934, emphasising that the 1916 exhibition should be curated and mounted by National Museum staff, the work, which would embrace 'earlier movements along similar lines', to be part of the 'normal functions of the Museum'. He did concede that 'taking into consideration the fact the origin of the 1916 collection [the first use of an expression that has endured for three-quarters of a century now] is entirely due to the patriotic and voluntary efforts of the 1916 Club', a subcommittee including one of their members would be helpful. The first major 1916 exhibition seems to have been in the Centre Court in the Kildare Street building on the twenty-fifth anniversary of the Rising in 1941, and like its successors in 1966, 1991 and 2006 must bow to its origins in 1932, when Westropp (assisted by L.S. Gogan) and Mahr (respectively a retired British Army officer and a Nazi sympathiser), in one of the few occasions in its history, when it was asked bowed to political pressure to do something of enduring worth.

Overview of Mahr's Impact on Archaeology and the National Museum

For all his mistakes, arrogance and attitudes and despite the shortness of the time he was to spend in Ireland, Adolf Mahr, by his sheer energy and output, transformed Irish archaeology and had a huge impact on the National Museum. He guided and influenced the first generation of native archaeologists, whose influences are with us to this day. Through the network of his contacts, both scholars and institutions, he internationalised archaeology and the museum and brought the collections to the widest international audience. In recognition of this, he was made President of the (British) Prehistoric Society in 1937, the only Irish-based scholar ever to achieve this eminence. He underpinned his rôles as Keeper and later as Director with philosophically informed direction and purpose and had a vision for the development and rôle of the museum. He implemented the then best practices of museology. He professionalised archaeological practice and excavation methodology, especially by his enthusiastic championing of the Harvard archaeological mission to Ireland; got involved in relief schemes (for unemployment); was involved in drawing up the 1930 National Monuments Act; and deftly dealt with various ministers, the OPW and the civil service in the delivery of new exhibitions and in planning a 'museum city' in the Phoenix Park, which was only realised at another site in 1997 with the opening of the Collins Barracks complex.

Mahr brought the scientific publication of archaeological research to a new level and, at the same time, was involved in the popularisation of the subject by co-operating with the media, particularly the newspapers, for which he both wrote and supplied information, and the radio, which he invited to the museum. Outside archaeology, Mahr was responsible for the accession of Albert Bender's oriental collection and played a great part in highlighting the relevance of the folk life collections to archaeological artefacts. Folk life accessions and contacts with collectors of traditional items from J.H. Delargy/Seamus Ó Duilearga down occupy a large proportion of his diaries, almost as much as archaeological accessions. He was among the first to seek a national folk life museum. Apart from his insistence on the training of his assistants whom he sent abroad, Mahr set up what he termed a 'local school' (as in a letter to Bender in August 1934), populated by both professionals and informed local correspondents and supporters like P.J. McGill in Ardara, Co. Donegal, Donal Ó Ríordáin in Maree, Galway (Bay), Dr T.B. Costello in Tuam, Patrick J. Tohall in Co. Leitrim, J.N.A. Wallace in Limerick and T.J. Barron in Bailieborough, Co. Cavan. He built and cultivated a nationwide network of contacts and supporters of the museum, a tradition the museum tries to cultivate to this day. He himself implemented the recommendations of the 1927 government-commissioned Lithberg Report on the museum and changed around the exhibitions, bringing the Irish archaeological collection into a more prominent position than it had enjoyed in the old days of empire. He tried to get the museum's collections into international exhibitions, including the Wilibrod commemoration at Utrecht and the 1938 New York exhibition. He put on frequent temporary exhibitions on subjects as diverse as 1916, Czech glass and ceramics and excavation finds of various years.

Mahr's interest in localities and building up a 'local school' led to him supporting regional and provincial archaeological societies, notably the Thomond or North Munster Society in Limerick, which seems to have been founded (or, more properly, revived) because of his friendship with local antiquarians who, in turn, coaxed Mahr to write for the first issues of their new journal, which were later reissued as a combined offprint.

All of this was achieved in twelve years, of which Mahr only spent six in the director's office. Above and beyond the various activities just sketched (some of which have been developed already), one of Mahr's main contributions to the National Museum is that no director before or since wrote more about his concerns or more badgered the Taoiseach, the minister and senior civil servants about his hopes and ambitions for the place. In addition, he had a vision for the future expansion of the institution at a new site, in his case the Phoenix Park and the (then) Vice-Regal Lodge (now Áras an Úachtaráin).

DAVE WALTER

The Unsaintly Sir St George Gore:
Slob Hunter Extraordinaire[1]

E ach fall, thousands of out-of-state hunters invade
Montana. They pay dearly in licence fees for the privilege of stalking Montana's game. Montana's Department of Commerce estimates that each visiting hunter
spends an average of $1,800 while here. And every fall the
media carries stories of hunters who wound their guides,
marksmen who drop a rancher's pet cow near the barn and
game hogs who unconscionably slaughter wildlife. In fact,
it is hard to top the 1999 saga of a Sun Prairie hunter who
killed and tagged a three-hundred-pound llama on the Cas-
cade Hutterite Colony near Fort Shaw – and then took the
carcass to a game processor.

But these sportsmen all compare poorly with that paragon
of the foreign nimrod: the Irishman Sir St George Gore.
On an 1854–7 expedition, Gore hunted lands now located
in Colorado, Wyoming, Montana and the Dakotas. He
hunted in a style and to an extreme *never* duplicated on the
Great Plains. In fact, Sir St George Gore funded the largest
private expedition into the Rocky Mountain West, either
before or since.

Gore was an Irish commoner who succeeded to a hereditary title in 1842. This windfall gave him access to the in-

come from substantial estates in north-west Ireland, concentrated around Manor Gore, near Sligo. Gore had been born in Dublin in 1811. He was educated at Winchester School and at Oriel College, Oxford. At the age of thirty-one, he received the title of the Eighth Baronet of Manor Gore, in County Donegal.

Soon Gore established his residence in the family's Victorian mansion. This manor house was located on fashionable Brunswick Square in the seaside resort of Brighton, East Sussex, about fifty miles south of London. Gore's annual income exceeded $20,000, primarily from the family's substantial Irish land holdings.

The Eighth Baronet was a stocky, hearty bachelor, fully bearded and prematurely balding. A contemporary described him as 'a fine built, stout, light-haired, and resolute-looking man'. Gore meshed an appreciation of classical literature, music and art with a real love of the outdoors. He was a member of England's élite Turf Club and he earned a reputation as a skilled horseman, marksman and fisherman. He also proved an excellent judge of Irish whiskey and gained notoriety for his fiery temper. Indeed, he was the Victorian aristocrat to the hilt.

Gore followed another hunter, Sir William Drummond Stewart, into the American West. A Scotsman, Stewart had toured the West from 1833 to 1838; he returned in 1843, again to hunt the Great Plains. Stewart and Gore had met in European hunting circles and become friends. Stewart recommended the American West to Gore as a bountiful hunting ground, replete with an infinite supply of wildlife.

On Stewart's recommendation, Sir St George Gore arranged his Great Plains tour through the London office of the American Fur Company (AFC). This corporation operated home offices in New York and St Louis, as well as trading posts throughout the American West, most notably in the Missouri River Valley.

Gore arranged for the AFC to provide him with the most current maps of the Rocky Mountain West and to use its St Louis office to hire experienced frontiersmen for his entourage. The company also agreed to supply the Gore expedition from its posts throughout the West and to exchange United States currency at any AFC office or post for drafts on Gore's Baring Brothers' London bank account.

In January 1854, the Gore party sailed from Southampton, England, for America: the forty-three-year-old Gore, his personal valet, his dog-handler and fifty hunting hounds; huge amounts of crated supplies and equipment; and Gore's personal carriage.

Gore's party arrived in New York in February, passed through Pittsburgh in early March and reached St Louis on 12 March 1854. Here, as arranged, Gore outfitted for the two-year expedition through the AFC office. In addition to topping off his cache of supplies and purchasing some Indian trade goods, Gore's AFC agents hired forty experienced frontiersmen – the very best – to make up his retinue. Besides general labourers, the AFC enlisted cooks, camp tenders, interpreters, guides, hunters, teamsters, bullwhackers and such specialists as wheelwrights and blacksmiths.

The company's hiring *coup* was engaging fifty-year-old Jim Bridger, already a living legend in the Trans-Mississippi West. One biographer called Bridger 'the ablest hunter, mountaineer, and guide in the West'. Bridger had covered the Rocky Mountains for thirty years; he had discovered the Great Salt Lake in 1823; he had led fur expeditions all through the West; he had established Fort Bridger on the Oregon Trail in 1843. Gore paid Bridger the prime $5-per-day wage to serve as his personal guide and companion on the two-year trek. Somewhat surprisingly, Gore and Bridger would become fast friends, despite their real differences of background, education and experience.

Once Gore had supervised the branding of his stock and the painting of his vehicles, the expedition was ready. Gore carried in his leather satchel a licence to travel in 'Indian country' from the federal Superintendent of Indian Affairs, Colonel Alfred Cumming.

The party left Westport (Kansas City), Missouri, in mid-June 1854, travelling west on the Oregon Trail, 'in quest of anything that walked, bawled, flew, or swam'. The caravan was unlike *anything* before seen in the West. In addition to the forty experienced frontiersmen, it included about 110 horses, twenty yoke of oxen, fifty hunting dogs and a line of twenty-eight vehicles.

The lead vehicle was Gore's two-horse carriage – the one he had freighted over from England. The specially made carriage converted into a sleeping compartment by cranking up its fitted top from the carriage bed. It had been re-painted a bright yellow and its chassis incorporated a series of coil springs to soften the ride for the aristocrat.

Strung out behind the carriage, in increasingly thick clouds of trail dust, were twenty-one modified Red River carts. These two-wheel, single-horse Metis vehicles (*charrettes*) had been painted a shocking red. Their loads were covered with white canvas. Sixteen of the carts carried Gore's personal baggage; five carts contained the gear of the forty hired men and some 'Indian trade goods'.

Four large Conestoga wagons trailed the Red River carts. Six-horse-draft hitches pulled each of these vehicles. They packed all manner of foodstuffs and a full set of carpentry tools. Because vehicle breakdowns could delay travel, the Conestogas also carried a complete blacksmith shop and an extensive array of wheelwright's equipment for on-the-spot repairs.

Deep in the choking dust rolled the last two vehicles: commercial freight wagons, hitched in tandem and hauled by eight yoke of oxen. Each wagon carried ten tons of bulk supplies. Horsemen wrangled the expedition's stock behind the procession. The seventy-five-head herd contained extra horses, extra oxen and several milk cows – the suppliers of milk for Gore's breakfast.

And everywhere skittered Gore's fifty hunting hounds – sniffing, exploring, digging and chasing birds and small animals. The pack included eighteen purebred English fox-hounds (trained for tracking) and thirty greyhounds (bred for the chase).

Gore's personal arsenal filled one entire Red River cart – although Bridger quickly had him disperse the weaponry through the entire train so that if the party lost a vehicle in a river crossing, they would not lose all of their firepower. In addition to huge amounts of ammunition, kegs of gunpowder and the materials to fabricate all types of shells and cartridges, it included ninety custom-made pistols, rifles and shotguns.

The Irishman's fishing equipment filled another Red River cart. His valet doubled as his fly-tier. Upon reaching a stream that he wished to fish, Gore would detail the man to check the hatch on the water and then to fashion feathered lures to match.

Other travellers that season on the Oregon Trail included Mormons on their way to the Great Salt Lake, families headed for the lush valleys of Oregon and single men travelling to various placer-gold strikes in the Rocky Mountains. They all must have stood in absolute amazement as Gore's cavalcade passed, looking most like a medieval procession on its way to a shrine. Their bewilderment would have increased when they learned that Gore had travelled so very far from home simply to chase and hunt game. The same amazement would engulf any Oregon Trail traveller who witnessed the pitching of Gore's camp. They would not, of course, have seen Gore. He would have been out hunting.

The hired men first erected a sixteen-foot by twenty-foot green-and-white striped canvas wall tent. Within, they laid a full, fitted India-rubber pad and covered it with thick French carpets. Workers then hauled from the freight wagons and erected the tent's furnishings: two wood-burning heater stoves; an oval steel bathtub, with the Gore family crest embossed on both sides; a portable iron table and a matching washstand; an ornamental brass bedstead and a feather bed; two lounge chairs; an oak dining table and chairs; dinnerware of the finest English pewter; heavy trunks containing Gore's extensive wardrobe and his large collection of leather-bound classics; a fur-seated commode with removable pot.

Ever the aristocrat, Sir St George Gore ate alone – rather than with the hired help. (He literally never messed with his men.) A personal cook prepared Gore's meals, which were served by three frontiersmen who doubled as waiters. The menu combined fresh game, fish and the high-quality staples he had brought along. The meals were complemented by fine French wines, English gins and brandies and Irish whiskeys. Gore frequently stayed up until midnight, reading and sipping his imported liquors. Although most of the hired help struck camp and hit the trail by five a.m., their leader usually slept until ten a.m., then bathed and ate a leisurely breakfast before beginning the day's hunt.

The procession reached Fort Laramie, on the North Platte River, in mid-July 1854. The Irishman stored some of his supplies at the AFC's nearby Gratiot's houses and then established a temporary camp two miles up the Laramie River from the fort.

Within a week, Gore had mounted a full-retinue hunting trip into the nearby Medicine Bow Mountains and the high mountain parks of Colorado. After this three-month foray – punctuated by buffalo chases, confrontations with grizzly and black bears, the shooting of trophy elk bulls and incredible trout fishing – Gore's caravan returned to Fort Laramie in mid-October. The aristocrat then paid off and discharged most of his employees.

In the middle of May 1855, Gore rehired his men and embarked on the next leg of the expedition. The party trailed through Wyoming into the Yellowstone Valley – Crow and Sioux strongholds. Jim Bridger would serve as Gore's scout, guide, carriage driver and companion for the next seventeen months.

Gore hunted constantly – most frequently from his favorite horse, Steel Trap – a big, grey Kentucky thoroughbred that he had purchased in St Louis and trained himself. But he also shot from 'hunting stands'. He shot bison, elk, grizzlies, black bear, wolves, deer, antelope and bighorn sheep. A bit of that meat went to the camp to feed the men, but, unless they appeared to be trophies, Gore left the rest of the carcasses to rot where they dropped on the prairie.

Although isolated in a vast prairie wilderness, this consummate hunter always maintained his elegant Victorian lifestyle. But aside from his valet and servants, only Jim Bridger was allowed in the aristocrat's green-and-white-striped tent.

In fact, frequently, following a sumptuous dinner, Gore would summon Bridger to his tent. Here they would drink Irish whiskey or English brandy into the night, while the nimrod read Shakespeare, Charles Dickens and Robert Burns's poetry to the frontiersman. In return, Bridger – by all accounts a consummate storyteller – would relate tales of the American West, many of which he had lived.

When the hunting party reached the Yellowstone River, Bridger headed the procession upstream to the mouth of the Tongue River (the current site of Miles City, Montana). He then pushed up the Tongue about ten miles to the mouth of Pumpkin Creek, where he located a site for their new quarters: the hundred- by hundred-and-twenty-foot stockade to be known as Fort Gore.

Gore supervised the beginning of construction and then began hunting forays through the Yellowstone Valley – upstream as far as present-day Forsyth and downstream to the current town of Terry. In the course of these travels, he met and traded with local Crow bands. But he remained focused on the hunt. During the summer and fall of 1855, the Irishman devastated local herds and flocks and individual trophy beasts.

Gore continued to hunt almost daily through the winter of 1855–6, too. He broke his aristocratic pattern of separation only at Christmas, when he ate dinner with the men. And what an incredible menu it was: roasted prairie chicken; broiled elk steaks; candied sweet potatoes; creamed corn; hot cinnamon buns; molasses; plum pudding; mincemeat pies; strong coffee; fine French wines; Irish whiskey.

During that winter, a Blackfeet raiding band stole about forty horses from the company's herd. Gore's men pursued the party north for several days but lost them in a blizzard. In response, Gore doubled his night guard and the party suffered no additional losses. He would replenish the herd in the spring by trading with local Crow bands in the Rosebud Valley.

Gore and his men lived at Fort Gore from July 1855 until May 1856. During this ten-month period, watchful Crows estimated that his hunting tally included 105 bear, more than 2,000 bison and 1,600 elk and deer. Crow leaders complained about the devastation of their meat supply to the AFC's factor (boss) at Fort Union, located near the confluence of the Yellowstone and Missouri Rivers.

Factor James Kipp forwarded those charges to federal authorities in St Louis. Although Superintendent of Indian Affairs Alfred Cumming became angered, he could do little to curtail the foreigner's activities – he was removed almost two thousand miles from Fort Gore. Still, Cumming promised to talk with Gore when he finally returned to St Louis.

In the spring of 1856, Gore ordered his men to build two flatboats, each ten feet by twenty-four feet, to transport his trophy heads, animal hides, antler sets and bison robes down the Tongue and Yellowstone Rivers to Fort Union. He and Bridger and the rest of the caravan would trail down the Yellowstone and hunt.

Gore's plan, when he reached Fort Union, involved paying off about half of his men, selling his surplus goods, livestock and vehicles to the AFC 'at a fair price' and floating down the Missouri River with the remainder of his retinue to St Louis. Gore had a date in October 1856 to join his aristocrat friends to hunt stag in the Scottish Highlands.

Gore's men torched Fort Gore in mid-May so locals could not use it. But because of his many hunting side trips, his cavalcade did not reach the Fort Union area until the end of June. The fish, birds and game in the lower Yellowstone Valley were extremely plentiful and Gore followed his usual pattern of slaughter. When the overland vehicles finally reached the mouth of the Yellowstone, trophy heads and hides were tied to the sides of all the wagons and Red River carts. Gore established his camp on the south side of the Missouri River, almost directly opposite Fort Union.

By reaching Fort Union, Gore had survived the American Great Plains for two years and, more importantly, for two winters. And he had never once lowered his standards of Victorian elegance. But Gore was also the epitome of the 'slob hunter': killing for the sake of killing, or for the thrill of the chase, or for the trophies – seldom touching carcasses unless they had trophy value. His actions were so extreme that they offended both Native Americans and the white frontiersmen who worked for him.

In the mid-1850s, Fort Union served as the hub of the AFC's trade network in the upper Missouri River Valley. Its factor was the experienced seventy-year-old James Kipp, who ran the daily activities at the fort. To honour the Gore–AFC agreement, Factor Kipp was prepared to provide Gore with US currency to pay off some of his men and to purchase Gore's surplus goods, livestock and vehicles 'at a fair price'. He also agreed to build two mackinaw boats – sixty feet long, with twenty-foot beams – to transport the remainder of the party, its residual goods and its trophies downriver to St Louis.

Kipp performed these tasks with little enthusiasm, since he had fielded the 'slob hunter' complaints from Crow and Blackfeet leaders that winter. These tribes were vital to the AFC's upriver trade. However, Kipp also was a solid 'company man' so he performed his prescribed duties. Kipp estimated that it would take his men six weeks to construct the two sixty-foot mackinaws. Gore received this news with pleasure, for he had hunted little around the confluence of the Yellowstone and Missouri Rivers. Gore paid off twenty-seven of his men, providing sizeable bonuses. The party's remaining members maintained the camp across the river from the fort. Gore split his time between hunting or fishing with Jim Bridger and separating his goods for sale to Kipp.

With some difficulty, the nimrod's men moved their camp and wagons and livestock herd to the north side of the Missouri. Here, Gore stockpiled those supplies and equipment that he wished to reserve for his return trip to St Louis. His men stacked the 'surplus goods' on the prairie, within fifty feet of the fort's front gate. They pulled the extra wagons and Red River carts – even Gore's carriage – to a spot nearby and drove the livestock herd close to the fort. Gore spent the midday drinking whiskey and he then informed Kipp that he was ready to negotiate.

But the talks went badly. Kipp seemingly believed that the foreigner was asking too much for the European staples; Gore apparently thought that the factor was taking advantage of him because of his isolated circumstances. The two men argued. Kipp retreated through the fort gates. The intoxicated Irishman returned to his camp in a rage and fumed for several hours, punctuating his rantings with generous draughts of Irish whiskey.

By late afternoon, Gore ordered a few of his men to drive the expedition's livestock several hundred yards away from the fort. Others he detailed to pull the twenty-one Red River carts, the four Conestoga wagons and the two freight wagons in concentric circles around his elegant bright-yellow imported carriage, parked right in front of the fort's main gate. Gore himself climbed into the mass of vehicles, doused the yellow carriage with lamp oil and touched it off. Soon flames were licking at all the carts and wagons and a huge plume of smoke was rising into the blue prairie sky. His intent was clear: he would destroy these valuable vehicles rather than sell them to the AFC, at *any* price.

As the fire grew, Gore became crazed. He ordered his men to help him throw all of the 'surplus goods' into the conflagration: the green-and-white striped tent, the brass bedstead and feather bed, the trunks of clothing and leather-bound books, the India-rubber pad and French carpets, the sextants and chronometers and barometers, all of the fishing equipment, kegs of gunpowder, casks of fine liquor – even the oval bathtub with the Gore family crest embossed on both sides. From a historian's point of view, the greatest loss was Gore's leather satchel containing his Baring Brothers' London bank drafts, his US passport, his licence to travel in 'Indian country', his letters of introduction, his expedition maps and even his personal journal of the expedition – everything!

The fire raged all night and into the next day. It scorched the front gates of the fort. When Gore's anger finally cooled, as did the fire, he still ordered his men to rake the ashes to recover any scrap of metal and to hurl those fragments as far as possible into the Missouri's muddy waters. That way no one from the AFC could reuse them. In the upper Missouri wilderness, removed by hundreds of miles from factories and supply warehouses, the wanton destruction of such precious goods and equipment was absolutely unforgivable. Not surprisingly, the contractual ties between Sir St George Gore and the AFC disintegrated in the flames of the pyre.

Now the Irishman had to reassess his situation. Without bank drafts, he could not purchase the two mackinaw boats from Kipp. So he decided to send his trophies downriver to St Louis on his two Yellowstone River flatboats. He and Bridger and the remaining men would ride the well-travelled Missouri River trail, 1,760 miles to St Louis, on horseback. At least he could hunt the river corridor all the way downstream.

The story could end here. However, for believers in retribution – for Gore's hunting excesses, for his fit of temper that destroyed valuable goods in the wilderness and for his wanton arrogance – this tale will deliver it. In fact, the Gore story contains elements of Greek tragedy, for the mighty protagonist first holds sway and then plunges to the depths because of a character flaw or a personal indiscretion. Shortly after the bonfire episode, Jim Bridger rode downriver to Fort William, run by an 'opposition' competitor of the AFC. Here he obtained an area map, which he and Gore studied carefully. The map depicted a mountain range to the south of Fort Union, labelled 'unexplored'. Despite his circumstances, the huntsman in Gore could not be suppressed. He proposed to Bridger a side trip to investigate and hunt this intriguing uncharted territory – which turned out to be the Black Hills. They then planned to exit east, following the Cheyenne River to its confluence with the Missouri. Bridger agreed to the plan.

Gore sent his two flatboats downriver the 580 miles to the mouth of the Cheyenne, near Fort Pierre. There the expedition would reunite early in October. In the meantime, the nimrod would convert his predicament into a special adventure. So, in August 1856, the reconstituted Gore procession began its ascent of the Little Missouri River Valley – this time without carriage, or Red River carts packed with supplies, or Conestoga or freight wagons carrying camp luxuries. Rather, the party consisted of Sir St George Gore, Jim Bridger, sixteen hired men, sixty-five saddle and pack horses and the fifty hunting dogs.

After the party passed through a 'badlands' section, game in the Little Missouri Valley proved bountiful. Gore reverted to his hunting pattern of chasing and shooting bison, elk, deer, antelope, grizzlies and black bear at will. Although Gore now ate with the hired men, slept on the ground and took a regular turn on night guard duty, meat and other staples remained plentiful.

Despite advice from experienced traders, the headstrong aristocrat penetrated deep into the heart of hostile Teton Sioux country. After almost three weeks on the trail, the hunting party had moved three hundred miles off the Missouri and was approaching the mysterious Black Hills. More important, they were violating lands long held sacred by regional Sioux bands. Suddenly, the eighteen-man party was surrounded by a war party of a hundred and eighty Teton Sioux, led by Bear's Rib. This warrior's usual practice when he found whites in the sacred Black Hills was simply to kill them.

However, possibly fearing retaliation by the US Army, Bear's Rib issued Gore an ultimatum. Either the party could stand and fight, at the obvious ten-to-one odds, or the men could abandon their weapons, their equipment, their horses, their clothing and their foodstuffs and just walk away by the route they had entered the 'unexplored' Black Hills. Gore may have been an arrogant aristocrat but he was no fool. He fully understood the situation. He chose to surrender and walk out. All the men hoped that Bear's Rib would not subsequently pursue such a vulnerable quarry. Now the Irish sportsman *really* had been reduced to the basics of wilderness life.

For the next five weeks, Gore's band of naked men and their dogs struggled back down the Little Missouri drainage, living on roots, berries, lizards, insects, birds' eggs and small game, cutting their feet on prickly-pear cactus, toasted and chilled by the September weather. Left defenseless with the loss of their weapons, the party travelled at night to avoid detection by hostiles. For the same reason, the men lived without warming or cooking fires.

After almost three hundred miles of excruciating overland travel, Gore, Bridger and the hired men stumbled into a hunting band of friendly Hidatsa tribesmen near the mouth of the Little Missouri River. The natives fed the survivors and led them to their camp near Fort Berthold on the Missouri. It was the end of October 1856 and the English gentry were assembling to hunt stag in the Scottish Highlands – this year *without* Sir St George Gore.

Reclothed, Gore bought passage for Jim Bridger and eleven of the men on a fur-company mackinaw bound for St Louis in mid-November. Bridger was to instruct the crews on the two flatboats – still waiting at the mouth of the Cheyenne River – to proceed to St Louis and he would supervise the storage of Gore's spoils. Then Gore, his valet and his dog-handler and three other members of the original party settled into one of the Hidatsa earthen lodges in the village of Crow's Breast, near Fort Berthold. Hence, during the winter of 1856–7, the erudite aristocrat lived like a Hidatsa native, without lavish resources, without the amenities of European life, without any of his familiar camp luxuries.

In July 1857, Gore and his two servants boarded a steamboat at Fort Berthold bound for St Louis. Gore recovered the substantial trophies and curiosities produced from his Great Plains safari. In late summer, the Gore party (including the pack of hunting dogs) travelled to New York City and then returned to Britain – in time for the 1857 Scottish stag hunt.

Gore never did marry. He never did return to the American West – although he spent a portion of 1876 in the Florida Everglades. He died in 1878 at Inverness, Scotland, aged sixty-seven.

This sporting foray of Sir St George Gore into the North American heartland – and specifically into Montana – is one of the first lavishly supplied and organised expeditions mounted solely to hunt and fish. The three-year trip cost an estimated $50,000 in mid-nineteenth-century dollars. However, cost was never a factor for Gore. What was important was the chase, the hunt, the kill and his ability to maintain his lifestyle, even in the wilderness.

Sir St George Gore has earned full 'jerk' status: for his wanton waste of precious supplies; for his demonstrable arrogance; for his treatment of his hired men; for his hunting excesses. Historians estimate that Gore killed, over the course of the three-year expedition: 4,000 bison, 1,500 elk, 2,000 deer, 1,500 antelope, 500 bear, at least 100 of them grizzlies, and scores of other assorted animals and birds. Without question, those figures alone – Gore's personality aside – earn him the title of a consummate 'Jerk in Montana History'.

Notes

The Life and Opinions of Leonard MacNally (1752–1820), Playwright, Barrister, United Irishman, and Informer

[1] A longer version of this paper appeared in Hiram Morgan (ed.), *Information, Media and Power through the Ages* (Dublin, 2001), pp. 113–36.

[2] As a Catholic, MacNally's grandfather was barred from undertaking transactions in property and liable to heavy penalties if discovered: Fitzpatrick, *Secret Service under Pitt* (London, 1982), p. 210n. Fitzpatrick is also the source for MacNally's conversion but there is no record of this in the published lists: Eileen Byrne (ed.), *The Convert Rolls* (Dublin, 1981).

[3] R.R. Madden, *United Irishmen*, second series, second edition (Dublin, 1858), p. 569.

[4] *Ibid.*, iii, pp. 351–2; for details of productions, see Ben Ross Schneider Jr *et al.*, *Index to the London Stage, 1660–1800* (Carbondale, 1979), p. 534.

[5] Leonard MacNally, *An Address to the Whig Club* (Dublin, 1790), pp. 7, 11.

[6] R.B. McDowell (ed.), *Proceedings of the Dublin Society of United Irishmen* (Dublin, Irish Manuscripts Commission, 1998), p. 7.

[7] *Ibid.*, pp. 11, 12, 24–5.

[8] James Kelly, *'That Damn'd Thing Called Honour': Duelling in Ireland 1570–1860* (Cork, 1995), p. 203. Needless to say, Barrington's account of his duel with MacNally is almost entirely unreliable: Barrington, *Recollections of Jonah Barrington* (Dublin, n.d.), pp. 307.

[9] See Marianne Elliott, *Partners in Revolution: The United Irishmen and France, 1793–1815* (New Haven, 1982), pp. 62–8.

[10] 'Proceedings in the Court of King's Bench…against the Reverend William Jackson' in Thomas McNevin (ed.), *Lives and Trials* (Dublin, 1846), p. 209.

[11] JW to Pollock, 24 September 1796, National Archives, Rebellion Papers 620/25/108.

[12] JW to —, 17 September 1795, 26 July 1796, 30 May 1797, 2 January 1798, National Archives, Rebellion Papers, 620/10/121/29, 32, 35, 42.

[13] In a memorandum written in late 1800, Edward Cooke recommended MacNally for a pension of £300: Charles Ross (ed.), *Cornwallis Correspondence* (London, 1859), iii, p. 320. See also 'Pensions to Loyalists' c. 1800, Public Record Office, London, Colonial Office Papers 904/7/9-11. MacNally pronounced this sum to be a 'handsome remuneration … [though] I am ignorant when it commenced and when and where I am to apply': JW to —, n.d., National Archives, Rebellion Papers, 620/10/118/23. For MacNally's applications for further funding, see below.

[14] See 'Account of Secret Service Money, 1797–1804' in J.T. Gilbert (ed.), *Documents Relating to Ireland, 1795–1804* (Dublin, 1893), pp. 26, 40 for payments by Pollock to JW. I would suggest that earlier payments by Pollock of £50 (15 November 1797), £100 (10 November 1797) and £300 (11 December 1797) to an unidentified person went almost certainly to MacNally (pp. 6, 7).

15 Burrowes wrote to the Earl of Clare, the Irish Lord Chancellor, distancing himself from radical politics (and Wolfe Tone): Burrowes to Clare, 1795, in T.W. Moody, R.B. McDowell and C.J. Woods (eds), *The Writings of Theobald Wolfe Tone, 1763–1798* (Oxford, 1998), i, pp. 519–21. (My thanks to C.J. Woods for calling this letter to my attention.)

16 John Larkin (ed.), *The Trial of William Drennan* (Dublin, 1991); Maureen Wall, 'John Keogh and the Catholic Committee' in Gerard O'Brien (ed.), *Catholic Ireland in the Eighteenth Century* (Dublin, 1989), pp. 163–70. But see also the memorial of barrister Edward Purdue to the lord lieutenant, Lord Whitworth, in which he claimed that because he was a strong government supporter in 1798 his 'Roman Catholic' clients left him and he lost business subsequently: National Archives, Official Papers 432/14, c. 1815.

17 Drennan to McTier, 17 May 1806, in D.A. Chart (ed.), *The Drennan Letters* (Belfast, 1931), p. 361.

18 W.E.H. Lecky, *A History of Ireland in the Eighteenth Century*, Vol. 3 (London, 1892), p. 376.

19 John Bossy, *Giordano Bruno and the Embassy Affair* (Yale, 1991), p. 143.

20 JW to —, n.d. (early 1798), National Archives, Rebellion Papers, 620/10/121/152.

21 JW to —, 14 July 1798, National Archives, Rebellion Papers, 620/12/121/120.

22 'The Castle is surrounded by emissaries; every person who goes in or comes out is reported and it is probable there are enemies in its offices for the party certainly have very minute intelligence': JW to —, 14 May 1797, National Archives, Rebellion Papers, 620/10/121/56. See also the report of the informer B[oyle], 1 Feb 1797: 'Some of the Castle servants have been sworn and also

the greater part, if not the whole of the workmen employed in the Ordnance yard', National Archives, Rebellion Papers, 620/18/3.

[23] JW to —, 30 December 1802, National Archives, Rebellion Papers, 620/10/121/24.

[24] See for example the handwriting in JW to —, 20 May 1797, National Archives, Rebellion Papers, 620/10/121/57. It is possible MacNally was drunk on this occasion.

[25] Perhaps not everyone was taken in by MacNally. A live snake was reportedly sent to him from the convict colonies in Australia in 1804: Kevin Whelan, *Fellowship of Freedom: The United Irishmen and 1798* (Cork, 1998), p. 49.

[26] Lecky, pp. 379–80.

[27] JW to —, 7 July 1797, National Archives, Rebellion Papers, 620/10/121/34, 69.

[28] Laurence Sterne, *The Life and Opinions of Tristram Shandy, Gentleman* (London, 1978), p. 345.

[29] 'Pensions to Loyalists', c. December 1800, Public Record Office, London, Colonial Office Papers, CO 904/7/9-11; a similar document published in *Cornwallis Correspondence*, iii, p. 320 has 'faithful' in place of 'useful'.

[30] See the letters in the Pitt Papers, March–April 1795, Public Record Office, London, 30/8/327/307-10.

[31] Fitzpatrick, *Secret Service*, pp. 197–200; see also MacNally's discussion of anti-union sentiment among Irish Catholics in 1810: JW to —, 6 June, 18 September 1810, Public Record Office, HO 100/158/168; HO 100/159/160). MacNally's post-union activities would repay further investigation.

[32] Camden to Portland, 26 February 1798, Public Record Office, HO 100/75/128-9; Portland to Camden, 2 March 1798, Public Record Office, HO 100/75/142; Cooke to Pelham, 26 December 1797, BL Add. Mss 33105/307.

[33] JW to —, 17 September 1795, National Archives, Rebellion Papers, 620/10/121/29.

[34] JW to —, 22 September 1797, National Archives, Rebellion Papers, 620/10/121/77.

[35] JW to —, 3 July 1797, National Archives, Rebellion Papers, 620/10/121/69.

William Ewart Gladstone

[1] J.L. Hammond, *Gladstone and the Irish Nation* (London, 1938), p. 738.

[2] *Proceedings of the British Academy*, vol. LXII, 1977 (London, 1978), p. 231.

[3] J.G. Swift MacNeill, *What I Have Seen and Heard* (London, 1925), p. 247.

[4] H.C.G. Matthews, 'Gladstone, O'Connell and Home Rule' in R.V. Comerford and Enda Delaney (eds), *National Questions: Reflections on Daniel O'Connell and Contemporary Ireland* (Dublin, 2000).

[5] *Hansard*, series 3, vol XVII, p. 513; Thomas E. Webb, *Ipse Dixit or the Gladstonian Settlement of Ireland* (Westminster, 1886).

[6] A South Hants Liberal Conservative, *The Goblin of Crotchets in the Gladstone Mind: Being a Reply to Mr Gladstone's Autobiographical Apology for a Propensity to Wild Innovation which Renders His Holding the Helm of State a Dangerous Pilotage for the Vessel of England's Weal* (Salisbury, 1869).

[7] *Dublin Evening Express*, 8 November 1877.

[8] Thomas Lough, *England's Wealth and Ireland's Poverty* (London, 1896), p. 50.

[9] J.R. Vincent (ed.), *The Diaries of Edward Henry Stanley, 15th Earl of Derby 1826–1893, Between 1878 and 1893* (Oxford, 2003), p. 817, diary entry for 22 October 1885.

[10] Jonathan Parry, *Democracy and Religion: Gladstone and the Liberal Party 1867–75* (Cambridge, 1986), p. 269; P.M.H. Bell, *Disestablishment in Ireland and Wales* (London, 1969), pp. 198–9.

[11] Lord Redesdale, *Some of the Arguments by which Mr Gladstone's Resolutions Are Supported Considered* (London, 1868), p. 1.

[12] Thomas MacKnight, *Ulster as It Is*, Vol. I (London, 1896), p. 184.

[13] Parry, p. 271.

[14] *Spectator*, 11 May 1867.

[15] P.M.H. Bell, *Disestablishment in Ireland and Wales* (London, 1969), pp. 110–212.

[16] *The Speaker's Handbook of the Irish Question by an Irish Liberal* (no date), p. 70.

[17] Desmond Bowen, *Paul Cardinal Cullen* (Dublin, 1983), p. 208.

[18] Paul Cardinal Cullen (1803–78) was Roman Catholic Archbishop of Dublin and Primate of Ireland. His opposition was mainly responsible for the failure of Gladstone's Irish Universities Bill (1873).

[19] *Freeman's Journal*, 30 September 1874. Gladstone's 'theological diversion' certainly enhanced his popularity with English nonconformity: T.A. Jenkins, *Gladstone, Whiggery and the Liberal Party* (Oxford, 1988), p. 36.

[20] *Northern Whig*, 25 February 1875; MacKnight, Vol. 1, p. 303.

[21] Swift MacNeill, p. 248.

[22] O'Connor Morris, *Ireland from 1798–1898* (London, 1898), p. 345.

[23] Vincent (ed.), entries for 1 October 1885, p. 818, and 13 January 1886, p. 826.

'The Machine Will Work without Them': Kevin O'Higgins and the Jury Bills of 1924 and 1927

[1] Maurice Manning, 'Women in Irish National and Local Politics 1922–1977' in Margaret MacCurtain and Donncha O'Corrain (eds), *Women in Irish Society: The Historical Dimension* (Dublin, 1978), p. 92.

[2] *Irish Citizen*, 27 September 1913.

[3] Constance Markievicz, *Women, Ideals and the Nation* (Dublin, 1909), p. 4.

[4] *Bean na hÉireann*, April 1909.

[5] *Irish Citizen*, 2 May 1914.

[6] Hanna Sheehy Skeffington, 'Reminiscences of an Irish Suffragette' in A.D. Sheehy Skeffington and Rosemary Owens (eds and publs), *Votes for Women: Irish Women's Struggle for the Vote* (Dublin, 1975), p. 18.

[7] *Irish Citizen*, December 1918.

[8] *Sinn Féin, An Appeal to the Women of Ireland* (Dublin, 1918).

[9] P.S. O'Hegarty, *The Victory of Sinn Féin* (Dublin, 1924), pp. 56–8.

[10] Diarmaid Ferriter, *The Transformation of Ireland 1900–2000* (London, 2004), p. 269.

[11] O'Hegarty, pp. 104–5.

[12] Manning, p. 92.

[13] John P. McCarthy, *Kevin O'Higgins, Builder of the Irish State* (Dublin and Oregon, 2006), pp. 1–2.

[14] *Ibid.*, pp. 4–5.

[15] Maryann Gialanella Valiulis, *Portrait of a Revolutionary: General Richard Mulcahy and the Founding of the Irish Free State* (Dublin, 1992), p. 184.

[16] See Sinead McCoole, *Hazel, A Life of Lady Lavery 1880–1935* (Dublin, 1996), chapter VIII; also McCarthy, pp. 243–8.

[17] *Dáil Debates*, 1 March 1923.

[18] *Dáil Debates*, 13 March 1924.

[19] Cited in Diane Norman, *Terrible Beauty: A Life of Constance Markievicz* (Dublin, 1987), p. 260.

[20] *Dáil Debates*, 5 March 1924, cited in Maryann Gialanella Valiulis, 'Defining Their Role in the New State: Irishwomen's Protest against the Juries Act of 1927' in *Canadian Journal of Irish Studies*, 18, 1 (July 1992), p. 43.

[21] *Dáil Debates*, 5 March 1924.

[22] *Dáil Debates*, 13 March 1924.

[23] *Ibid.*

[24] *Ibid.*

[25] *Ibid.*

[26] *Ibid.*

[27] *Ibid.*

[28] Letter to the Editor, *The Irish Times*, 12 March 1924, cited in Valiulis, 'Defining Their Role', p. 44.

[29] Letter to the Editor, *The Irish Times*, 10 March 1924, cited in Valiulis, 'Defining Their Role', p. 44.

[30] *Dáil Debates*, 15 February 1927.

[31] *Dáil Debates*, 23 February 1927.

[32] *Dáil Debates*, 15 February 1927.

[33] *Dáil Debates*, 23 February 1927.

[34] *Ibid.*

[35] *Dáil Debates*, 15 February 1927.

[36] *Ibid.*

[37] *Ibid.*

[38] *Ibid.*

[39] *Ibid.*

[40] *Ibid.*

[41] *Ibid.*

[42] *Ibid.*

[43] *Ibid.*

[44] *Ibid.*

[45] *Dáil Debates*, 23 February 1927.

[46] *Ibid.*

[47] *Ibid.*

[48] *Ibid.*

[49] *Ibid.*

[50] *Seanad Debates*, 30 March 1927.

[51] *Seanad Debates*, 8 April 1927.

[52] *Dáil Debates*, 23 February 1927.

[53] *Ibid.*

[54] *Ibid.*

[55] *Dáil Debates*,15 February 1927.

[56] *Ibid.*

[57] *Seanad Debates*, 30 March 1927.

[58] *Ibid.*

[59] *Ibid.*

[60] *Ibid.*

[61] *Ibid.*

[62] *Seanad Debates*, 8 April 1927.

[63] *Ibid.*

[64] *Ibid.*

[65] *Ibid.*

[66] *Seanad Debates*, 30 March 1927.

[67] *Ibid.*

[68] *Ibid.*

[69] *Ibid.*

[70] *Ibid.*

[71] Letter to the Editor, *Voice of Labour*, 12 March 1927, cited in Valiulis, 'Defining Their Role', p. 48.

[72] *Dáil Debates*, 23 February 1927.

[73] *Seanad Debates*, 8 April 1927.

[74] *Ibid.*

[75] *The Irish Times*, 28 February 1927, cited in Valiulis, 'Defining Their Role', p. 50.

[76] Rosemary Cullen Owens, *A Social History of Women in Ireland 1870–1970* (Dublin, 2005), p. 85.

[77] *Seanad Debates*, 17 December 1925.

[78] *Dáil Debates*, 23 April 1935, cited in Mary Clancy, 'Aspects of Women's Contribution to the Oireachtas Debate in the Irish Free State 1922–1937' in Maria Luddy and Cliona Murphy (eds), *Women Surviving: Studies in Irish Women's History in the 19th and 20th Centuries* (Dublin, 1990), p. 208.

[79] *Seanad Debates*, 8 April 1927.

[80] *Ibid.*

[81] *Seanad Debates*, 30 April 1927.

[82] *Seanad Debates*, 30 March 1927, cited in Clancy, p. 222.

[83] Editorial, *Dundalk Democrat* quoted in the *Irish Independent*, 14 February 1917, cited in Valiulis, 'Defining Their Role', p. 53.

[84] Editorial, *Irish Independent*, 11 February 1927, cited in Valiulis, 'Defining Their Role', p. 53.

[85] Editorial, *Kilkenny People*, quoted in *Irish Independent*, 1 March 1927, cited in Valiulis, 'Defining Their Role', p. 53.

[86] Valiulis, 'Defining Their Role', pp. 52–3.

[87] *Ibid.*, p. 53.

[88] *Seanad Debates*, 8 April 1927.

[89] *Dáil Debates*, 12 May 1927.

[90] Mary Robinson, 'Women and the New Irish State' in MacCurtain and O'Corrain, p. 63.

[91] *Ibid.*

[92] *Ibid.*

[93] *Ibid.*

[94] Caitriona A. Beaumont, 'Women and the Politics of Equality, 1830–43', MA thesis, University College Dublin (Dublin, 1989), p. 3.

[95] Rosaleen Mills, 'Women on Juries' in *The Irish Housewife* (Dublin, 1955), p. 99.

[96] *Ibid.*

[97] Robinson, 'Women and the New Irish State', p. 64.

[98] *Ibid.*

[99] *Irish Citizen*, October 1919.

[100] Helena Molony, 'James Connolly and Women' in *Dublin Labour Year Book* (1930), p. 31.

[101] Margaret MacCurtain, 'The Historical Image' in Eilean Ni Chuilleanain (ed.), *Irish Women: Image and Achievement* (Dublin, 1985), p. 49.

[102] Other measures introduced included the Censorship of Films Act (1923) and the Censorship of Publications Act (1929), both of which empowered male censors to decide the suitability of a film, book or periodical on moral grounds, including any information on birth control; civil divorce was banned in 1925; the sale, advertising or importation of contraceptives was prohibited by Section 17 of the Criminal Law (Amendment) Act; 1932 saw a ban on married women teachers, followed by a ban on married women in the civil service. The 1934 Criminal Law (Amendment) Act legislated on the age of consent, contraception and prostitution; the Conditions of Employment Act (1936) limited the number of women working in any given industry, while a number of Articles in the 1937 Constitution limited the role and status of women, particularly Articles 40, 41 and 45.

[103] Clancy, p. 226.

[104] Caitriona A. Beaumont, 'Women and the Politics of Equality: The Irish Women's Movement, 1930–1943' in Maryann Gialanella Valiulis and Mary O'Dowd (eds), *Women and Irish History: Essays in Honour of Margaret MacCurtain* (Dublin, 1997), p. 175.

[105] *Irish World*, 16 July 1927, cited in Margaret Ward, *Hanna Sheehy Skeffington: A Life* (Cork, 1997), p. 287.

St Richard of Dundalk

[1] Katherine Walsh, *A Fourteenth-Century Scholar and Primate: Richard FitzRalph in Oxford, Avignon and Armagh* (Oxford, 1981).

[2] W.A. Pantin, *The English Church in the Fourteenth Century* (Cambridge, 1955), p. 116.

[3] Walsh, p. 112.

[4] *Ibid.*, p. 119.

[5] *Ibid.*, p. 223.

[6] *Ibid.*, p. 256.

[7] *Ibid.*, p. 211.

[8] T.P. Dolan, 'Richard FitzRalph's *Defensio Curatorum* in Transmission' in Howard Clarke and J.R.S. Phillips (eds), *Ireland, England and the Continent in the Middle Ages and Beyond: Essays in Memory of a Turbulent Friar, F.X. Martin, O.S.A.* (Dublin, 2006), chapter 11, pp. 177–80.

[9] Pantin, p. 165.

[10] T.H. Aston, 'Oxford's Medieval Alumni' in *Past and Present* 74 (1977), pp. 3–40.

[11] T. Wright (ed.), *Political Poems and Songs*, Rolls Series 14, 2 vols (London, 1859–61).

[12] Terry Jones, Robert Yeager, Terry Dolan, Alan Fletcher and Juliette Dor, *Who Murdered Chaucer? A Medieval Mystery* (London, 2003).

Additonal material from:

Geoffrey Chaucer, *The Riverside Chaucer*, Larry D. Benson (gen. ed.), 3rd edn (Boston, 1987).

Aubrey Gwynn, 'The Sermon Diary of Richard, Archbishop of Armagh' in *Proceedings of the Royal Irish Academy* 44 C (1937), pp. 1–57.

Notes

Mrs Markievicz

[1] The biographies of Constance Markievicz that I used most were Sean O'Faolain's *Constance Markievicz* (London and Toronto, 1934), Anne Marreco's *The Rebel Countess: The Life and Times of Constance Markievicz* (Philadelphia, 1967), Jacqueline Van Voris's *Constance de Markievicz in the Cause of Ireland* (Massachusetts, 1967) and Diana Norman's *Terrible Beauty: A Life of Constance Markievicz* (London, 1987). This was prepared as a light-hearted talk and could not felicitously be transformed into an academic paper, so though I have amplified it somewhat and added a few source references, it remains essentially a script and a *jeu d'esprit*.

[2] Sinn Féin Ard Fheis, 23 March 1996.

[3] *Irish Independent*, 22 April 2003.

[4] I wrote an article about her in the *Sunday Independent* of 2 April 2006 which is reproduced on my website: www.ruthdudleyedwards.com.

[5] Joe McGowan, *Countess Markievicz: The People's Countess* (Sligo, 2003) has an account of the background of Casimir Markievicz and the to-ings and fro-ings over his bogus title.

[6] Donal Nevin, *James Connolly: 'A Full Life'* (Dublin, 2005).

[7] Kathleen Clarke, *Revolutionary Woman: An Autobiography, 1878–1972* (Dublin, 1992).

[8] Maude Gonne MacBride, *A Servant of the Queen* (Dublin, 1938).

[9] Sean O'Casey, *Drums under the Window* (London, 1945).

[10] Charles Townshend, *Easter 1916: The Irish Rebellion* (London, 2005) is the most up-to-date source for what Constance Markievicz did during and immediately after the Easter rebellion.

[11] General Blackadder was both indiscreet and sympathetic. He reported contemporaneously to Countess Fingall that he had done one of the hardest things he had ever had to do in condemning to death Patrick Pearse – 'one of the finest characters I have ever come across': Ruth Dudley Edwards, *Patrick Pearse: The Triumph of Failure* (London, 1979).

[12] Although there have been attempts to discredit William Wylie's evidence, he was distinguished by his fairness: he fought unsuccessfully to have the trials held in public and to have the prisoners allowed defence lawyers. See Townshend.

[13] Frank Sherwin Jr (ed.), *Frank Sherwin: Independent and Unrepentant* (Dublin, 2007).

[14] Available at http://historical-debates.oireachtas.ie.

Walter Long: Irish Revolutionary

[1] For Long's family background, see the two essential sources for this chapter: Alvin Jackson's deeply researched entry in the new *Oxford Dictionary of National Biography* (Oxford, 2004–5) and James Kendle, *Walter Long, Ireland, and the Union, 1905–1920* (Dun Laoghaire, 1992), a most useful assessment of the man as well as his Irish career.

[2] Long died in 1924.

[3] See Robert Blake, *The Conservative Party from Peel to Major* (London, 1997), in which he is mentioned exactly once.

[4] See, for example, David Dutton, *Austen Chamberlain: Gentleman in Politics* (Bolton, 1985).

[5] Neal Blewett, *The Peers, the Parties and the People* (London, 1972), p. 75.

[6] Alvin Jackson, *The Ulster Party: Irish Unionists in the House of Commons, 1884–1911* (Oxford, 1989), pp. 303–4.

[7] Alvin Jackson, *Home Rule: An Irish History 1800–2000* (London, 2003), p. 166.

[8] *Ibid.*, p. 166.

[9] Vernon Bogdanor, 'The Selection of the Party Leader' in Anthony Seldon and Stuart Ball (eds), *Conservative Century* (Oxford, 1994), pp. 72–3.

[10] Patrick Buckland, *Irish Unionism 1: The Anglo-Irish and the New Ireland, 1885 to 1922* (Dublin, 1972), p. 72.

[11] R.F. Foster, *Charles Stewart Parnell: The Man and His Family* (Hassocks, 1976), p. 207.

[12] Kendle, p. 19.

[13] Jeremy Smith, *The Tories and Ireland, 1910–1914: Conservative Party Politics and the Home Rule Crisis* (Dublin, 2000), pp. 125–54.

[14] Jackson, *Home Rule*, pp. 117–32.

[15] Peter Hart, *The I.R.A. at War, 1916–1923* (Oxford, 2003), ch. 4.

[16] Kendle, p. 85.

[17] *Ibid.*, p. 79.

[18] *Ibid.*, p. 88.

[19] Taylor was Catholic but also the sole exception to the rule.

[20] Alvin Jackson, *Colonel Edward Saunderson: Land and Loyalty in Victorian Ireland* (Oxford, 1995), pp. 232–42.

[21] Eunan O'Halpin, *The Decline of the Union: British Government in Ireland 1892–1920* (Dublin, 1987), p. 164.

[22] One of his informants was J.M. Wilson, a unionist activist and brother of Field Marshal Sir Henry Wilson. For an example of one of his reports to Long, see Patrick Buckland (ed.), *Irish Unionism 1885–1923: A Documentary History* (Belfast, 1973), pp. 364–6.

[23] Kendle, p. 167.

[24] Charles Townshend, *The British Campaign in Ireland: The Development of Political and Military Policies* (Oxford, 1975), p. 25.

25 Ironically, he claimed it had been a cabinet commitment – almost certainly wrongly – just as Lloyd George had overstated his authority during the 1916 home rule negotiations that Long had opposed. Kendle, p. 191.

26 *Ibid.*, p. 147.

27 *Ibid.*, p. 168.

28 *Ibid.*, pp. 90–1. He wrote this in 1914.

29 The absence of British movements based on this identity analogous to those in Ireland does not mean such an ethnicity did not exist. It means, instead, that it already held power.

Sir Edward Carson and the Last-Ditch Stand of the Ascendancy

1 A.T.Q. Stewart, *The Ulster Crisis: Resistance to Home Rule, 1912–14* (London, 1969), p. 44.

2 *The Irish Times*, 28 October 1935.

3 Maurice and Jane O'Hea O'Keeffe (eds), *The Premier County of Tipperary: Living Voices* (Tralee, 2006), p. 100.

4 Richard Ellmann, *Oscar Wilde* (London, 1987), pp. 423–4.

5 Stewart, p. 226.

6 'What fools we were not to have accepted Gladstone's Home Rule Bill,' he told Ramsay McDonald in 1930. 'The Empire would not have had the Free State giving us so much trouble and pulling us to pieces.' Kenneth Rose, *King George V* (London, 1983), p. 242.

7 Patrick Geoghegan, 'The Making of the Union' in Dáire Keogh and Kevin Whelan (eds), *Acts of Union: The Causes, Contexts and Consequences of the Act of Union* (Dublin, 2001), pp. 41–5.

8 Patrick Buckland, *Irish Unionism 1: The Anglo-Irish and the New Ireland, 1885–1922* (Dublin, 1972), p. 28.

9 *Notes from Ireland*, No. 18, Vol. 1, Second Series, 6 May 1893 (from the *Bradford Daily Argus*, 26 April 1893). Published by the Irish Unionist Alliance.

10 'The Religious Difficulty under Home Rule: (1) The Church View' in G. Rosenbaum (ed.), *Against Home Rule: The Case for the Union* with introduction by Sir Edward Carson, KC, MP and preface by A. Bonar Law, MP (London, 1912, reprinted 1970), pp. 204–5.

11 'To those who think Roman Catholicism intolerant & productive of clerical tyranny & Protestantism as the reverse, a visit to N.E. Ulster would be a revelation. No such ferocious intolerance or such clerical tyranny exists, I believe, in Christendom. I heard a sermon on Sunday from a Presbyterian which [could] be matched only by the ravings of a mad Mullah. I really trembled for the small Catholic minority in Belfast, for incitements like this are only too likely to lead to a pogrom. All the Prot. clergy are politicians denouncing Home Rule from every pulpit, standing alongside Carson on the platforms and at the saluting point … I honestly know nothing like this in Catholic Ireland which is remaining silent under the most savage & intolerable insults and provocation.' Letter to Molly Childers, 7 October 1913, Childers Papers 1100, Wren Library, Trinity College, Cambridge. Whereas the Presbyterian Church in Scotland has in recent years through its moderator made a handsome apology for anti-Irish sentiments of the 1920s, which effectively called for the expulsion of Irish Catholics from Scotland, neither the Church of Ireland nor the Presbyterian Church in Ireland have ever accepted any accountability for the consequences of the rampant politically partisan and sectarian behaviour of many of their leading members in the 1912–14 period, nor has the subject yet been properly investigated by historians.

[12] 'Partition', *Forward*, 21 March 1914, in P. Beresford Ellis (ed.), *James Connolly: Selected Writings* (Harmondsworth, 1975), p. 276.

[13] Cited in Geoffrey Lewis, *Carson: The Man Who Divided Ireland* (Hambledon and London, 2005), p. 91.

[14] *Ibid.*, p. 99.

[15] 'The Ultimate End of Terrorism' reprinted in Norman St John Stevas (ed.), *The Collected Writings of Walter Bagehot*, Vol. VIII, pp. 89–92. See also Lord Northcliffe's opinion, March 1914, cited in G.K. Peatling, 'Unionist Identity, External Perceptions of Northern Ireland and the Problem of Unionist Legitimacy', *Eire–Ireland*, 39: 1 and 2, Spring/Summer 2004, p. 225.

[16] p. 115.

[17] Brian Inglis, *Roger Casement* (London, 1974), p. 360.

[18] Ian Colvin, *The Life of Lord Carson* (London, 1936), Vol. III, pp. 242–50.

[19] *Sunday Independent*, 12 March 2006. 'Orange banners commemorate William III as an enlightened monarch as they commemorate principled men like that Dubliner, Edward Carson, who so desperately wanted to keep Ireland united.'

[20] Nicholas Mansergh, *The Irish Free State: Its Government and Politics* (London, 1934).

[21] Dorothy Macardle, 'James Connolly and Patrick Pearse' in Conor Cruise O'Brien (ed.), *The Shaping of Modern Ireland* (London, 1960), p. 195.

[22] Notes for a debate on Ireland's influence on British politics in the Historical Society, Trinity College, 5 November 1965, by Nicholas Mansergh, reproduced in Martin Mansergh, *The Legacy of History for Making Peace in Ireland* (Cork, 2003), p. 288–9.

[23] Speech at Orange rally at Finaghy, cited in Michael Farrell, *Northern Ireland: The Orange State* (London, 1980), pp. 27–8. One of the most detailed accounts of Carson's

role in inciting the expulsions from the shipyards is contained in Paddy Devlin, *Yes We Have No Bananas: Outdoor Relief in Belfast 1920–39* (Belfast, 1981), pp. 46–50.

[24] H. Montgomery Hyde, *Carson: The Life of Sir Edward Carson, Lord Carson of Duncairn* (London, 1974), pp. 486, 490–1.

[25] Garret FitzGerald, 'Celebrating a Debt to Churchill', review of Roy Jenkins's *Churchill* in *The Irish Times*, 27 October 2001, quoting a Churchill speech of 28 October 1948, praising Ireland as 'an orderly Christian society, with a grace and culture of its own and, a flash of sport thrown in' and expressing the hope that there would one day be a united Ireland, which he would regard as 'a blessing for the whole of the British Empire and also for the civilised world'.

Sean MacBride: The Assassin's Cloak

[1] Since the broadcast I have been contacted by Professor John A. Murphy, who wished to point out that he was the first person to make critical remarks about Sean MacBride on that day. I have checked the record and this is certainly true. However, he was listened to respectfully, while my robust contribution was almost entirely drowned out by interruptions, cat calls and hissing.

An Error of Judgment: Rescuing Adolf Mahr's Contribution to the National Museum of Ireland

[1] I am indebted to writers Gerry Mullins and David O'Donoghue for discussion and to Paul Gosling, Gustav Mahr, Hilde Strasburger (neé Mahr), Ingrid Reusswig (neé Mahr) and Mary Cahill for additional information.

The Unsaintly Sir St George Gore: Slob Hunter Extraordinaire

[1] This text is a composite of both articles and speeches about St George Gore prepared by the late Dave Walter over a twenty-year period. First published in *Montana Magazine*, 74, November–December 1985, Walter subsequently revised his work for publication in *Montana Campfire Tales* (Guilford, 1997) and in *Speaking Ill of the Dead* (Helena, 2000). Walter continued revising this work for a Montana Committee for the Humanities Speakers' Bureau presentation and, finally, for presentation by video for the 2006 Speaking Ill of the Dead conference in Ireland.

Sources

Two accounts, covering limited aspects of the Gore expedition, appear in the ten-volume series *Contributions to the Historical Society of Montana*: F. George Heldt, 'Sir George Gore's Expedition' in Vol. I (Helena, 1876), pp. 128–31; James H. Bradley, 'Sir George Gore's Expedition, 1854–1856' in Vol. IX (Missoula, 1923), pp. 245–51.

Some of the principals in the story – e.g. Jim Bridger and James Kipp – are the subjects of biographical sketches in the ten-volume set. See also LeRoy R. Hafen (ed.), *The Mountain Men and the Fur Trade in the Far West* (Glendale, 1968). The standard work on Bridger remains J. Cecil Alter, *James Bridger: Trapper, Frontiersman, Scout, and Guide* (Salt Lake City, 1925), often in its numerous, subsequent editions. Although the work contains some erroneous information, the Gore tale is addressed in John I. Merritt, *Baronets and Buffalo: The British Sportsman in the American West, 1833–1881* (Missoula, 1985). Somewhat marred by similar inaccuracies, see also Clark C. Spence, 'A Celtic Nimrod in the Old West' in *Montana: The Magazine of Western History*, Vol. IX, 2, 1959, pp. 56–66.

The very best source is the excellent work by Jack Roberts, *The Amazing Adventures of Lord Gore* (Silverton, 1977). Based on some imaginative, thorough research, this account is rich in context, reasonable in its attribution of motives and replete with maps, photographs and illustrations. Where other authors have fumbled or fabricated or exaggerated the events of the expedition, Roberts tells a measured tale with verve and expertise.

Notes on Contributors

THOMAS BARTLETT has been Professor of Modern Irish History at University College Dublin since 1995. He was Parnell Fellow in Irish Studies at Magdalene College, Cambridge (2001–2) and was elected a member of the Royal Irish Academy in 1995. He is the author of *Fall and Rise of the Irish Nation: The Catholic Question, 1690–1830* and co-editor, with Keith Jeffery, of *A Military History of Ireland*.

PAUL BEW has been Professor of Politics at Queen's University Belfast since 1991. He has been a notable commentator on Northern Irish politics for many years and in March 2007 became Baron Bew when he was elevated to a life peerage in the British House of Lords. Among his publications are *Ideology and the Irish Question: Ulster Unionism and Irish Nationalism 1912–1916*. He has also written biographies of Charles Stewart Parnell and John Redmond.

ROSEMARY CULLEN OWENS is a lecturer in the Women's Education Research and Resource Centre in University College Dublin. She is the author of *Smashing Times: A History of the Irish Suffrage Movement 1889–1922* and *A Social History of Women in Ireland 1870–1970*.

Notes on Contributors

TERENCE DOLAN is Associate Professor of Old and Middle English in the School of English and Drama at University College Dublin. He is co-author (with Terry Jones, among others) of *Who Murdered Chaucer? A Medieval Mystery* and is the author of *A Dictionary of Hiberno English*. He also makes regular appearances on a variety of radio programmes.

RUTH DUDLEY EDWARDS is an historian, crime novelist and journalist who for more than a decade has written about Northern Ireland. She won the National University Prize for Irish Historical Research in 1978 for *Patrick Pearse: The Triumph of Failure* (reissued 2006) and in 1988 the James Tait Black Memorial Prize for her biography of the publisher Victor Gollancz. Her other books include *The Faithful Tribe: An Intimate Portrait of the Loyal Institution*.

PETER HART holds the Canada Research Chair in Irish Studies at Memorial University of Newfoundland. He is the author of *Mick: The Real Michael Collins*, *The IRA and Its Enemies*, *The IRA at War 1916–1923* and *British Intelligence in Ireland*. He is currently working on his next book, *The Michael Collins Papers*.

MARTIN MANSERGH, historian and politician, is a member of Dáil Éireann for South Tipperary. He was educated at King's School, Canterbury and Christ Church, Oxford, where he obtained a doctorate in French history. He is the former Head of Research with Fianna Fáil, was special adviser to three Taoisigh and a significant figure in the Northern Ireland peace process. His speeches and essays have been collected in the volume *The Legacy of History*.

MARGARET O'CALLAGHAN teaches modern Irish history and politics in the School of Politics, Philosophy and International Studies at the Queen's University of Belfast and has taught at Cambridge University and the University of Notre Dame, Indiana. She has published on nationalism and unionism in modern Ireland and on the politics of cultural identity in the Irish Free State, the politics of the Parnellite period and British policy towards Ireland between the 1880s and 1925. She and Professor Mary Daly of UCD have been co-directors of a major North–South research project, funded by the Higher Education Authority, on the commemoration of the 1916 Rising in 1966 in both Irish political jurisdictions. Their co-edited book on the politics of the commemoration will be published by the Royal Irish Academy in 2007.

DAVID NORRIS is a member of Seanad Éireann and was a senior lecturer in the English Department at Trinity College, Dublin, from 1968–94. He is renowned internationally as a Joycean scholar and has published widely on a variety of literary, sociological and legal topics. He is also Founding Chairman of the James Joyce Cultural Centre in Dublin

DR PAT WALLACE has been the Director of the National Museum of Ireland for nineteen years. Before that, he was the archaeologist in charge of the museum's excavations of the Viking site at Wood Quay, Dublin. He has served on international reference committees for urban excavations. Well known as a lecturer and for popularising Ireland's heritage, he has also made several radio and television programmes. He was awarded with a Knighthood by the Queen of Denmark and an honourary doctrate from the University of Roskilde.

Notes on Contributors

DAVID WALTER, who died in July 2006, was an historian with the Montana Historical Society and the author of a number of works on the history of Montana, including an examination of the state's Second World War conscientious-objector camps and the 1920s Ku Klux Klan movement. He was one of a group of historians who originated the concept of Speaking Ill of the Dead: Jerks in Montana History as an annual session of the Montana Historical Society conference.

Speaking Ill of the Dead